# MICHAEL HANEKE'S CINEMA

The Ethic of the Image

Catherine Wheatley

*Berghahn Books*
New York • Oxford

Published in 2009 by

*Berghahn Books*

www.berghahnbooks.com

**Library of Congress Cataloging-in-Publication Data**

Wheatley, Catherine.
  Michael Haneke's cinema : the ethic of the image / Catherine Wheatley.
    p. cm. --  (Film Europa ; v. 7)
  Includes bibliographical references and index.
  ISBN 978-1-84545-557-6 (hbk) -- ISBN 978-1-84545-722-8 (pbk)
  1.  Haneke, Michael, 1942---Criticism and interpretation.  I. Title.

  PN1998.3.H36W44 2009
  791.43023'3092--dc22

                          2008047813


**British Library Cataloguing in Publication Data**

A catalogue record for this book is available from
the British Library.


Printed in the United States on acid-free paper


ISBN 978-1-84545-557-6 (hardback), ISBN 978-1-84545-722-8 (paperback)

*To my parents*

# CONTENTS

# LIST OF ILLUSTRATIONS

# DECLARATION

All translations from German and French in this book are, unless otherwise indicated, my own. Italicised film titles indicate original release titles. Film titles that are not italicised indicate a literal translation (by myself) of the original title in those cases where no English release title exists, or alternatively where no English release title could be traced.

Some of the material from this book has appeared elsewhere in various forms. A summary of this book's aims has been published as 'Ideology, Ethics and The Films of Michael Haneke', in *Philosophy and Film*, ed. Barbara Gabriella Renzi and Stephen Rainey, Cambridge Scholars Press: New Castle, 2006. Material on *La Pianiste* from Chapter Five appears in extended form in two articles: 'Unseen/Obscene: the (non) framing of the sexual act in three French films', in *Framed!*, ed. Ann Lewis, Michael Seabrook, Lucy Bolton and Gerri Kimber, Peter Lang: Reading, 2006; and 'The masochistic fantasy made flesh: Michael Haneke's *La Pianiste* as melodrama', in *Studies in French Cinema* vol. 6 no. 2 (2006). The analysis of *Caché* in Chapter 6 is developed from a short article entitled 'Secrets, lies and videotape: Michael Haneke's *Hidden*', which featured in *Sight & Sound* Magazine, vol. 16. i.12, (February 2006).

I am grateful to the editors of each of these publications for their kind permission to reproduce this material, and for their comments and criticisms, which enabled me to improve upon it for this book.

# A Note on the Titles

After the first mention of each film, where the titles are given in both the original language and the English translation (if applicable), each of Michael Haneke's films is referred to by its original title (defined as the title by which it was released in its country of production, rather than its English translation) as follows:

*Der Siebente Kontinent* (1989)
*Benny's Video* (1992)
*71 Fragmente einer Chronologie des Zufalls* (1994)
*Funny Games* (1997)
*Code inconnu* (2000)
*La Pianiste* (2001)
*Le Temps du loup* (2003)
*Caché* (2005)
*Funny Games U.S.* (2007)

There is little consensus amongst insitutions and authors over the correct form of reference to some of these works. *Benny's Video* and *Funny Games* – made in Austria but given English-language titles – are always referred to as such and the early Austrian films are regularly referred to in English-language publications and institutions by their English titles. However, *Code inconnu* and *Caché* are sometimes translated into their English versions, sometimes not; and confusion abounds regarding *La Pianiste* and *Le Temps du loup*, which despite being produced in France are often referred to by both their English and, more mysteriously, German titles. In the case of *La Pianiste* in particular the choice of appelation has rather serious implications, since the German title (*Die Klavierspielerin*, from Elfriede Jelinek's novel of the same name) is a cumbersome, semi-invented word which deliberately references the awkwardness of its protagonist, Erika Kohut, and her position in Viennese society. This title also emphasises her gender, as well as her agency as a piano *player*, rather than her facilitating of agency to others as a *teacher*. Both these latter nuances are retained in the French title (although not the intentional awkwardness), but lost in the English *The Piano Teacher*.

With so many discrepancies, the choice to retain the original working title for each project within this book is in some ways a matter of convenience. But there are two other reasons for the decision. Firstly, that two of the films (*Benny's Video* – note the apostrophe – and *Funny Games*) are deliberately given English-language titles despite the fact that they were produced in Austria. I believe this is an intentional reference on Haneke's part to the dominance of the English language (in its Americanised version) in the cinematic domain, and a deliberate ploy to invite comparisons with U.S. (that is, Hollywood) product. Had I translated all the titles, the specific Englishness of these titles would have been lost. Which leads me to my second point: when viewed in sequence the original language of each title and indeed each film tells us something about Haneke's trajectory from the national platform to the international. One could perhaps write a paper on the titles of the films alone – they are certainly not chosen lightly – and what was his latest project at the time of writing, a U.S. remake of *Funny Games*, released under the same title, only serves to lend a fascinating circularity to the list of Haneke's films.

# ACKNOWLEDGEMENTS

This book is developed from my doctoral research, and this being the case, my first debt of gratitude is to the Arts and Humanities Research Council and to the University of Oxford Faculty of Medieval and Modern Languages, without whom it would not have been financially possible for that research to have been undertaken. My deepest thanks go to my supervisor, Dr Reidar Due, for his unwaning enthusiasm for the project over a four-year period and for his guidance and support throughout the conception and writing of this work; and for coming to my rescue, and doing so with good humour, when an early draft of the work was lost on a stolen laptop. I would also like to thank Film Studies at the University of Southampton, in particular Tim Bergfelder, for encouraging me to turn my thesis into this book, and Lucy Mazdon for making time available for rewrites. I am much indebted to the staff at the Film Archiv Österreich and the Film Bibliothek in Vienna, especially to Mr Thomas Ballhausen for his ability to source some apparently unlocatable materials and for his willingness to send numerous copies of television films to the U.K. Thanks to Guido Bonsaver, Robin Fiddian, Ben Morgan, Andrew Webber, Wes Williams, Lucy Bolton, Jim Morrissey, Alison Roberts and particularly William Brown, for reading through various drafts. Finally, and especially, my thanks go to my family, Ann, Les and Robert Wheatley, for their endless encouragement and astonishing patience throughout.

# INTRODUCTION

*The cinema seat is of greater assistance than the analyst's couch. Sitting in a cinema seat we are left to our own devices and this is perhaps the only place where we are so bound and yet so distant from each other: that is the miracle of cinema.*

*In cinema's next century, respect of the audience as an intelligent and constructive element is inevitable. To attain this, one must perhaps move away from the concept of the audience as the absolute master. ...*

*For one hundred years, cinema has belonged to the filmmaker. Let us hope now the time has come for us to implicate the audience in its second century.*

Abbas Kiarostami

This book began life as a result of the peculiar response that I became aware of having when watching the films of Austrian film-maker Michael Haneke. I first saw one of Haneke's films in 1999, and the experience of watching *Funny Games* was a distinctly unpleasant one for me: over the course of the viewing I was overwhelmed by a feeling of unease, of discomfort. I wanted to leave the cinema, but I couldn't bring myself to do so – such was my fascination with the film. Subsequent viewings of Haneke's other works were characterised by a similar ambivalence on my part. Some were more distressing than *Funny Games*, others less so, but all affected me profoundly in a way that I struggled to account for.

Surveying some of the critical reception of the film, it became clear to me that I was not alone in responding to Haneke's films in this way. The works clearly present a problem for spectators in terms of how to respond to them: 'gruelling', 'punitive', 'aggressive' – these are terms frequently used to describe the films. In my attempts to understand what it is about them that is so discomfiting, I turned to spectatorship theory. But while I found there a litany of writing on why it is we enjoy certain films, I was surprised to discover almost nothing had been said about why we *do not* enjoy others. My task was therefore clear: to examine Michael Haneke's films with a view to understanding something more about the unpleasurable cinematic experience and, ultimately, to discovering why Haneke's films reverberate so strongly with so many viewers. Working in parallel on a sustained textual analysis of Michael Haneke's films and a critical reflection on the history of spectatorship, the problem crystallised for me as a one of *ethical reflexivity*.

This book is therefore concerned to a large extent with ethics. This is perhaps not unusual: as Simon Blackburn comments in his *Introduction to Ethics* all aspects of our daily life are coloured by ethical questions.[1] Almost every choice we make, every act we undertake, as human beings in a social world has moral implications. What we might term the moral or ethical environment – the climate of ideas about how to live, which contains both the norms of our actions and the implicit criteria by which we live – surrounds us as we go about our daily lives. It constitutes what we find acceptable or unacceptable, admirable or contemptible. It constitutes our conception of when things are going well and when they are going badly; our conception of what is due to us, and what is due from us, as we relate to others. It comprises our emotional responses: what is a cause of anger or gratitude, or pride or shame, or what can be forgiven and what cannot. It makes up, and is made up of, our standards – our standards of behaviour and of belief. In the eyes of some thinkers, most famously perhaps G.W.F. Hegel, it shapes our very identities: even our consciousness of ourselves is largely, or perhaps essentially, a consciousness of how we stand for other people.[2]

And reflection upon this ethical environment is by no means the private preserve of philosophers. Drama, literature, poetry and film all work out ideas of standards of behaviour and their consequences. After all, the satirist and cartoonist, as well as the artist and the novelist, comment on and criticise the prevailing climate just as effectively as 'philosophers'. Blackburn puts it thus: 'The impact of a campaigning novelist, such as Harriet Beecher Stowe, Dickens, Zola or Solzhenitsyn, may be much greater than that of the academic theorist. A single photograph may have done more to halt the Vietnam War than all the writings of moral philosophers of the time put together'.[3]

When Peter Watkins, in *The War Game* (1965), asked the spectator to consider the consequences of nuclear war he did it by enacting an ethical situation for us. When Steven Spielberg gave us *Saving Private Ryan* (1998), he likewise used film as an illustration of the ethics of war. Less polemically, but no less engagingly, Alfred Hitchcock depicts, in each of his films, a moral problem. Is it worse to honour a promise to murder, or to go back on one's word and risk endangering one's loved ones? Is it acceptable to seek revenge on someone who has manipulated you, harmed you or your family? Is murder ever justifiable? Should we lie, or prostitute ourselves, for the good of our country? Our friends? Our family? In fact, a vast majority of films – like literature – take an ethical dilemma as their central narrative pivot. Suspense, melodrama, action, even romance – all centre, to a greater or lesser degree, upon moral choices with which we are more or less familiar.

It is clear that philosophy is not alone in its engagement with questions of ethics, and that film regularly concerns itself with the ethical climate in which live. But what attempts have been made to understand film's relationship with ethics? Generally speaking, we can divide those critics and theorists who have brought questions of ethics to bear on film studies into two camps. The first, which we can refer to as the 'American moralist critics',[4] is comprised of academics and critics working within a tradition which stems from literary criticism and which generally privileges content over form. These critics give readings of specific films, oeuvres and genres focusing on the questions of morality played out within a narrative context. Typical of the approaches they take is Raymond Carney's analysis of Frank Capra's *It's A Wonderful Life* (1946).[5] Carney's discussion of this film is particularly interested in plot, character and action, and it focuses almost exclusively on the moral trajectory of the film's protagonist, George Bailey (played by James Stewart). Regarding the spectator's relationship to the film, Carney makes the assumption that by watching George's progression through the film, the viewer can 'learn' something about their own sense of moral responsibility as they empathise with the character's suffering and redemption.[6]

If the American moralists are concerned with the ethics of a film's content, other thinkers are concerned with the ethics of film form. The second category of theorists who marry ethics and film analysis are those, from Jean-Louis Baudry and Christian Metz to Peter Wollen and Laura Mulvey, whose film theory is interested in what the ethics of film as a medium are.[7] The relationship of film to ethical thinking is not merely one of narrative illustration: film does not only reflect on the ethical environment, but it is also of course part of it. And if the workings of the ethical environment in which we live can be strangely invisible, so too can the workings of cinema. Apparatus theorists such as Baudry and Metz claim that the very mechanics of the cinematic institution are ethically coercive, while participants in what D.N. Rodowick terms 'the discourse of political modernism',[8] including Wollen and Mulvey, argue that the cinematic apparatus manipulates the spectator watching a film like Capra's into unthinkingly accepting the system of values that the film promotes. These theorists believe that Hollywood film is morally suspect because it is politically coercive: that by offering a narrative based on principles of unity, continuity and closure, such films efface the constructedness of the filmic medium and promote an identification with, and unquestioning acceptance of, the fictional world offered by the film, which frequently promotes specific political values. Its system of representation often involves, they argue, the objectification of women, the vilification of homosexuals and the idealisation of capitalist society, all of which the spectator is persuaded to accept as 'normal' or 'natural'.

For these theorists, then, the filmic institution may have its own implicit ethics. They may not explicitly state their moral take on film and its workings, but it is there, if we are willing to look closely enough, in a set of underlying ethical assumptions within the politicised discussion of film form about what is 'right' and what is 'wrong'. However, in subordinating moral problems to political problems, theorists like Mulvey and Wollen do not address the moral questions, as such. The ethics of film that emerges out of the discourse of political modernism is, de facto, embedded in a political argument. Ethical concerns are unresolved here because they are inessential. The position is perhaps best summarised by a line from Bertolt Brecht's *The Threepenny Opera*, 'Food first, then morals'.[9]

For some critics of Austrian director Michael Haneke's work, politics remains a primary concern. In this book, however, we shall allow ourselves what Brecht might see as the 'luxury' of leaving politics to one side. In part, this is a strategic move, for within philosophy an ethical problem, while it may have social implications, is not normally couched in terms of political ideology or power but in terms that are specifically moral, concerning for instance sentiment, responsibility, shame or guilt – terms conspicuously absent from the discourse of political modernism. But it is also a necessary move. For the language of philosophical ethics is the language in which Haneke himself discusses his work. And more significantly, I believe, it is also the language in which these films think about *themselves*.

Ethical concerns sculpt the themes and forms of Haneke's work. Each of his feature films presents an ethical problem within its narrative – suicide, murder, conspiracy and rape are recurring themes, for example – and they also demonstrate an underlying concern with questions of guilt and responsibility. But this concern does not only take place on a narrative level, as characters struggle with and against their responsibility for past and present actions: it is also demonstrated on an extra-diegetic level. The content of each of these films presents us with a series of ethical problems which echo or mirror a set of ethical problems that Haneke sees as inherent to the viewing situation. These problems revolve around the spectator's complicity with the cinematic apparatus and their tacit acceptance or denial of this complicity, and the key focus of Haneke's films is on the spectator's responsibility for their own involvement in the spectator–screen relationship. While the questions of complicity, responsibility and guilt raised within the narratives of Haneke's films then provide in themselves ample material for consideration, they also represent by analogy Haneke's concerns with the acts of film-going and film-viewing.

Philosophical reflections on ethics contain a distinctive ambition. The ambition is to understand the springs of motivation, reason and feeling that move us. It is to understand the networks of rules or 'norms' that sustain our lives. The ambition is often one of finding a system in the apparent jumble of principles and goals that we respect, or say we do: it is an enterprise of self-knowledge. By analogy, Haneke's work stands in a tradition of films that reflect upon their own construction, attempting to understand the rules or norms that govern and sustain them. These films are formally reflexive – they reflect on their own construction. They are the films produced by Samuel Peckinpah, Oliver Stone, Jean-Luc Godard, Chantal Akerman – just a few of the directors who have tried to investigate the workings of film *through* film (albeit more often than not with political concerns as their focus).

Haneke draws on many of the formal techniques present within the work of such directors, techniques analysed within the discourse of political modernism and mobilised for the purposes of political polemic. But he also develops them and refocuses them. Within the following six chapters, I shall demonstrate that in Haneke's works aesthetic reflexivity is conducive to the spectator's moral reflexivity. By placing reflexive techniques within new frameworks, I argue, Haneke is able to co-opt the spectator into a uniquely moral relationship to the film. Reflexivity within his films is used not, as in the works of these earlier directors, to create a form of cinema which is a vehicle for a political and moral agenda, but to encourage a more open-ended reflection on the spectator's part about moral questions. On an implicit level, the films prompt their spectators to ask: How are we complicit with the apparatus? What are the moral consequences of this? Why, upon watching Haneke's films, do we so often feel irritated, cross, even guilty?

These are the questions that make Haneke's work so problematic and so provocative. We will seek the answers to them – or at least some potential responses – over the course of the book. But in order to do so, we need a new way of thinking about the film viewing experience: an ethical theory of spectatorship. My analysis of what I shall call Michael Haneke's 'critical aesthetic' will attempt to account for what precisely the relationship between formal reflexivity and moral reflexivity is; how exactly Haneke radicalises the spectator's relationship to the screen, and what the implications of this radicalisation are for film theory at large. In doing so, I hope here to make some initial steps towards an examination of film's relationship to ethics, both in Haneke's films and in a larger sense.

At the time of writing, Haneke has made eight feature films, (nine if we include his adaptation of Kafka's *Das Schloß*, originally filmed for television but subsequently given a cinematic release; ten if we include the remake of his own *Funny Games*, released in 2008 under the title *Funny Games U.S.*). This corpus of eight films – starting with *Der Siebente Kontinent/The Seventh Continent* (1989) and including *Caché/Hidden* (2006) – will constitute the empirical object of this book. Surprisingly, given Haneke's critical and commercial success, they have received little academic attention to date.[10] To this author's knowledge, only two academic books exist devoted entirely to the director's work, both anthologies edited by celebrated Austrian film scholar Alexander Horwath: *Der Siebente Kontinent, Michael Haneke und Seine Filme*, published in 1991, and *Michael Haneke* (co-edited with Giovanni Spagnoletti), published in 1998.[11] What is remarkable about these books is that both were published prior to Haneke's move to France, which marked his transition onto the international film stage. Likewise, Willy Riemer devotes an entire section of his book *After Postmodernism: Austrian Film and Literature in Transition* (2000) to Haneke, but his approach centres on Haneke as a national film-maker, the flag bearer for an industry that otherwise sees little international recognition.[12] Only Fatima Naqvi, in her 2007 study of the pervasive rhetoric of victimhood since 1968, *The Literary and Cultural Rhetoric of Victimhood*, attempts a comprehensive analysis of Haneke's films in their entirety, in a chapter devoted to his articulation of questions of sacrifice and oppression within his body of work.[13]

It seems that the early academic interest that Haneke's films inspired has not quite developed in keeping with his work. Outside these four (or two and two halves of) books, the literature on Haneke is limited to articles in scholarly journals and – more frequently, it must be noted – the popular press. The principal points of interest that these articles raise are usually linked to questions of violence within Haneke's cinema or to the socio-political content of Haneke's films, with a few critics such as Robin Wood and Christopher Sharrett reading Haneke's films as 'contemporary morality tales'.[14] In their treatment of ethics, such approaches are typical of the 'American moralist' school of criticism involving, for the main part, a predominantly narrative focus. In other words, they focus on the morality *within* the hermetically sealed filmic world, rather than between the film and the viewer. In thus doing they overlook, to my mind, a crucial aspect of the experience of watching a Haneke film: the spectator's experience of the film as it is pertinent to themself.

It is with a sample of spectatorial responses to Haneke's films that I shall begin the book, examining the critical reception of his films and the perceived problems that arise from Haneke's work in Chapter One, paying particular attention to the authorial figure of Michael Haneke. I discuss how this authorial figure arises through the films, and argue that, as such, we cannot take the director's intentions alone as our starting point for an analysis of the ethics of spectatorship: although we may, and indeed will, refer to the director as the intentional origin of the films in order to understand them, we should also take into account the director as the product of the films. For what we are concerned with here is not decoding the 'objective' meaning of Haneke's oeuvre, so much as understanding the subjective experience of it. To better understand the stylistic rendering of questions of morality and film-viewing arising from Haneke's films, I propose a theory of ethical spectatorship, one that is rooted in the history of the spectatorship theory, going from Sergei Eisenstein via André Bazin to Jean-Louis Baudry and Christian Metz, but which also moves beyond it.

As we have already noted, the various positions which more recent theories of spectatorship see as both existing and potential are dominated by concerns with the problem of ideology. By reframing these arguments in terms of ethics, we can discern an implicit ethical problem within ideology critique, which centres upon a set of tensions between activity and passivity, emotion and reason. A similar set of tensions has been articulated conceptually in the moral philosophy of Immanuel Kant, who discusses the ethical conflict between the human, or as he terms it, 'man's' 'instinct' or 'inclination', and one's 'considered' or 'intellectual' awareness of his situation in the world. I therefore introduce Kantian ethics as a model for analysing Haneke's critical aesthetic, in order to discuss how Haneke's films make the underlying ethics of ideology critique explicit and primary. I argue that, above all, they bring into play the Kantian conception of the ethical agent as caught between two impulses: the impulse towards rationality and responsibility on the one hand, and the impulse towards pleasurable experience and away from unpleasure on the other. The experience of these conflicting impulses is characteristic, I shall argue, of responses to Haneke's films.

The individual films which illustrate how this is the case are treated in the following four chapters. Chapter Two explores Haneke's early Austrian films – *Der Siebente Kontinent, Benny's Video* (1992) and *71 Fragmente einer Chronologie des Zufalls/71 Fragments of a Chronology of Chance* (1994) – in relation to existing cinematic models. The three films experiment with modernist technique, both in the sense of a pure, aesthetic modernism as in the films of Chantal Akerman, and of a more politicised, aggressive modernism, as in the later films of Jean-Luc Godard. Consequently, here I introduce the terms 'first generation modernism' (or benign modernism) and 'second-generation modernism' (or aggressive modernism) in order to distinguish between these models. The distinction between the two forms will become significant in later analyses of Haneke's film-making. However, although Haneke makes some attempts in the early films to rework modernist techniques – employing them for moral rather than political effect – they nonetheless remain highly derivative, never really stepping out of the shadow of counter-cinema. The films thereby reiterate the position of ethical spectatorship that counter-cinema offers the spectator, or rather fails to offer. The chapter thus examines how the film-historical frameworks that the early films draw upon preclude them from producing a radically different position for the spectator.

Following this examination of the trilogy's operating aesthetic, Chapter Three looks at Haneke's subsequent development of benign and aggressive modernist techniques, and his superimposition of an additional cinematic framework onto them. In *Funny Games* (1997) the director brings generic convention to bear on the spectator's relationship to the screen. Providing an extended analysis of the relationship between first- and second-generation reflexivity in creating 'unpleasure', and the implications of the unpleasurable effect upon the audience in Haneke's films, the chapter raises questions concerning narrativity and impact. I examine how the experience of unpleasure upon watching *Funny Games* parallels the Kantian conception of morality as a struggle between emotion (or instinct), and reason (or intellect). We can compare the position created for the spectator of *Funny Games* to that of the Kantian moral agent: in both cases the individual must choose between a desire for pleasure and an acknowledgement of their moral responsibilities. Drawing an analogy between the cinematic viewing situation in which people seek entertainment and critical oblivion, and Kant's conception of humanity as always and naturally drawn to seek pleasure and avoid unpleasure, I claim that, in both cases, an ethical imperative arises at the point at which rational awareness of self and society operates in contradistinction to the pleasure drive. This would account for the feeling of unpleasure that Haneke's films give rise to, manifested as discomfort, anger, even shame or guilt.

Looking back to the Eisensteinian notion of 'impact', I also elucidate the difference between the impact produced by Haneke's films and that reached through montage cinema. For the impact that arises out of Haneke's films differs from that which arises out of Eisenstein's in its creation of an individuated spectator response, rather than a collective response. In Haneke's films, impact does not consist in the spectator having specific thoughts and ideas that are directly related to the film image, as it does in Eisenstein's propaganda films. Rather Haneke uses first- and second-generation modernism, operating in tension with a generic framework, to encourage an open-ended form of moral reflection upon the film, whereby each spectator must strive to find their own position. In this respect, I shall contend, moral spectatorship of Haneke's films can be seen as a case of coming to terms with one's personal moral relationship to the film.

Chapter Four looks at the resolution of the generic framework with first and second-generation modernism in the three films which follow *Funny Games*: Haneke's first three French-language works, *Code inconnu*, *La Pianiste* and *Le Temps du loup*. Here, I examine how the shift that Haneke makes from a national to an international context is reflected by developments in both extra-cinematic strategies (such as marketing, promotion) and intra-cinematic strategies (such as the narrative and reflexive techniques discussed in the previous chapter). I look at how Haneke's positioning of the spectator as an ethical subject is further developed within this body of work, as well as discussing some of the problems that arise as he negotiates the three frameworks. The key problem in the post-*Funny Games* films is situated at the border between coercion and spectatorial autonomy. On one level, Haneke's films become more controlling of their spectators in order to preclude over-simplistic or aggressive responses to the films; that is, to preclude what we might term the 'wrong' responses. But at the same time Haneke attempts to avoid over-determining what the alternative to these 'wrong' responses should be; that is, to render the spectator autonomous. He does not offer a 'right' response, for the only correct response to Haneke's films is to reach one's own conclusion. How Haneke seeks various solutions to this somewhat paradoxical situation is the prime focus of Chapter Four.

In Chapter Five, I return to the 'moral' emotions of shame and guilt, introduced in Chapters Three and Four. Drawing on psychological research into these emotions, I specify the way in which they are specifically linked to self-awareness and self-appraisal but also to aggression, which perhaps offers some explanation for strong negative reactions to Haneke's films. I then turn to an extended analysis of *Caché* as both exemplifying Haneke's project of placing the spectator in a specifically moral relationship to the cinematic image, and of representing this project on a diegetic level. *Caché*, I shall argue, represents the most complete harmonisation of form and content in Haneke's body of works, in addition to functioning as a comment on Haneke's cinematic project, its strengths and weaknesses.

The chapter concludes by analysing the link between Kantian ethics, the 'moral spectator' of Haneke's films and the notion of moral perfectionism, as taken from Stanley Cavell's philosophical writings on film. As will be demonstrated in earlier chapters, Haneke's films refuse clear answers to the problems they pose, both within the narrative and in relation to how we perceive them. Instead, they encourage an individual engagement with these problems. Haneke's project of moral spectatorship relies precisely on each viewer having a different relationship to the film, and so creates a cinematic form to which the spectator's response is personal and subjective. At this point, the Kantian analogy ceases to be useful, for the spectator's relationship to Haneke's film does not result in a moral output, as Kant would have the experience of morality do. Instead we find in Cavell a model of how ethics can be experienced as a constant striving to understand the moral questions raised in any given situation, to see these clearly and to take responsibility for one's part in that ethical situation. This Cavellian model of spectatorship credits the viewer with an unprecedented autonomy. But it also carries with it a considerable burden of responsibility, and it thereby refuses the spectator any possibility of seeking refuge from the world in the darkness of the cinema. This refusal of flight from one's ethical position in the world is precisely, I argue, the endpoint that Haneke's films strive towards.

As this brief description of my methodology demonstrates, throughout the book I simultaneously proceed on a film-analytic and a theoretical level in order to fully integrate textual considerations with theoretical ones. Individual films are examined with reference to the particular issues and problems which they raise, and I trust this dual approach clarifies the ethical issues that arise from Haneke's oeuvre and their theoretical context while simultaneously stressing the changing nature of Haneke's moral project.

The study is thus organised along two axes. On the one hand, it attempts to provide a context for the theoretical problems that arise from Haneke's films, and so moves from existing theoretical and film-historical models to an analysis of Haneke's place in relationship to these models. Within this context, Kant and Cavell serve as our two philosophical guides to the ethics of Haneke's model of film-making and the position that it offers the spectator. Kant allows us to understand the way in which ethical questions present themselves and the manner in which we respond to them psychologically and morally, by providing us with an analogy in the form of his moral agent. Cavell helps us to see why it is important that Haneke is working today – what benefits and responsibilities it offers the modern spectator, living in a post-political society in which individualism is prized above all else. As a contemporary writer with an acute awareness of the unique tensions which make up twenty-first century life, Cavell can help us understand the significance of Haneke's model of ethical spectatorship to us as spectators.

On the other hand, the book discusses how Haneke's own approach to the positioning of the spectator develops in the course of his career. It considers the manner in which, as Haneke moves from national to international film-maker, his audiences change alongside his films. Without straying too far into the terrain of reception studies, some interesting insights offer themselves as we analyse the changing nature of both film and audience, and consider to what extent one affects the other. Haneke's films engage in an ongoing dialogue with their audiences. As we will see in some detail, Haneke particularly targets specific film-going publics, the spectators he feels are most in need of the position of ethical spectatorship that his films offer. Through extra-cinematic factors, his films lure these spectators in; and once they are sitting comfortably inside the cinema he attempts to teach them something about their relationship to the film-going experience. In this manner his films (in their formal construction and their self-representation outside the cinema) are extremely manipulative, positioning the spectator in a rather determined manner. But at each step in his oeuvre, Haneke at least appears to take into account the way in which responses to the previous films were formulated, offering the most recent film as *his* response. Spectatorial reception thus comes to influence the film, as well as vice versa. And, in this way, the position of ethical spectatorship that Haneke's films offer their spectators is reformed and refined, tailored to what the director terms the 'willing consumers of the cinema of distraction'.[15]

The project's focus necessarily imposes boundaries. I do not systematically cover all of Haneke's feature films in depth. Are some of the films more worthy of attention than others? I do not believe so, although there are critics who would undoubtedly disagree with me. But some do have a greater relevance to the main concerns of this book than others. *Funny Games* and *Caché* stand out as two high points within Haneke's project of positioning the spectator morally. For this reason, I devote an entire chapter to each of these films. At the other end of the spectrum, *Das Schloß* was originally made as a television film, receiving a cinematic release only after Haneke's growing reputation made that a financially astute move. A period adaptation of sorts, it notably moves away from the world of modern technology, and with it Haneke's critique of the cinematic medium, which is one of the lynchpins in his ethical positioning of the spectator. Accordingly, this film does not receive extended treatment here.

Nor, for that matter, do any of Haneke's earlier works made specifically for television. While Haneke's early style informs his later work, his television films present a very different position for the spectator since they are produced specifically for home audiences rather than the cinematic spectator. The director himself has stated that, on a formal level, there is little consistency between the television productions and the later films.[16] An inquiry into how accurate this claim is would certainly yield some fascinating insights; unfortunately, however, it is outside the scope of this book.[17]

Given the limited nature of this study's focus, it also does not deal with other, vital aspects of Haneke's work. His French films – particularly *Code inconnu* and *Caché* – can be, and have been, considered as socio-political inquiries into the dynamics of modern European society and its multicultural integration. As mentioned, this territory has been explored by Robin Wood and Christopher Sharrett amongst others. Haneke's remarkable ability to elicit superlative performances from his actors is evident in the outstanding work contributed to his films by Ulrich Mühe, Susanne Lothar, Arno Frisch, Juliette Binoche, Annie Girardot, Benoît Magimel, Isabelle Huppert and latterly Naomi Watts, amongst others. Although I will consider the director's use of stars briefly, I do not devote substantial attention to performance or characterisation. A detailed assessment of the production history of Haneke's collaboration with producers Veit Heiduschka and Marin Karmitz, cinematographers Christian Berger and Jürgen Jürges, and editors Nadine Muse and Andreas Prochaska also falls outside the purview of this study.

It is similarly impossible within the restrictions of this work to extend my inquiry into the ethics of spectatorship very far beyond Haneke's films and the light that they can shed on conventional cinematic practices. This is unfortunate, since the inquiry into the ethics of spectatorship has only just begun, and a great deal more work on the subject is required.[18] Hopefully this book is one step in the right direction. What it offers, of course, is just one way of conceptualising the ethics of the viewing situation. But I hope that it can perhaps open the way for a systematic inquiry into the ethics of film spectatorship, and suggest a new direction for research in the field of ethics and film.

# Notes

1. Simon Blackburn, *Ethics: A Very Short Introduction* (Oxford: Oxford University Press, 2003), p. 2.
2. G.W.F. Hegel, *The Phenomenology of Spirit*, trans. A.V. Miller (Oxford: Oxford University Press, 1967).
3. Blackburn (2003), p. 5. In the case of the photograph, Blackburn is referring here to Hung Cong ('Nick') Ut's 'Accidental Napalm Attack, 1972'.
4. I use this term to refer to a school of thought that comes primarily from the United States. However, it should not be taken too literally, for its members are not exclusively American: for example, Robin Wood, who sometimes (although not always) writes in this tradition, was born in the U.K. and is presently based in Canada.
5. Raymond Carney, *American Vision: the Films of Frank Capra* (New York: Cambridge University Press, 1986).
6. Carney (1986).
7. See, for example, Jean-Louis Baudry, 'Ideological Effects of the Basic Cinematographic Apparatus,' *Film Quarterly* 28(2): 39–47 (1974–5); Christian Metz, *Film Language: A Semiotics of the Cinema*, trans. Michael Taylor (New York: Oxford University Press, 1974); Peter Wollen, 'Godard and Counter-Cinema: Vent d'Est' (1972), in *Readings and Writings* (London: Verso, 1982); and Laura Mulvey, 'Visual Pleasure and Narrative Cinema' (1973), in *Visual and Other Pleasures* (London: MacMillan, 1989). Further discussion of the slippage between the political and the ethical that takes place around this time is in Chapter Two.
8. D.N. Rodowick, *The Crisis of Political Modernism: Criticism and Ideology in Contemporary Film Theory* (Berkeley: University of California Press, 1994).

9.  Bertolt Brecht, *The Threepenny Opera*, trans. J. Willet and R. Mannheim (London: Methuen, 2000[1929]), p. 55.
10. A situation which is thankfully – and not before time – beginning to alter as a result of *Caché*'s critical success: at the time of writing both BFI Publishing and Wallflower Press had anthologies devoted to Haneke in the pipeline, and the 2007 Society of Cinema and Media Studies conference had several panels devoted entirely to Haneke's films.
11. Alexander Horwath (ed.), *Der Siebente Kontinent, Michael Haneke und Seine Filme* (Wien: Europeverlag: 1991); and Alexander Horwath and Giovanni Spagnoletti, *Michael Haneke* (Torino: Edizioni Lindau, 1998).
12. Willy Riemer (ed.), *After Postmodernism: Austrian Film and Literature in Transition*, Riemer (Riverside, CA: Ariadne Press, 2000).
13. Fatima Naqvi, *The Literary and Cultural Rhetoric of Victimhood* (Basingstoke and New York: 2007).
14. Christopher Sharrett, 'The World That Is Known: An Interview with Michael Haneke', *Cineaste* 29(3): 28–32 (Summer 2003), p. 28.
15. Haneke, in Anon., 'Beyond Mainstream Film: An interview with Michael Haneke', in Riemer (2000), p. 161.
16. See, for example, the interview with Michel Cieutat: 'Entretien avec Michael Haneke', *Positif* 478: 22–29 (December 2000), p. 24.
17. I devote some consideration to this question, as well as to the question of how Haneke's films are experienced differently by home audiences and cinema audiences, in an essay to be featured within an anthology on Haneke edited by Ben McCann and David Sorfa, to be published by Wallflower early in 2009 under the provisional title *The Films of Michael Haneke: Europe Utopia*.
18. Although one giant leap has been made recently: see Daniel Frampton, *Filmosophy* (London: Wallflower, 2006). Published too late to inform this book, Frampton's work is a significant intervention in contemporary dialogue around film and ethics.

*Chapter 1*

# THE LAST MORALIST?

In an essay he contributed to a compendium on the films of Robert
Bresson, Michael Haneke describes the reaction of the audience at the
1983 Cannes Film Festival to the decision to award Bresson that year's
Special Jury Prize. As Bresson, called up by Orson Welles, stepped on to
the stage, 'an acoustic battle broke out between those booing and those
acclaiming him'.[1]

Haneke's description of the event might just as easily be applied to
the audience's reaction when Haneke himself was called up to receive
his prize for Best Director at the 2005 Cannes Film Festival: some
audience members booed; others stood for an ovation, but the noise
did not subside until Haneke had left the stage. What could have
caused this uproar? The bleak vision of contemporary society that
Haneke's films present is not always easy to stomach, but it cannot be
the content of Haneke's films alone that is responsible for the outrage
his films inspire. As the director puts it, 'films that tell of the lamentable
state of the world are in abundance at every festival; the more cosily
and stylishly they settle themselves in our anguish, the greater the
chance the jurors and journalists will thank them for it'.[2] Indeed,
perhaps this is more the case now than ever before: the numerous
awards and critical acclaim garnered by *La Pianiste*, and more recently
*Caché*, have cemented Haneke's status as one of a new generation of
*auteurs* currently leading European cinema, alongside (amongst others)
the Dardenne brothers, Catherine Breillat, Lars von Trier, Gaspar Noé
and François Ozon, all of whom have been known to offer dismal –
even nihilistic – perspectives on the current state of society. But
although these directors have their admirers and detractors, none of
them, arguably, provokes the intensity of feeling that Haneke's films do.
Today, he seems to be one of the most contentious directors working in
European cinema, and one of its most divisive.

Despite the controversy that surrounds Haneke's films, there have
been curiously few attempts to engage in depth with what it is that
makes his films so provocative. This book is in part aimed at trying to
redress this imbalance, to counter the visceral responses to Haneke's

films with an intellectual, analytical response, and over the course of this enquiry I hope to legitimise Haneke's films as objects open to further study, to bring them to the attention of other scholars and theorists. I am of course aware of the contradiction in using a theoretically oriented study to discuss the visceral responses that Haneke's films give rise to, for in describing these responses, and the aesthetic structures that give rise to them, we deprive them of their immediacy and therefore their power. This reservation is increased by Haneke's own scepticism about scholarly interpretation – or indeed any interpretation – of film, especially of a biographical or *auteur*ist approach. For instance, in an interview released as part of the pressnotes to *71 Fragmente einer Chronologie des Zufalls*, he dismisses the idea of having recourse to the author's biography in order to explain a film's deeper meaning, stating that he, 'provide[s] a construct and nothing more – its interpretation and its integration into a value and belief system is always the work of the recipient'.[3] But some understanding of who Haneke is will be essential to an understanding of his unique work as a film-maker and of two essential aspects of his work: the cinematic and historical traditions which influence both the form and the effect of his films; and the apparently accusative stance his films takes toward their spectators. It is for this reason that we shall begin with a brief look at Michael Haneke's biography.

## Haneke, Cinematic Traditions and Historical Contexts

Biographical information on Haneke is very limited. The few published biographical sketches are usually the result of direct demands from journalists and are thus 'composed' and schematic, and would require additional contextual support. Fortunately, Alexander Horwath, a prodigious academic but also an acquaintance of Haneke, provides a very detailed account of Haneke's personal and professional development in his book *Der Siebente Kontinent*.[4] I am deeply indebted to Horwath for most of the biographical information concerning Haneke's personal life that I have reproduced below.

   Haneke's background is that of the left-leaning bourgeoisie. Born on 23 March 1942 in Munich to Beatrix von Degenschild, a Catholic actress, and Fritz Haneke, a Protestant theatre director, the young Michael Haneke was raised by one of his aunts in Wiener Neustadt, a working class suburb of Vienna where he attended the Gymnasium, the Austrian equivalent of a British grammar school. Perhaps naturally in the light of his parents' professions, his main academic interests were drama, music and literature, and he hoped to become an actor or concert pianist (film and music, he agrees with Tarkovsky, have a surprising amount in

**Figure 1.1** Michael Haneke.
*Courtesy of the BFI stills department. Permission graciously supplied by WEGAfilm.*

common). Lacking sufficient talent for his first and second choices of career, however, he enrolled to study Psychology, Philosophy and Drama at the University of Vienna.

His studies completed, Haneke worked as a film and literary critic for various regional newspapers and the national *Die Presse*. Horwath points out that he was, in many ways, a walking cliché of a young bourgeois intellectual in the early 1960s: interested in philosophy (above all existentialism), in modernist literature (Lawrence Durrell, D.H. Lawrence and Thomas Bernhard), and the so-called 'art cinema' of Fellini, Bergman, Antonioni, Bresson and the directors of the French *nouvelle vague*, in particular Jean-Luc Godard.[5] Like those directors, it was by writing about film that Haneke discovered film-making; like them, he was a cinephile before he became a cineaste. And it is clear that he was very impressed by the films that were being released around this period: his nominations for *Sight & Sound*'s 2002 poll of several hundred directors' and critics' top ten best films include Robert Bresson's *Au hasard Balthasar* (1966), Pier Paolo Pasolini's *Salò o le centoventi giornate di*

*Sodoma* (1975), and Michelangelo Antonioni's *L'Éclisse* (1962).[6] Echoes of these works reverberate throughout Haneke's own films: as we will see in due course, his early influences evidently stayed with him.

Haneke's directing career, however, began not in cinema but in the theatre, in Germany. In 1967, after staging several plays as a student, he began working for the Südwestfunk Television Company. In the meantime, he continued to write as a critic and as a screenwriter, although he saw more success with the former: having been subsidised 300DM by the Austrian equivalent of the Film Council to write his first screenplay *Wochenende/Weekend*, no producer was willing to option it, and it eventually fell by the wayside. Frustrated, he left Südwestfunk at the beginning of 1970 and began to direct plays independently. First was a production of Marguerite Duras's *Ganze Tage in den Bäumen/Whole Days in the Trees* at the Stadttheater Baden-Baden. There followed engagements in Darmstadt (for example Kleist's *Der zerbrochene Krug/The Broken Jug*) and Düsseldorf (Hebbel's *Maria Magdalene*, Strindberg's *Der Vater/The Father*), then later throughout Germany – in Berlin (Bruckner's *Krankheit der Jugend/Sickeness of Youth*) and Hamburg (Enquist's *Die Nacht der Tribades/The Night of the Tribades*) – as well as Austria (such as Goethe's *Stella* in Vienna's renowned state theatre).[7] By the early 1970s he had established a name for himself as a talented and capable director, and envisioned a long lasting career within the theatre.

Then in 1973 Südwestfunk contacted him again, offering him the chance to direct his first television film for them. *After Liverpool*, from a screenplay by James Saunders, marked the beginning of Haneke's career as a cine-televisual director, and he went on to write a total of twelve more television films, of which he directed ten, including an adaptation of Josef Roth's *Die Rebellion/The Rebellion* (1993). In fact Haneke continued to make films for television right up until the end of the 90s, when he adapted Kafka's *Das Schloß/The Castle*, although Haneke's producers, Wegafilm, also gave the film a cinematic release, an attempt to cash in on Haneke's increased profile as a Euro-*auteur*, much to his apparent displeasure.[8] Since I am concentrating here on the films made for cinematic exhibition, I do not intend to treat *Das Schloß* or any of these television works in much detail.[9] However, as mentioned in the introduction, clear precursors of Haneke's mature style exist in the television work: the reflexivity of *After Liverpool* (1974); the sparse, cool, adaptation of *Drei Wege zum See/Three Ways to the Lake* (1976); the intensely personal appraisal of a generation in *Lemminge/Lemming* (1979); in *Wer war Edgar Allen?/Who was Edgar Allen?* (1984), a game of reality, cinematic reproduction and identity; in *Fräulein/Madam* (1986), a demythologising of 1950s melodrama. Already Haneke's early cinematic influences can be perceived in the television films: Andrea Lang, for example, describes the collective works as demonstrating a concern with 'isolated individuals and understated relationships', portrayed, 'in a style reminiscent of Robert Bresson'.[10]

*Der Siebente Kontinent*, Haneke's first cinematic feature, was released in 1989 to a warm reception. It was selected for presentation at Cannes, shown in the 1990 New Directors/New Films series at the Museum of Modern Art, New York and selected that year as the official Austrian entry for 'Best Foreign Language Film' at the Academy Awards. Following this success, *Der Siebente Kontinent* became the first part of a trilogy, followed by *Benny's Video* (1992) – winner of a Felix, the European Film Award, for Best Film, and shown in competition at the New York Film Festival that year – and *71 Fragmente einer Chronologie des Zufalls* (1994), again a Cannes Film Festival selection and winner of a Golden Hugo award. Over the course of these three films the director developed the formal style that had come to characterise his work,[11] a very precise, controlled aesthetic that minimises cutting and camera movement, introducing, in Lang's words, 'a new aesthetic paradigm into Austrian cinema'.[12] Haneke followed the trilogy with *Funny Games* (1997), another German language film. The last film he was to make in the German language (although not in Austria – the film was shot in Italy), the critical response to *Funny Games* was much more mixed than for previous films, as it was attacked for exploiting the violence it supposedly deplores. But doubtless as a result of its controversial nature, the film was a commercial success and brought the director international recognition. Haneke was subsequently courted by actress Juliette Binoche and producer Marin Karmitz to make a film in France, which became *Code inconnu* (2000). Returning to Austria, but this time with (predominantly) French backing, he then made *La Pianiste* (2001) – set in a Vienna where the inhabitants speak French and starring acclaimed French actress Isabelle Huppert. The film garnered prizes at Cannes and numerous other festivals, and Haneke was to work with Huppert again for the less successful (in both commercial and critical terms) *Le Temps du loup/The Time of the Wolf* (2003) – a 'surprise' non-selection at Cannes[13] – before collaborating once more with Binoche on *Caché* (2005), which won him the Best Director prize at Cannes and has been by far the most profitable of Haneke's films to date.[14]

This biographical material – taken, as I mentioned above, mainly from Horwath – opens out onto two fields of contextualisation that inform our understanding of Haneke's films. The first is particularly prominent in Horwath's own reading of social and political concerns in Haneke's films, having to do with Haneke's status as an Austrian director, raised in a specific national cultural climate. The second is historical, relating to Haneke's formative artistic influences and the cultural debates that surrounded them. I have already commented on the influence of Bresson, Antonioni and Pasolini, amongst others, on

Haneke's film style, and indeed, in his sixties at the time of writing, Haneke seems to belong in temperament and spirit with this earlier generation of European film-makers. In the pages that follow, I shall treat each of these influencing factors in turn, starting by placing Haneke's work within a tradition of Austrian film-making, very much influenced by Austria's political history, before moving on to examine the resonances of 1960s and 1970s film and theory in Haneke's work.

## An Austrian Film-maker

Film historian and theorist Thomas Elsaesser perhaps best sums up the international perception of Austrian cinema when he writes that Haneke's fatherland, 'is not a film-producing nation, and – its cinema being no exception – that Austria's fate has been to be overshadowed by Germany, the powerful neighbour to the north'.[15] There is some irony in the fact that the above quote is taken from Elsaesser's rather short entry on Austrian cinema in the *Bfi Companion to German Cinema*;[16] nonetheless, Elsaesser goes on to point out two important factors that complicate this apparently self-evident assessment. Firstly, Austria has, almost since the beginnings of the cinema, nurtured an indigenous 'commercial' cinema production sector which had its golden age in the first half of the century but was revived, to some extent, by Ernst Marischka's hugely successful *Sissi* trilogy (1955–1957), starring Romy Schneider (a childhood friend of Haneke's). This production sector may be comparatively small (1,009 silent films between 1907 and 1930, 197 sound films between 1930 and 1945); even so, it amounts to a distinct cinematic tradition, and certainly in its early years it boasted a distinct set of themes and genres over a lengthy period. Secondly, Elsaesser explains, since the 1960s Austria has developed a unique cinematic voice in the area of experimental and art cinema, associated with names such as Peter Kubelka, Kurt Kren, Peter Weibel and Valie Export, demonstrating a pronounced antagonism to postwar Austrian society and the Austrian state apparatus, which the young film-makers of the 1960s castigated as corrupt, hypocritical and mired in its fascist past.[17]

More pertinent to an understanding of Haneke's work, however, is the group of film-makers that Elsaesser describes as following in the wake of Kren, Weibel, Kubelka et al.: the 'New Austrian Cinema' of Franz Novotny and Peter Patzak. While less formally extreme than their antecedents, these directors also focused narratively on their country's relationship to its fascist past. Their films, psychological studies of socially representative individuals, depict an urban underclass at odds with the values, but also deprived of the benefits, of the prosperous Austrian 'Second Republic' (Novotny's *Die Ausgesperrten/The Excluded*,

1982). Or else they go to the countryside, where the Alpine idylls of summer tourists and skiing instructors peel away to reveal still lifes of brutalising everyday existence in the provinces, as traditional peasant structures make way for Mafia-like agribusiness and political wheeler-dealing (Christian Berger's *Raffl*, 1984).[18] Some combine the Nazi past with the traditional Austrian provincial theme, such as Wolfram Paulus's *Heidenlöcher* (1986). A key term of this cinema is *abreagieren* (giving vent to frustration), encompassing violence within the petit-bourgeois family, silent rages and sexual humiliations, a culture of resentment that leads to racism, xenophobia and anti-semitic aggression, all phenomena which have marred Austria's liberal self-image.[19]

These films stand at a mid-point between the twin poles of mass entertainment and extreme 'art' cinema that preceded them in Austria. Peter Patzak, for example, works the above ideas into popular genre films, such as *Kassbach* (1979): fascist attitudes in everyday life, hatred of foreigners and political corruption are the film's primary subjects, while Patzak's use of dialect and lower-class heroes, as well as borrowings from classic cinematic genres such as action thrillers, attract wide audiences.[20] His films, like those that make up the New German Cinema movement, can also be said to reflect a wider thematic concern with complicity in Austrian culture from the 1960s onwards. The writers Thomas Bernhard and Elfriede Jelinek, and the modern artists Marlene Haring and Hans Schabus, have examined their society's complicity in the spread of National Socialism, women's oppression and the perpetuation of the class system.[21]

Haneke's films are thus a continuation of an ongoing tradition of social criticism and popular art that has a specifically Austrian slant to it. In the cinema, this tradition is represented by the films of Berger, Novotny, Patzak and Paulus; in literature, by Bernhard, Peter Handke and Jelinek. The latter in fact notes the similarities between her own work and Haneke's, 'I, like Haneke, in so far as I know his work, am better able to criticise society from a negative perspective ... [p]recisely because even the positive clichés are so stifling'.[22] And indeed, Haneke's adaptation of Jelinek's *Die Klavierspielerin* (*La Pianiste*) doubly underlines his standing in these filmic and literary traditions, for it was also shot by New Austrian Cinema director (turned cinematographer) Christian Berger.

Robert von Dassanowsky claims Haneke as a distinctly Austrian filmmaker, arguing that we can also see in the form of Haneke's films the fragmentary, subjective concept of Viennese impressionism. He furthermore situates Haneke's work within a broader context of Germanic culture, making a link between reflexivity within Haneke's films, the distancing effects of Brechtian theatre, and the rejection of the false totality of art that Benjamin saw as a strong contribution to the aesthetic/political aim of Fascism.[23] This reflection of the Benjaminian view in which mankind's self-alienation has reached such a degree that it can experience its own destruction 'as an aesthetic pleasure' leads us back into a consideration of Haneke's interest in complicity and cinema. And, with its references to Fascism, it also leads us to Austria's elephant in the corner: the country's complicity with the Nazi regime. While Haneke may have never tackled this subject directly, its undertones resonate throughout his films. For example, the violence that occurs in each of his films is (superficially at least) polite, rational, almost genteel. Relegated for the most part to the off-screen space, it is a violence with a peculiarly fascist resonance, for it is chilling, cold and calculated, rather than cathartic. More profoundly, his use of reflexive devices to expose the spectator as complicit with the cinematic apparatus (which we will discuss in depth over the course of this book) is analogous with the ongoing exposure of Austrian society's collaboration with the Nazi regime, as Dassanowsky claims.[24]

It is perhaps no surprise, then, that a number of critics have hastened to posit Haneke as a specifically national film-maker – that is, a film-maker concerned primarily with his home nation – and to argue for readings of his Austrian-language films in particular as a comment on contemporary Austrian society. Brigitte Peucker, for example, in her article 'Fragmentation and the Real: Michael Haneke's Family Trilogy' describes *Der Siebente Kontinent, Benny's Video* and *71 Fragmente einer Chronologie des Zufalls* as, 'a body of texts concerned at the thematic level with the situation of the bourgeois family in contemporary Austria … reflected at the level of cinematic style [by] strategies used to fragment or attenuate narrative'.[25] But while Peucker's analysis of the trilogy affords many insights, Haneke has long railed against his films being seen as treatments of specific national situations. Ever since a journalist asked him, at the Cannes screening of his debut feature, whether 'Austria is really that bad [as it seems in Haneke's films]?' the director has stressed the universality of his films' 'messages', stating that, 'my films don't specifically target Austria,' but 'have to do with the entire advanced industrialised world'.[26] He explains: 'That's the classical means of defense [sic] against my desire to make people aware of certain problems. It's the typical sweeping under the carpet of uncomfortable elements. It has nothing to do with the nationality of the film'.[27] While this 'sweeping under the carpet' is certainly a phenomenon familiar to Austrians – one which Robert von Dassanovsky sees as characteristic of postwar Austrian cinema – Haneke is keen to stress that it is by no means confined to his fatherland. Rather, he claims, it is characteristic of a European bourgeois approach to all that is problematic, be it political or personal. This brings us, then, to the second context in which we must consider Haneke's work, that of European cinematic and cultural-theoretical traditions, most significant amongst which, in this context, is modernism.

## A Modernist Film-maker in a Postmodern Era

Alexander Horwath and Paul Arthur have both written about the importance for Haneke of the European film-makers he admired in his youth, especially Bresson, Antonioni and Pasolini. References to the great modernist film-makers abound in his work as in his conversations, and examination of Haneke's innovative work over the past two decades readily reveals his connection to the modernist tradition. On a superficial level, his films recall the utopianism of John Cassavetes (*Variation*), the spirituality of Bresson (*Der Siebente Kontinent*) and Tarkovsky (*Le Temps du loup*), the visual metaphors of Antonioni (the child who pretends to be lame/blind in *Il Deserto rosso/Red Desert* (1964) and *Der Siebente Kontinent*; the destruction of material objects at the climaxes of *Zabriskie Point* (1970) and *Der Siebente Kontinent*). He even goes so far as to 'quote' the first scene from Bresson's *Une femme douce* (1969) in *Wer war Edgar Allen?* (the scarf of a suicide victim floats slowly down a river). Formally, modernism is reflected, for example, in the early films through the withholding of narrative information and of psychology, ellipsis, fragmentation and foregrounding of the medium, all of which conspire to provide a 'clarifying distance' that will transform the viewer from 'simple consumer' to active evaluator.

Like the great modernist film-makers, Haneke clearly defines himself against the dominant conventions of mainstream (Hollywood) film. He describes the trilogy of *Der Siebente Kontinent*, *Benny's Video* and *71 Fragmente* as 'a polemic against the American cinema of distraction',[28] and in his notes to *71 Fragmente* he writes:

> I attempt to provide an alternative to the totalising productions that are typical of the entertainment cinema of American provenance. My approach provides an alternative to the hermetically sealed-off illusion which in effect pretends at an intact reality and thereby deprives the spectator of the possibility of participation. In the mainstream scenario spectators are right off herded into mere consumerism.[29]

In this statement, there are clear echoes of modernism's hostility to mainstream culture and the Althusserian position that sees dominant cultural forms as vehicles of ideology, positioning the spectator as its unwitting victim – a position that we will discuss in more detail in subsequent chapters. Such statements make it explicit that Haneke is not drawing on the formal conventions of modernism, but allying himself with its fundamental theoretical principles. His films belong to a modernist tradition both in form and intention, conforming to many of the categories that Peter Wollen sets out in his call for a modernist 'counter-cinema',[30] as we shall discuss in Chapter Two.

To call Haneke a 'modernist' then is not only to connect the formal qualities of his work with the formal qualities of an earlier school of film-making, but also to understand that his work has a relevance to its time, to comprehend the precise ways in which it connects with the modern-day social climate in which he is working. And it is true that at the same time as they look back to an earlier age, Haneke's films are very much tied to the currents of the social era in which they are produced, the connections between the films and this social era being complex and multifaceted.

These connections occur on a thematic level: in the later films' concerns with European integration (*Code inconnu*), post-9/11-style disasters (*Le Temps du loup*), and postcolonial aftermaths (*Caché*). But they are also present in the more generalised depiction of an alienated Western society, in which communication has broken down and our lives are mitigated by the media of television and film. If Haneke's films are critiques of Western society's emotional glaciation, as Brigitte Peucker claims, then it is clear that he sees this society as being defined in no small part by the way in which television and cinema have eroded our ability to connect with the real. In an interview with Michel Cieutat, Haneke explains that he has been witness to television's invasion of the domestic sphere and its hijacking of the cinema's unique pleasures.

> I am part of a generation which was able to grow up without the continual presence of television. So I was therefore able to learn about the world directly, without any intermediary. Today, by contrast, children learn how to perceive reality through television screens, and reality on television is shown in one of two ways: on the one hand there are documentary shows, and on the other fiction. I think that the media has played a significant role in this loss of any sense of reality. ....[31]

Over the course of his lifetime, Michael Haneke has seen television supplant cinema, and eventually transform it. He is a child of the modernist era, and yet he is working in a postmodern period (or perhaps even a 'post-postmodern period'): a time when the joys of the cinema, as celebrated by Truffaut and the young Godard, are past; when the ideologically pernicious potential of the cinema has been discovered, dismantled and discussed; when critics such as Jean Baudrillard and Slavoj Žižek can write of the disruption between the 'virtual' and the 'real'. The very etymology of media suggests something of the mediation of perception that has now become a norm. Cine-televisual representation is no longer a new and exciting phenomenon, but something quotidian: we take for granted its presence in homes, hotels, aeroplanes and arenas, public houses and public spaces.

Of course, cinema and television are not the same thing, but they influence each other, ape each other. The brute power of the impression created by the larger-than-life dimensions of the screen upon a one-off visit to the cinema has been matched and indeed overtaken by the mass of impressions and their permanent presence. The rapid editing and jump cuts that were so innovative when Godard first introduced them, when Arthur Penn and Sam Peckinpah developed them into their cinema of 'ultraviolence',[32] are now the hallmarks of MTV and television shows such as *ER*. Likewise, Peckinpah's slow motion montages are now a standard means of stylising gunplay in film and television alike. Little matter that when Peckinpah first introduced this aesthetic of violence into cinema it was intended to shock audiences into a realisation of violence's true horror, it has now become the norm. Television can take what is most strange, captivating and unique from the cinema and turn it into something domesticated, ordinary, even *boring*, simply through its ubiquity.

So any director working today – notably those working within Hollywood – faces the challenge of how to respond to this set of cine-social circumstances, in which film constantly has, to borrow Ezra Pound's phrase, to 'make it new', in order to grasp the spectator's attention by distinguishing itself from television. Some film-makers, such as Quentin Tarantino, have made a return to a joyous celebration of cinematic spectacle for its own sake. For Tarantino and his ilk, the imperative is to always go one better, and this has led to a constant striving for intensity. Others, such as Oliver Stone and Peter Weir, have attempted to use cinema to comment on our mediatised culture, in which reality and representation have lost all sense, with varying degrees of success.[33] Like these directors, Haneke wants his films to be reflexive, to theorise themselves. But he also wants them to break with dominant cine-televisual forms.

One way in which he attempts to forge this break is by looking back towards an earlier moment in film history, to the modernist techniques of deconstruction and distanciation that operate in the works of Michelangelo Antonioni and Chantal Akerman, for example. The director's first three films – *Der Siebente Kontinent*, *Benny's Video* and *71 Fragmente einer Chronologie des Zufalls*, dubbed the 'emotionale Vergletscherung Trilogie' or the 'emotional glaciation' trilogy[34] – are concerned thematically with narcissism, abjection and the coldness of personal contacts in the age of video, themes that echo those of the German films *Die Angst des Tormanns beim Elfmeter/The Goalkeeper's Fear of the Penalty* (Wenders, 1972) and *Warum läuft Herr R. Amok?/Why Does Herr R. Run Amok?* (Fassbinder, 1970), in which sudden violence interrupts into otherwise quotidian existences. They are marked by a disciplined, sparse style predicated on ellipsis and fragmentation, the eschewal of narrative information and developed character psychology, and the foregrounding of the cine-televisual medium. As mentioned above, references to the films of Antonioni, Akerman and Robert Bresson proliferate: for example, Haneke's first film, *Der Siebente Kontinent*, alone draws on scenes from *Il Deserto rosso*, *Jeanne Dielman, 23 Quai du Commerce, 1080 Bruxelles* and *Pickpocket* (Bresson, 1959), as we shall discuss further in due course. Conforming to many of the 'cardinal virtues' that Peter Wollen sets out in his call for a 'counter-cinema' that will negate dominant mainstream forms of representation, these three films belong firmly, then, to a modernist tradition in theme, form and intention.

But while the films making up the trilogy were critically acclaimed, they were not particularly commercially successful outside Austria and Germany,[35] and it is worth noting that of the three, only *Benny's Video* saw a public theatrical release in the U.K. (although not in the U.S.), and with the exception of a U.S. VHS release of *Der Siebente Kontinent* none of the three early films were available for home viewing in the U.K., the U.S. or France until late 2006.[36] Perhaps as a result of the lack of commercial recognition that his early films saw, Haneke appears to develop an increasing awareness of contemporary audience expectations. Around the time of the release of *Funny Games*, increasing references to television begin to appear in his press statements and interviews. He claims that 'works of art which carry a message are regarded with contempt by a younger generation influenced by American mass culture,' and states: 'You can't pick your audience, and an audience has an education behind it, especially if you have an audience that's from the school of television ... I think you are really naïve with the first film because every film prompts different reactions, and you often get the opposite from what you expect because the audience is very different. ...'[37] One of the ways in which Haneke's later films distinguish themselves from his early, Austrian-language work is in their awareness of mainstream audience expectations, and in their deliberate courtship of them. Specifically, the two films immediately following the trilogy – *Funny Games* and *Code inconnu* – both introduce a new aspect of commercialism into Haneke's films, which will be more thoroughly integrated into his subsequent works. In the case of *Funny Games*, commercial concerns take the form of generic conventions; and in *Code inconnu*, the use of stars. Subsequently, the films are loosely based on genre forms and feature star actors in the lead roles.

These aspects become key characteristics of the marketing campaigns for each film. Pitching to a wider audience as he moves from the national forum to the international, Haneke's films become more seductive, apparently changing tack in order to lure in a wider, more international audience. The technique appears to be effective, for his stylistic development coincides with an increase in distribution and viewing figures for Haneke's films that occur after his move to France.[38] And indeed, the move to France might in itself be seen as part of an attempt to court a wider audience, for French-language films are more widely distributed, and consistently perform better, in the international market than German-language films.[39]

This developing commercialism has led to accusations of 'selling-out'. However, some careful attention to the films themselves, as well as to the industrial metatexts surrounding them (such as distribution, exhibition and promotion contexts), reveals that Haneke deploys generic convention and star power carefully, circumscribing them within the modernist framework that operates within his earlier films. Not for Haneke the cinephilia and homage of Tarantino, nor the youthful aggression of Gaspar Noé, the sarcasm of Todd Solondz or the apocalypticism of David Fincher: Haneke's later films continue to be marked by an austerity and maturity that appears the result of age and education. He clearly seeks to distinguish himself from the younger generation of directors who are influenced by television, and aligns himself firmly with the professionals of a past era: 'The younger generation is more and more influenced by American films and television so there is a huge difference between them and the generation that grew up without television'.[40] So in his early work, Haneke embarks upon a cinematic project that echoes the modernist strictures of deconstruction and alienation, before making a key shift from a position in which he completely rejects the dominant conventions of mainstream cinema in the same manner that Godard and Bresson do, to one that reflects the views of Hans Eisler, an equally radical critic of the culture industry, that the interaction of audience and cinema contains revolutionary potential: 'There is an ingredient of truth in what the public expects of cinema: ... [B]ehind the shell of conventionalised behaviour patterns, resistance and spontaneity still survive'.[41] And this resistance is to be found in part in the legacy of early cinema: 'To the extent that the motion picture in its sensationalism is the heir of the popular horror story and dime novel and remains below the established standards of middle-class art, it is in a position to shatter those standards, precisely through the use of sensation, and to gain access to collective energies that are inaccessible to sophisticated literature and painting'.[42] Haneke's later films still mobilise the modernist reflexivity of the earlier films, and they moreover introduce a more aggressive form of reflexivity, characteristic of the later work of Jean-Luc Godard for example. Coupled with the seductive structures of genres and stars, this deployment of reflexivity bridges a gap between the modern and the postmodern. Or, put otherwise, the films are an attempt to put together the two potentials of bourgeois high culture and popular film culture. Haneke, like Brecht and Eisler before him, rejects the arrogance of experts who prevent modern works from reaching a wide audience because they presume to know in advance what the masses want and can understand.[43] Rather, in order to highlight the spectator's complicity with the cinematic apparatus, he *asks them* what it is that they want and they understand.

> As soon as the spectators find themselves alone with the questions posed by the story, without instructions for their ready interpretation, they feel disturbed and begin to assemble their defenses. A productive conflict, I would think. The more radically the answers are withheld, the sooner they will have to find their own.[44]

His incorporation of commercial convention into his films is thus indicative of an aggressive strategy, a desire to lure in his audiences and a willingness to argue with them rather than merely trying to please them. In this respect, his position once more echoes that of Brecht, Eisler and Adorno: an artist must try to make the best art possible; to make things less well than one could so as to be popular leads nowhere, ethically or aesthetically. His approach is perhaps best summed up in Walter Benjamin's much-cited dictum: 'The public must always be proved wrong'.[45]

## Responses to the Films

If Haneke sets out to contradict the audience's assumptions about his films, his approach in the films from *Funny Games* onwards is not without its own contradictions. Haneke's later films have passionate defenders: for Robert Horton (writing of *Funny Games*) he is a 'modern master'.[46] Peter Matthews (on *Le Temps du loup*) claims that his flaws 'put the successes of other directors to shame',[47] and for Paul Arthur (on *Caché*) his films, although they may offer unwelcome sights, are to be avoided 'at our peril'.[48] Haneke, Arthur states, may be the only director working today who 'possesses a creative sensibility befitting our contemporary climate of dread, disgust and rage'.[49] However, others feel his films go too far, and are too concerned with 'extreme' cases. While Haneke's early works brought some moderate criticism along with the critical acclaim they received, ('Haneke has always been called "cold", "distanced", "intellectual", "analytical"', says Christian Berger,[50] Haneke's cinematographer on *La Pianiste*) his later films produce much more vitriolic responses. For Tony Rayns (on *La Pianiste*), he is 'conspicuously humourless',[51] for Fiona Morrow (on the same film), 'aggressive'.[52] Always seen as somewhat gruelling, following *Funny Games* – and then *La Pianiste* – his work has become synonymous with rigorously controlled, punitive scenes of pain and alienation, and has earned him the dubious sobriquet 'The Master of Everyday Horror'.[53] And at times, the controversies that have swirled about his films threatened to overshadow his achievements. Jonathan Romney – writing in 1998 – sees Haneke's films as constituting 'a terrorist attack on the audience'[54] – a remark which, post 9/11, becomes heavily loaded. Mark Kermode, on *Funny Games*, goes even further: 'rarely has a filmmaker exercised such perverse precision in his desire to torment an audience who have paid to watch his work, but for whom he clearly harbours unbridled contempt'.[55]

Kermode's comments exemplify a set of critical attitudes to Haneke, and in particular (although not exclusively) to *Funny Games*. These attitudes take the position that the director occupies *within his films* to be authoritarian, sadistic and morally suspect, with critics claiming that there is a paradox in the director's regular insistence that the spectator work out the answers for themselves at the same time as he so vehemently asserts his own authority over his films. For does the knife not cut both ways? If Haneke's work is meant, at least in part, as an indictment of the viewer's complicity in the cinematic spectacle, then what does this say about the director who incites this complicity? The apparent hypocrisy of a director who criticises those who collude with the cinematic spectacle while leaving those who put it on screen untouched has been most precisely articulated by J. Hoberman in his 1998 review of *Funny Games* for the *Village Voice*, in which he writes:

> Symptomatic of the fascist mind-set is the self-righteous application of a strict code of civility from which the ruler himself is naturally exempt. Thus, Haneke despises the mass audience's vicarious pleasure in make-believe mayhem while demonstrating his own capacity to dish it out. The most honest aspect of Haneke's movies is the evident satisfaction the director derives from the authoritarian aspects of his position – demonstrated most spectacularly in Funny Games when the worm, as it were, finally turns. The wheel is rigged so that only Haneke can win.[56]

## Haneke's Authorial Persona

What Hoberman's remark has in common with the vast majority of negative responses to Haneke's films is the way in which he focuses upon the question of the director's intentions. This approach to the analysis of a film-maker's work is somewhat surprising, for it runs counter to dominant trends in critical analysis. For some years now, theories of film criticism have been marked by anti-intentionalist attitudes, disdaining or at least downplaying the relevance of the intentions (and related mental states) of the makers of art objects. Nonetheless, the particular attention that such responses pay to the director's intentions, the peculiarly personal attack that Haneke's opponents make on him – rather than on his films – merits some consideration. What is it that diverts the critics' attention away from the films and towards the film-maker?

Perhaps, one might argue, Haneke's authorial persona is so visible because his films are marketed as 'Michael Haneke' films. It is a consequence of the cinema's 'youth', when compared to literature and the classical arts, that the director, so often still alive at the time that their work is being written about, is frequently able to inform critical reception of their own films. And of course today, television and increased media circulation allow interviews with those involved in a film's production to be published and read around the world at the time of a film's release – often before – and the publicity machine that surrounds not only Hollywood, but also European productions, encourages and even enforces a film's stars and directors to speak out about it as much as possible. No doubt, the *politique des auteurs* has never really ceased to be prominent within film theory and criticism. As David Bordwell has put it, if the author really is dead, critics regularly perform séances in order to speak with them.[57] Indeed it is true that *auteur*ism has in no small part influenced the content of this book which, after all, is about the films of Michael Haneke, or at least those works made under the aegis of an authorial function 'Michael Haneke'.

Yet it is unlikely to be wholly due to metatextual concerns that criticism tends to focus so often on Haneke's intentions, for he is notoriously publicity shy and reticent to discuss the 'meanings' of his films, telling Christopher Sharrett, for example, that: 'I have no interest in self-interpretation. It is the purpose of my films to pose certain questions, and it would be counterproductive if I were to answer these questions myself'.[58] While he is willing to discuss the concerns that inform his films, as is illustrated by the comments on the previous pages, Haneke becomes silent when asked for an 'explanation'of any of the works. We could make the argument that this hard-nosed rejection of traditional interview practice and reputation for evasiveness contributes, in a Salinger-esque manner, to how we perceive the director. So Nick James, interviewing Haneke for *Sight & Sound*, describes the director as 'convivial, relaxed', but 'guarded', and goes on to conclude that as a director, Haneke is 'reluctant to play anybody's game but his own'.[59] Or Fiona Morrow, in the *Guardian*, claims that: 'There is something cynical in [his] refusal to engage in discussions of the meaning of the work, made more acute in his enjoyment in stirring up an audience for the sake of it'.[60]

Doubtless there is some truth to Morrow's claim. Nonetheless, the biographical reticence of Haneke, who refuses to comment on his personal life or history, is also likely to be the result of his modernist effort to efface the author in favour of the work. Biographical information about artists in general, Haneke has said, is 'not very interesting'.[61] He expounds:

> My films irritate and provoke some people; critics then look for an explanation that will allow them to safely put the films aside … [T]hey could say, the *auteur* who made this film is a negative person, he is pathological, and that's why his films look this way. That is one possibility. But since my private life is not available to the public – I have never published anything about myself – they can't say what I'm like, so this reason does not apply, they can at best speculate about it.[62]

The more significant effect of this refusal to discuss the content of his films is then to push us back towards the films themselves in order to seek answers. His reticence about his own biography is therefore also connected to a position his work takes regarding authorship and subjectivity. With his 'real' presence largely effaced, 'Michael Haneke' emerges as author first and foremost through his films.

To illustrate how this is the case, let us reconsider Kermode and Romney's views that Haneke 'torments' and 'attacks' the spectator. The choice of verbs here implies that the spectator is victim, the director the torturer. These negative perceptions of Haneke take not the *real* person as their target then, but the *reel* person. Such responses are based on two perceived factors within Haneke's films: authorial authority (the director as torturer) and spectatorial unpleasure (the spectator as tortured). The two points are inextricably linked. The unpleasurable effect of Haneke's films ruptures the pleasure drive that Haneke sets in motion through his use of generic structures and brings the spectator into a position of awareness. This allows the spectator a dual form of knowledge about the film. At once, they become aware of themself, sitting in the auditorium, as a consumer of the film. But at the same time, they become aware of the film as a construct, the product of a director. The *auteur* is a spectator effect linked to unpleasurable film viewing: the spectator, made uncomfortable by the cinematic experience that they participate in, sees not just the film, *but also its author*, as the source of this unpleasure.

So the author emerges through the film: indeed as an imagined figure he is a product of the film – the *reel* Haneke – just as, as a real object, the film is a product of an individual film-maker – the *real* Haneke. The tendency to equate the two is perhaps natural. Indeed the figure of 'Michael Haneke' of which we speak within this book is an institutional figure in which personal intention is certainly a component but in which the status of the director's statement is at the same time not that simply of a source or document but that of an element in the discursive construction of the films. When analysing spectatorial response to the film, it is important to bear in mind how this spectator-based figure of the *auteur* is different from a conventional intentional *auteur*. For whereas conventional *auteur* theory takes the figure of the director and uses it as a key to unlocking a film's iconography and meaning, here the spectator watches the film, and through their experience of it they construct a notion of the director.

Succinctly put, the brutality of Haneke's films prompts spectators to ask themselves a question which centres on two points of awareness. Why, they ask, is *the director of this film* doing this *to me*? This is precisely the question that this book will engage with. But we cannot take the figure of the director that arises through the films as an intentional origin to explain the films, for it is through the films themselves that this figure arises. Although throughout this book we will refer to the director as the intentional origin of the films in order to understand them, we must also take into account the director as the product of the films. For what we are concerned with here is not decoding the 'objective' meaning of Haneke's oeuvre, so much as understanding of the subjective experience of it; that is, the experience of Haneke's films for their spectator.

## The Critically Aware Spectator

Critical responses to Michael Haneke's oeuvre make it clear, then, that there is something problematic about his films for the spectator. This problem is perhaps best articulated by Amos Vogel, when he writes that, 'the extremities to which Haneke goes in withholding information are ultimately difficult to take or define'. Vogel claims that '[Haneke's] style and cinematic approach can lead to a kind of transcendence, a heightened sense of engagement on the part of the spectator',[63] but that nonetheless, 'Haneke's stated intention to have the viewer come to his own insights and explanations presupposes, in its purest form, a level playing field that cannot exist,' precisely because cinema is 'an inherently manipulative medium'.[64] It seems that the spectator of Haneke's films is at once manipulated and forced to be autonomous, and, as we saw in the last chapter, this creates a very peculiar position for them, one that is often experienced as uncomfortable, even distinctly unpleasant.

If Vogel's description of the paradoxical nature of Haneke's films is correct, then naturally it will be difficult for audiences and critics to know how to respond to the particular problem that Haneke's films present, whereby they are both subject to and responsible for the cinematic spectacle. Manipulation and autonomy seem to be diametrically opposed. How, we might ask, can one be both directed and independent at the same time? Film theory and film practice has tended to take the mutual exclusivity of the two for granted, basing itself upon an either/or principle: either a film is manipulative of its spectators, thereby conveying a 'message' or producing a unilateral audience effect; or it accords them choice, in which case it may be much more ambiguous in terms of meaning. This tendency to draw a clear line between manipulation and autonomy goes back to the roots of spectatorship theory and extends into its more recent articulations: for the history of film spectatorship also has at its heart a conflict between manipulation and choice, beginning with the opposition between the formative conception of film as put forward by Sergei Eisenstein and the realist view of the cinematic phenomenon advocated by André Bazin and extending into, and beyond, the apparatus theory of Jean-Louis Baudry and Christian Metz.[65]

The subject positioning that Baudry and Metz describe as taking place in classical narrative cinema makes it naturally impossible for the spectator to criticise his own habits of perception in film-viewing or the modes of perceptual intelligence that the films themselves display, and this is a key assumption with Haneke's cinema.[66] This is not a universally accepted conclusion, and there has been vigorous theoretical debate as to whether or not this is indeed the case. In particular, Noël Carroll has argued that the semiotic theory of illusion is based on a very dubious assumption: that the spectator mistakes the representation of an object for the real thing, confusing film and reality. Carroll states that if we believe this, then the argument that a film can emancipate the spectator from the constraints of interpellation by allowing them a position of awareness is self-contradictory. This is because, in the case of the theorist for example, the subject constructed in representation is supposed to be able to recognise the real character of representation, and hence his or her own constructed nature. If this is possible, Carroll argues, then Baudry's theory cannot be true, and film theory that weds a lack of awareness to the critique of modernity in a manner that is other than metaphorical is thus mistaken, based upon a profound over-valuation of the power of representations that indicates a misunderstanding of the way in which representation affects cognition, whether positive or negative.[67]

But Carroll's argument is not entirely convincing. Just because it is *possible* for a subject to recognise the illusory quality of cinema, it does not automatically follow that every subject will always be *capable* of thinking through its logical consequences (or for that matter, *willing* to – a matter to which I will return in due course). It is not inconsistent with Baudry's thought and subsequent appropriations of it by other theorists to state that the spectator is unaware of the way in which they are positioned by the cinematic apparatus *unless something happens to make them aware of it*. Once the subject has become aware of the manner in which classic realist cinema interpellates them – through watching an avant-garde film or reading Baudry's writings, for example – they may henceforth view films in a new light, 'free' from the subject positioning of which they were formerly the construct. This is a process of induction into thinking critically about films that many film critics, academics and genre fans alike will be familiar with, having gone through it themselves. But it is by no means a given.

Carroll's argument falls down, then, because he places too great an emphasis on the spectator's conflation of a representative image with what it represents. Various theories of spectatorship, developed from apparatus theory, have contended that we do not mistake what we see on screen for something real, offering instead a more nuanced view of what happens to the spectator's self-consciousness as they watch a film. Richard Allen, for example, has claimed that film is an efficient producer of what he calls a projective illusionism. This phenomenon involves no creation of a false belief. Instead 'you', as a viewer:

> do not mistake a staged event for actuality in the manner of a reproductive illusion; rather you lose awareness of the fact that you are watching a recorded event that is staged before the camera … When you imagine that you look upon the events of the film 'from within', the frame of the image circumscribes the limits of your visual field rather than signalling to you that what you see is a projection of a recorded image … In projective illusion, the spectator occupies the perceptual point of view of the camera upon the events of the film.[68]

Gregory Currie, in his more recent article 'Film, Reality, and Illusion', goes one step further. He argues for 'impersonal imagining', whereby the viewer imagines the events of fiction taking place, but does not imagine being in a specific spatio-temporal relation to these events. Taking the example of Mark Twain's novel *Huckleberry Finn*, he argues that the reader imagines Huck floating down river, but does not imagine being *there* with him. Similarly the film viewer of *Psycho* (1960) imagines Marion being attacked in the shower, but does not imagine being there in the shower to share the experience. Currie's account of impersonal imagining implies that we not only lose awareness of the artificial nature of film, but that we lose awareness of *ourselves* watching that film, so caught up are we in the narrative situations that it causes us to engage imaginatively with.[69]

What is common to the accounts offered by Allen and Currie, and to those offered by Baudry, of the spectator's relationship to the screen, is not a confusion between the real and the represented object (we do not believe the onscreen image is part of the reality in which we exist), but rather a perceived *lack of awareness* on the viewer's part of their actual circumstances – their physical situation within the cinema and their existential position in the world outside the cinema – while watching a film. The imaginative pull of classic realist cinema does not allow us to be caught up in on-screen events and at the same time to be aware of ourselves, as viewers, sitting in the cinema. This is why if we have a toothache, or are sitting in an uncomfortable seat, or if the person seated behind us is eating their popcorn very loudly, our pleasure in the film is diminished: we cannot be totally oblivious to our actual situation and so cannot submit ourselves totally to the images on screen. To Haneke, classic realist film positions the spectator as passive by inducing a total suspension of awareness on their part. The spectator, when prompted, would of course admit they are watching a film, they know it is not real, but while in the cinema – if the film is successful – they are conscious of nothing but what is happening on screen. In this sense, classic realist cinema merits its frequently given appellation the 'dream screen'. The spectator, immersed in the pleasure of film-viewing, ceases to be aware of their self or their situation; they do not confuse what they see with reality, but simply cease to be aware of the concept of reality or any other lucid concern, unless prompted to do so by something within the diegesis or by an external factor that breaks the spell that the film casts.[70]

## Ethical Film, Ethical Theory

The idea that the spectator was not thinking independently – or worse yet, not even thinking at all – but was being manipulated by the mechanisms of the cinematic apparatus, has been a cause of apprehension amongst film-thinkers and film-makers for several decades now. For the majority of theorists working in the 1970s and 1980s, the interpellative effect of the apparatus that Metz and Baudry describe assumed a negative value for, as Carroll has pointed out, the very concept of ideological interpellation has 'a pejorative force … ordinarily we do not want our ideas and our thinking corrupted by outside influences'.[71] The notion that one's thought processes could be 'corrupted' or at the very least 'influenced' in the manner we might associate more readily with hypnotism, subliminal advertising or, in more extreme terms, 'brainwashing', implied that the spectator must be prone to the machinations of an other, and the cinema was, therefore, perceived as either sinister or outright oppressive. The concerns of many were summed up by Joan Copjec, who makes explicit the implications of Baudry's description of the spectator as 'chained', 'captured', 'captivated': words which, Copjec exclaims, 'we ordinarily associate with imprisonment'.[72]

In spectatorship theory up until the late 1970s, the cinema is then conceived in one of two ways. On the one hand, it is seen as a form of mass culture whose effect is perniciously manipulative and which positions the spectator as passive, as in the writings of Metz and Baudry: in this account, the spectator of classic realist films is positioned as passive, but believes themself (according to Baudry) to be an active, unified subject.[73] On the other, it can be celebrated as a new art form with the potential not simply to model, but to engineer, a state of liberated active consciousness, of critical awareness, as in the formulations of post-1968 film theorists.[74] Characterised by a militant hostility to commercial, narrative cinema as well as a commitment to radical politics and formal experimentation/'counter-cinema' (a term coined Peter Wollen in his 1972 essay on Jean-Luc Godard's *Le Vent d'est*) is defined by two goals.[75] The first is to allow the spectator a position of critical awareness and thereby to reveal to them the inherent illusionism of the cinematic apparatus. The second is to involve the audience member in a political struggle by making them conscious of his interpellation by standard cinematic institutions; and indeed, in keeping with the ideological theory that precedes or coincides with them, counter-cinematic films are generally very political, two of the most frequently cited examples being Godard's *Le Vent d'est* (1970, made in conjunction with Groupe Dziga Vertov) and Chantal Akerman's *Jeanne Dielman, 23 Quai du Commerce, 1080 Bruxelles* (1976). But whatever specific causes might motivate the film-maker, counter-cinema always involves an attack on the cinematic apparatus *in its totality* as an instrument for perpetuating ideology. For once the subject is free from cinematic interpellation, Wollen claims, he or she will be able to see the 'truth' of their situation.[76]

This is the binary opposition that post-1968 film theory makes between classic realist cinema and counter-cinema, and these are the two positions that it sees as being open to the spectator. We can sum up our position at this point as follows: post-Baudry, political-modernist theory eventually reaches the position that classic realist cinema interpellates the unwitting spectator, holding them hostage to the apparatus effect. The cinema's own attempt to counter this is, as we have seen, to produce counter-cinema. And Michael Haneke's films are to some extent part of this counter-cinema, since they present an alternative to classic mainstream film.

Indeed, by opposing his cinema to mainstream offerings, the position that Haneke invites the spectator of his films to assume seems, in many ways, to reiterate that offered by counter-cinema. Certainly his comments on the contemporary culture industry echo many of the statements made within the discourse of political modernism. He writes, for example, that: 'the [Hollywood] film has succeeded in transforming subjects so indistinguishably into social functions, that those wholly encompassed, no longer aware of any conflict, enjoy their own dehumanisation as something human, as the joy of warmth. The total interconnectedness of the culture industry, omitting nothing, is one with social delusion'.[77] Likewise his approach within his films to this problem mirrors that of a number of counter-cinematic and modernist film-makers who have sought to make a political critique of modernity through an exposé of the ways in which the cinematic apparatus can interpellate the spectator, drawing heavily on reflexive devices to reveal something about the viewing situation to the spectator. And indeed, we have already noted that the influence of counter-cinema on Haneke's works is more than evident: today, there are numerous critics who hasten to align him with directors such as Godard and Akerman.

Yet Haneke doesn't quite fit into a position hitherto captured by the discourse of political modernism, for his films produce a drastically different response from those associated with the counter-cinema movement. This much is clear from the critical response to the films: when were film-makers such as Chantal Akerman or Jean-Luc Godard ever referred to as 'terrorists', 'hypocrites', or 'fascists'?

How then, does Haneke's critical aesthetic diverge from that of counter-cinema? An attempt to broach this question will expand over the pages of this book, but a first answer presents itself in terms of the object of Haneke's critique. Reflexive devices are employed within Haneke's films, as in counter-cinema, as part of an attempt to create a position of awareness, but in Haneke the object of this awareness is not primarily the ideology attached to the individual film, or even the cinematic apparatus as a whole: his films are not critiques of modernity in the most general sense, nor do they set out to bring the political reality of the spectator's situation to their attention. Rather, they prompt the spectator to think about their own participation in the cinematic institution. Their focus is the spectator's consumption of, and voluntary interaction with, this ideological vehicle. So, while in most counter-cinematic films reflexive techniques are intended to distance the spectator from the action of a film, to call them into awareness of themselves, and thus allow them to survey the film with a critical eye, Haneke instead appears to use the same devices not to reveal the reality behind ideology but to involve the spectator in a consideration of the relationship between film and film-viewer.

For despite being critically aware, the spectator of counter-cinema is still positioned as passive; that is, as an innocent 'victim' of the cinematic apparatus, whom it is the responsibililty of the counter-cinematic work to 'rescue'. Haneke however creates a third position for the spectator, revealing them as *willingly* passive, and asking them instead to be active – at least in a mental sense – and to take responsibility for their part in the workings of the cinematic institution. Here, formal reflexivity is mobilised in service of personal, rather than institutional, reflexivity; that is, in encouraging the spectator to think about themself, and their already existing moral principles. The films therefore offer a reorientation of counter-cinematic techniques, using them not to ask how we are victims of cinematic interpellation, but how we collude in it. And in so doing, they prompt a reorientation of the way in which we think about the spectator–screen relationship. The position Haneke offers the spectator is not to do with the subjectivity of *belief*, but rather the subjectivity of *moral choice*.

This being the case, the shift in focus which takes place between counter-cinema and Haneke's cinema cannot be fully accounted for by existing theoretical approaches to spectatorship, which confine themselves for the most part to questions of meaning-making and awareness. While there is a wealth of critical debate surrounding the question of how the cinematic apparatus controls and positions the spectator, this debate has, as we have seen, primarily taken place on a political level: while couched in ethical language (as any discussion involving value judgments needs to be), it does not take ethics as its primary concern. Apparatus theory and its variants are adequate for explaining counter-cinema, which is likewise concerned with political questions. But Haneke's films are concerned with ethics, and so something more, or at least something different, is needed in the discourse of spectatorship theory in order to discuss them. To fully understand the position that Haneke's films offer the spectator we need an *ethical* theory of film, a theory that disengages from the overt concern with politics which characterises ideology critique, and focuses instead on the morality of the viewing situation.

## The Ethical Imperative in Ideology Critique

One way in which we can begin to think about film in terms of ethics is by turning to the moral philosophy of Immanuel Kant. Why Kant? Primarily because the key set of relations that form the basis of Kant's conception of morality are those of activity and passivity, action and belief: the same relations with which, as we have seen, much of spectatorship theory is concerned. Secondly, as we will come to see, Kant also perceives a tension between reason and emotion as central to understanding morality. This tension is present within the discourse of political modernism, which perceives the two as diametrically opposed. But the subtle nuances of Kant's conception of the relationship between reason and emotion are more accurately reflected by Haneke's films. Basing our ethical spectatorship theory upon Kant's moral philosophy can then help us to understand something about the special way in which Haneke's films position their spectators, as well as allowing some insights into the ethics of other film-makers and other films.

Let us begin by attempting to reframe existing spectatorship theory in terms of Kantian ethics, in order to see what common moral underpinnings there are between Haneke's films and counter-cinema. Retaining the gendered terms of the original, for Kant man's capacity for rational thought is what allows him to make moral decisions upon which he acts, and so it is this capacity that allows him to be autonomous and therefore responsible for his actions and his beliefs. We have seen that the spectator of classical realist cinema exists, at least in the eyes of the apparatus theorists and political modernists, in a state of suspended awareness. This they saw as politically dubious, since it deprived the spectator of the possibility for rational engagement with the film, and allowed them to be interpellated by the cinematic institution. Since ideological interpellation posits a subject through coercion, the subject stands in a relationship to the cinema that they have not thoroughly considered. The state of suspended awareness that the spectator exists in when watching a classic realist film therefore points to an ethical problem inherent to the cinematic institution. Kantian ethics can clarify this problem for us. For if, as Kant claims, what makes moral agents is our power of *reason*, then the restrictions that classic realist cinema places on our faculty of critical awareness negate the spectator's capacity to be a moral agent.[78]

In this model, classic realist cinema, on the level of spectatorship, does not invite a moral response. Individual films may assert a particular set of values which we subconsciously accept – Leslie Brill and Raymond Carney are among those critics who have argued that many Hollywood films promote moral values on a narrative level[79] – but while the narrative level of a classic realist film might involve an ethical content, this is negated by the process of spectatorship itself. Hollywood cinema's interpellative effect is premised on our inability to make rational judgements while watching a film, and this suppression of awareness that characterises the viewing situation logically prevents us from having the ability to be morally aware. For how can one be aware of the ethical dimensions of a situation if one is not aware of that situation in the first place? The only way in which a film's moral content can be consistent with moral agency is if the spectator can assess that morality and make their own judgement about it, rather than reproducing the film's moral outlook as a result of being ideologically interpellated.

This is the basic ethical problem implicit within apparatus theory. And herein too lies the ethical imperative underlying the production of counter-cinema. If the faculty of critical awareness – within the Kantian framework – is a necessary condition of any kind of autonomous thinking, then any filmmaker seeking to create a film that positions the spectator as an independent thinker must break the spell of cinematic illusionism, just as advocates of political modernism suggest. Critical awareness is a necessary condition for ethical awareness, and although it is not the only condition it is the primary one. Counter-cinema's use of cinematic reflexivity to negate the cinematic illusion allows the spectator to become critically aware of the medium's workings and is a first step towards allowing the spectator to also become *ethically* aware of the medium's working.

For apparatus theorists and counter-cinema film-makers, then, the filmic institution may have its own implicit ethics. They may not explicitly state their moral take on the cinema, but it is there, if we are willing to look closely enough. In seeing critical awareness as a necessary criterion for spectatorship, political modernists oppose themselves to the ethical void of Hollywood cinema; and in granting the spectator rational awareness, counter-cinema opens the way for him to become morally aware. However, in identifying moral problems with political problems theorists such as Mulvey and Wollen also present a very definite agenda. So the ethics of film that emerges out of the discourse of political modernism is by its very nature politically conditioned, and the 'pure' pursuit of ethics is a secondary concern in the face of political imperatives: because they are inessential, ethical concerns are not fully worked through here.

## The Cinema as Refuge from the World

There is an ethical concern that is implicit, but unresolved, within apparatus theory and counter-cinema. However, this concern does not have to do with the act of spectatorship, but rather with the act of film-making. That is, it consists of the view that Hollywood cinema's positioning of the spectator in a position of suspended awareness is morally problematic, and that the film-maker therefore has an ethical imperative to produce a work that breaks with cinematic illusionism and thereby grants the spectator the opportunity to engage critically with the cinematic image. Haneke has another concern, as we have seen. This is not to do with the *fact* of the spectator's suspended awareness, but with the *act* of suspending awareness: that is, it is do with the spectator's own willing submission of their critical faculties to the pursuit of spectatorial pleasure.

For an elucidation of how this change in focus, from film to viewer, impacts on our understanding of Haneke's critical aesthetic and its relationship to ethics, we must turn away briefly from Kant and towards Stanley Cavell. But before we do so, a caveat of sorts is necessary, concerning Cavell's dual status as both a philosopher and a film analyst. The disjunction between Cavell's writings on individual films and genres in books such as *The Pursuit of Happiness: The Hollywood Comedy of Remarriage* and *Contesting Tears: The Melodrama of the Unknown Woman*,[80] and his philosophical works such as *The Claim to Reason*, is quite disconcerting. His film criticism is concerned principally with the analysis of narrative events and is uncritical of apparatus theory and the Hollywood institution.[81] In these instances, he uses film narrative in service of philosophy, as illustration. However, in *The World Viewed* (in which he discusses the ontology of film), Cavell takes a much more general, overarching approach to his subject, providing a model of how philosophical concepts can arise through film and its theory, and thereby sheds new light on both fields of enquiry. It is an enlightening text, and one to which we will return later in this book for further elucidation of what is so unique about the ethics of watching Haneke's films.

What is important for the moment is Cavell's conception of cinema's appeal to film-goers. For Metz and Baudry, cinema's appeal lies in the fact that it appears to grant the spectator a position of total knowledge and therefore total power. It offers a scopic pleasure, whereby 'all the viewer requires – but he requires it absolutely – is that the actor should behave as though he is not being seen, and so cannot see him, the voyeur'.[82] One of the ways in which political modernism and counter-cinema therefore responded to this perception of cinema's appeal was by attempting to rupture the spectator's illusion of power. But for Cavell the peculiar appeal of cinema lies in the fact that it grants us not the power of the pornographer, but *respite from our complicity in the structuring of the world*.[83] Throughout *The World Viewed*, in his discussion of issues concerning the troubling of epistemic relations to each other and to the rest of the world, both our desires and the blocks to their gratification are given by Cavell as *ours*; all of ours, as inhabitants of the modern, Western world, sharers of a particular culture. Cinema relieves us of this burden, granting 'not a wish for power over creation … but a wish not to need power, not to have to bear its burdens'.[84]

Cavell's theory of cinema's appeal underlines the spectator's agency as a consumer of films, a point which goes to the very heart of ideology critique. We might think here of Louis Althusser's celebrated claim that there is no ideology except '*by* the subject and *for* subjects'.[85] In this statement, Althusser underlines the manner in which the subject colludes with their own interpellation and theorises the manner in which social institutions repeatedly appeal to the narcissism of human beings by calling upon them to occupy a place in the social world. The question is not one of the indoctrination of one class or sub-class by another (spectator by director, for instance) as some theorists would have it, but rather – since interpellation takes place at an unconscious level and in all men and women – of a process of socialisation, an essential condition of communal existence within any economic order.

By responding to this call, human beings define themselves as individuals who believe that their place is freely chosen, while it is in fact determined by the system that interpellates the subject.

True to its roots in Althusserian thinking, one of the most radical aspects of apparatus theory was the the way in which it extended film theory from thinking about watching a given film to thinking about cinema-going as a whole. In Baudry and Metz, the spectator's relationship to the screen is no longer discussed with reference to pictorial representations alone, but also with reference to the institution itself. However, in the wake of apparatus theory, political modernism failed to engage fully with extra-cinematic concerns. Indeed, film theory throughout the 1970s was more than a little blinkered in its emphasis on what happens inside the movie theatre between spectator and screen, and its analysis of the components of cinematic signification without full consideration of how that situation arose in the first place. The nuances of Louis Althusser's conception of interpellation are then somewhat reduced by political modernism: instead of seeing the individual as a willing participant in their own subjection, political modernism imagines that the spectator is somehow hostage to the apparatus effect, and that it is therefore the responsibility of the director to 'liberate' them, by breaking with realist conventions and allowing them to engage rationally with the film. What this position overlooks is that, at some point, the spectator has paid money for their cinema ticket and *chosen* to watch the film, to submit to the spectacle's pleasures and powers. The role of the spectator in instigating, through a desire to see and a willingness to pay for, certain cinematic images and narrative devices, is crucial to the Hollywood institution's perpetuation, as is evidenced by the integral role of genre movies to the classic studio system, for example.[86] If the political modernists are correct in claiming that the spectator is a hostage to the cinematic apparatus, it is only because they engage in a kind of cinematic Stockholm syndrome: actively participating in, and even desiring, their own subjection.

Cavell's theory of cinema's appeal can therefore help us to understand the significance of the shift in emphasis from the film-maker to the film spectator. For Cavell and Haneke alike, no longer is the question one of how the filmic apparatus positions the spectator, or even (as in the writings of Laura Mulvey, for example) how it creates pleasure for the spectator, but how the spectator *chooses to involve themself* with the cinematic object: what they watch, what their motivations are, how this is borne out within the viewing situation. In this configuration, Kantian ethics is analogous not with the morality of the cinematic apparatus but with the morality of the spectatorial experience. For Cavell's theory of cinema's appeal can be seen to mirror Kant's view that most people privately wish to return to the 'ethical

state of nature', a state in which everyone pursues his or her own desires without constraint. [87]

Children, Kant writes, exist in this state: oblivious to the concept of responsibility to the self or to others, they become moral beings *only with the emergence of reason*.[88] And while the spectator remains under the spell of the narrative, unaware of themselves or the world around them, they exist in a state akin to the Kantian 'ethical state of nature', unaware of moral imperatives and unable to apply the notion of morality to themselves. It is perhaps for this reason that we are so much more able to accept, and even enjoy, onscreen scenes or scenarios of immorality – of violence, revenge, rape – which we would never stand for outside the cinema. The oblivion we choose precludes an awareness of our moral responsibilities and of our complicity with the spectacle; that is, we cannot perceive that we are participating in the act of spectatorship, and thus cannot take responsibility for that participation.

So the spectator finds in mainstream cinema a refuge from the world of responsibility. But the desire for escape from these responsibilities is not in itself morally reprehensible. According to Kant, it is our natural inclination to act immorally when that action promises pleasure: we are so attracted to pleasure and repelled by pain that we *all* initially choose to satisfy desire rather than obey the moral law.[89] The desire to sequester ourselves in the cinema is neither good nor evil; indeed, no single want – whether wanting to steal something, or to buy something, or to subject oneself to cinema's pleasures – is morally wrong, it simply lacks intrinsic moral worth. However, Kant writes, while we are not morally responsible for our desires, we *are* morally responsible for the manner in which we respond to them.[90] As rational, thinking adults we can recognise when our desires are in conflict with our sense of moral rightness, and so make an effort to overcome them. Living a moral life is a constant struggle, for we are always torn between the laws of morality and the allure of pleasure, but we must make a positive effort to act morally. And to act morally is to assert our reason over our instinctive desire for pleasure.[91] In this case, the spectator's choice to suspend their faculty for critical awareness must be seen as an ethically problematic act, for they *deliberately choose* to suspend their faculty of reason in favour of a total submersion in the pleasures that the cinematic apparatus offers.

## Pleasure and Reason

It is the spectator's willing entry into moral oblivion or, as Haneke puts it, moral 'distraction', that constitutes the primary focus of Haneke's cinema. His films encourage the spectator to consider their own participation in the act of film-going, to reflect upon why they enter the cinema and what it is they want from the viewing experience. They encourage them to look at their motivations and the ethics of these motivations. The reflexivity of Haneke's films motivates the reflexivity of the spectator, bringing the individual self into the picture in a very particular way, as yet unrealised in counter-cinematic models, encouraging the spectator to think first and foremost about their own self.

One way in which they do this is by forcing the spectator to become aware of their personal drive towards pleasure. For the spectator to reach this position, Haneke has firstly to encourage a pleasurable relationship to the on-screen image: the pleasure drive must be set in motion, in order that the spectator can eventually contemplate it, consider what it is they want to see, why they want to see it and why the cinema encourages (or discourages) this desire. In his later films in particular, Haneke draws on the conventions of mainstream cinema in order to do precisely this, setting up each of his films as a pleasurable experience before then asking the spectator to consider the ethics of this experience.

We will attempt to understand precisely how he does this in the following chapters. For now, it is important to acknowledge that this integrative approach marks a pivotal divergence from counter-cinema which, since it functions as a form of aesthetic resistance to classic realist cinema, denying the spectator all complicity and all emotional involvement.[92] Peter Wollen states that having been conceived as its antagonist, no element of the mainstream convention is reconcilable with counter-cinema if it is to be truly radical, and since scopophilic pleasure is perhaps *the* defining characteristic of the former, it is naturally inimicable to the latter.[93] In the 1970s, this may have been a necessary move: a ground-clearing exercise that would allow for a rebuilding of the elements of cinema. But today it seems somewhat reductive. For the anti-pleasure polemic, while informing a seminal body of works, forecloses the possibility of a more productive engagement with cinematic emotions, as they are dismissed as always and inextricably the effect of manipulation. While classic realist cinema prevents the spectator from engaging with film rationally, counter-cinema prevents them from engaging with it emotionally. And in creating two broad regimes of discourse (realism and modernism, ideological and theoretical practice) opposed to each other and thus complete in themselves, political modernism could not produce critical concepts sensitive to nuances of form or meaning. D.N. Rodowick explains it thus: 'As an epistemological relation, reflexivity can only be awkwardly considered here either according to a standard that equates visibility with self-evidence in the semiotic constructedness of art, or as the doubling of a reflexive situation in the spectator whose conscious activity *simply mirrors that of the text'*.[94] Rodowick's statement emphasises that there is no room for ambiguity in the spectatorial response to political modernism, and that this being the case, its films can be just as coercive in their use of rational argument as Hollywood films are in their use of emotional manipulation.

We will use two examples in order to explain this. First, let us consider the case of Frank Capra's *It's a Wonderful Life*. When watching a classic realist film, the moral conclusion the audience arrives at – if the film is successful – is generally the one promoted through the ideological apparatus by the use of emotional persuasion. So watching *It's a Wonderful Life*, and sharing the emotional trajectory of George Bailey, the spectator eventually concludes that the ruthless businessman Mr Potter is morally reprehensible and that family, friendship and community are worthy pursuits in themselves. For this is indeed the message played out in the film's narrative, and the audience is coerced into agreeing with it through emotional affect and the prompted withholding of critical awareness. As a second example, let us take a counter-cinematic film, Chantal Akerman's *Jeanne Dielman*. In this case, the audience is also coerced into reaching a fixed moral conclusion – for example that women's everyday experience is indeed worthy of our careful attention – through the effort of intellectual concentration required and unambiguous filming techniques employed. The film involves no emotional manipulation, but rather presents itself as 'objective truth'.

Haneke's films demonstrate none of the reductiveness inherent to Wollen's arguments for counter-cinema, for although Haneke sets his films up in contradistinction to Hollywood film, the ethical impact of his later works in particular depends as much on the spectator's emotional engagement with, as their alienation from, the filmic spectacle. Nor does he slide into the kind of moralism that classic Hollywood narrative offers. The narratives of *Funny Games* and *Benny's Video* may focus on very specific social and ethical problems, while more complex questions of how people live morally in the world are approached in *Code inconnu* and *Le Temps du loup*, but Haneke presents each of these situations with little narrative judgement, leaving the spectator, positioned as a moral agent, to consider them autonomously. For example, the plot of *Benny's Video* concerns the actions of a young man who films his seemingly motiveless murder of a school-friend, and of his parents who help him to conceal his crime. Although the scenario presents us with the material for a series of ethical problems or debates, these questions are not tackled within the film itself, at least not in the way that they might be in a Hollywood film with a similar plot premise, such as Max Ophüls's *The Reckless Moment* (1949): the film's murderer is neither vilified nor justified through camerawork, editing, dialogue or acting, and no resolution is offered.[95]

Haneke's films draw on techniques for spectatorial manipulation familiar from both Hollywood cinema and counter-cinema, as we will see over the following chapters. But within Haneke's films, we will come to also see that narrative cannot simply be targeted as the origin of ideological relations in the cinema and neither can cinematic reflexivity be identified unproblematically as a critical form. For in their juxtaposition with one another, both are reframed. Drawing on Hollywood convention, Haneke mobilises emotion in order to combine it with reflexive techniques which block the pleasure drive and give rise to a moment of critical awareness. He thus creates a dialectic between emotion and reason, re-enacting the Kantian crisis in which moral reason impacts on us as human agents with a moral life that is permeated by emotions.

Within cinema, our awakened reason asserts itself upon emotions that are usually mobilised by narrative cinema, and which Haneke plays upon within his films. Encouraged into a pleasurable relationship with the film, reflexive devices strike us with an unforeseen force, as they rupture the safe, secure position of refuge we have taken up. Discomfited, the spectator becomes aware of themself as someone sitting in the cinema, engaging in an escapist pursuit. They retain their earlier desire for pleasure, but it must now struggle against the rational awareness of the cinema's manipulative structures. Due to this conflict between emotion and reason, we may say that the object of critical awareness is then itself moral, involving both our emotional involvement with the film, and the ethical implications of that involvement.

As integrative works situated between intellectual projects and popular entertainments, Haneke's films break down a binarism that begins when Bazin opposes continuity editing to montage, and continues into counter-cinema's conception of itself as a negation of Hollywood film-making. And in this way, Haneke potentially opens up a way out of the paradox that counter-cinema faced, whereby the very structures intended to create a radically different position for the spectator end up positioning them in a similar, subjected manner to those that counter-cinematic films oppose, one persuading the spectator to accept a fixed conclusion through emotional manipulation, the other through rational logic.

For the object of a morally consequent film must be to work through the specific forms of spectatorial address which are functions of the binding of narrative and space, in a manner that disturbs and ultimately cannot be contained. This is precisely what Haneke's films do, prompting us to assume a position of moral spectatorship, in which we are able to consider the content of his films and the cinematic situation (and the relationship of the two) in accordance with our existing moral principles. More than just a narrative moral schema, Haneke's works comprise a certain conjunction of elements, diegetic and non-diegetic, which contribute to their overall moral effects. His cinema is not didactic, but it is educational, for it asks the spectator questions and places them in a position whereby they are able to make up their own mind about the possible answers. As he himself puts it,

> [T]hose who produce images and information need to find out how to make the images and information fresh and perceptible once again; how to restore to them the power that derives from their potential for critical engagement. Surely that is the challenge for the film-maker. Spectators are used to the programming of television and the entertainment cinema, which present a world that is explainable and whose contradictions can be resolved. To have their craving for pacification gratified, they are willing to pay a great deal of money to the imperialism of illusion. By telling the story in a manner that refuses to be part of this kind of collusion, a film can be irritating and also productive.[96]

'Irritating' is certainly an apposite description of Haneke's films; this much we have seen. And we have also seen that the crux of the problem that many of Haneke's critics perceive in his films lies in the fact that they are at once manipulative in the extreme, but that they simultaneously demand from the spectator an individual response. The problem that Haneke faces is how to negotiate these two opposing tendencies productively; for the reception of each of Haneke's films depends greatly on how successful he is with each film in attaining an equilibrium between Hollywood convention on the one hand and reflexivity, emotional response and rational response on the other. *Code inconnu*, for example, has been described as overly intellectual and lacking in emotional engagement by some critics,[97] while *Funny Games* has been compared by others to Wes Craven's *Scream* (1996), with some younger spectators so caught up in its patterns of suspense and stylised violence that they failed to maintain the emotional distance necessary for the position of moral spectatorship for which Haneke aims.[98]

In the following chapters we will analyse the ways in which Haneke's films constitute a process of experimentation, a 'working out' of his critical aesthetic and his methods of positioning the spectator morally so that they find their own answers to the questions his films pose. As we will see, Haneke's film-making starts off from a position very similar to that of counter-cinema. But over the course of his oeuvre, this position is modified as he revises and refines his technique, in search of a 'third way' between classic realism and counter-cinema that will allow the spectator to be positioned morally. Each film compensates for flaws in the previous one. At the same time, they grow more controlling of their spectators in order to preclude over-simplistic or hostile responses to the films, that is to preclude the *wrong* responses; and become less deterministic, in order to render the spectator autonomous. Haneke cannot offer a *right* response, since the only right response to Haneke's films is to reach one's own conclusion.

# Notes

1. Michael Haneke, 'Terror and Utopia of Form, Addicted to Truth: A Film Story about Robert Bresson's *Au hasard Balthasar*', in *Robert Bresson*, ed. James Quandt (Ontario: Wilfred Laurier Press, 1998), p. 556.
2. Haneke (1998), p. 556.
3. Haneke, Pressnotes for *71 Fragments of a Chronology of Chance* (1989 Cannes screening), reproduced in *After Postmodernism: Austrian Film and Literature in Transition*, ed. Willy Riemer (Riverside, CA: Ariadne Press, 2000).
4. Horwath (1991).
5. Horwath (1991), p. 15.
6. The *Sight & Sound* top ten survey was last carried out in 2002. Results are available at: http://www.bfi.org.uk/sightandsound/topten/poll
   Haneke's response is available at:
   http://www.bfi.org.uk/sightandsound/topten/poll/haneke (last accessed 8 July 2005).
7. I have given the names of the plays as they were performed in German, as well as the English translation where available.
8. This is according to producer Veit Heiduschka, in Riemer (2000), p. 65.
9. In an interview with Richard Porton for *Cineaste*, Haneke stresses that he considers making films for television to be something quite different from making films for cinematic release, especially in the current climate. See Richard Porton, 'Collective Guilt and Individual Responsibility: An Interview with Michael Haneke', *Cineaste* 31(1): 50–51 (Winter 2005), p. 51.
10. Andrea Lang, in *The BFI Companion to German Cinema*, ed. Thomas Elsaesser (London: BFI, 1999), p. 129.
11. Haneke's producer, Veit Heiduschka, must be given some credit for this development, since it was (according to Heiduschka, at least), his idea to remove all shots in these three films that diluted their precision or pandered to the audience through the set-up or lighting: 'each shot consistently needs to have the right tone' (Heiduschka, quoted in Riemer [2000], p. 63). We cannot know the exact extent of the producer's contribution to Haneke's oeuvre, but it is almost certainly the case that he mentored Haneke through his transition from television to film.
12. Lang, in Elsaesser (1999), p. 129.
13. Critics were quick to infer that the film's low profile at Cannes was an indication of poor quality, with many reviews referring to this fact – only *Variety* was astute enough to note that the film was ineligible for competition that year on account of the presence of Patrice Chéreau in the film, Chéreau being that year's Jury president.
14. See Appendix Two.
15. Elsaesser (1999), p. 26.
16. Elsaesser (1999), pp. 25–31.
17. Elsaesser (1999), p. 26.
18. *Die Ausgesperrten* was in fact based on a script by Elfriede Jelinek, and told the story of a juvenile who kills his family and the events leading up to the murders. The film subverts 'family values', and contains explicit sex and violence. Its thematic similarities with both *The Seventh Continent* and *Benny's Video* make for an interesting comparison with Haneke's works.

19. Elsaesser (1999), pp. 29–30.
20. Lang, in Elsaesser (1999), p. 189.
21. As Mattias Frey also points out, the self-referential violence of *Benny's Video* and *Funny Games* might also be connected to a contemporary movement in Austrian cinema, which saw a wave of ironic and often self-referential 'black comedies' appear in the late 1990s and the first few years of this century. *Funny Games* in particular can therefore also be seen in the context of films like *Die totale Therapie* (Christian Frosch, 1996), *Die Gottesanbeterin* (Paul Harather, 2001), *Komm, süßer Tod* (Wolfgang Murnberger, 2000), and *Der Überfall* (Florian Flicker, 2000), with their typically Austrian mix of comedy, violence and irony. See Mattias Frey, 'A Cinema of Disturbance: The Films of Michael Haneke in Context', *Senses of Cinema Online Film Journal*, http://www.sensesofcinema.com/contents/directors/03/haneke.html (last accessed 2 November 2006).
22. Elfriede Jelinek, in Artificial Eye's pressnotes for *The Piano Teacher*, 2001, p. 6. Available at the British Film Institute.
23. Walter Benjamin, 'The Work of Art in the Age of Mechanical Reproduction', in *Film Theory and Criticism: An Introduction*, eds Leo Braudy and Marshall Cohen (Oxford: Oxford University Press, 2004), p. 811.
24. Robert von Dassanowsky, *Austrian Cinema: A History* (Jefferson, NC: McFarland, 2005), p. 254.
25. Brigitte Peucker, 'Fragmentation and the Real: Michael Haneke's Family Trilogy,' in *After Postmodernism: Austrian Film and Literature in Transition*, ed. Willy Riemer (Riverside, CA: Ariadne Press, 2000), p. 176.
26. Haneke (2000), p. 170.
27. Porton (2005), p. 50.
28. Michael Haneke, 'Film als Katharsis,' in *Austria (in)felix: Zum österreichischen Film der 80er Jahre*, ed. Francesco Bono (Graz: Edition Blimp, 1992), p. 89. My translation.
29. Haneke (2000), p. 172.
30. Wollen (1982a).
31. Cieutat (2000), p. 28.
32. Stephen Prince, *Savage Cinema* (Austin: University of Texas Press, 1998).
33. Notably with *Natural Born Killers* (1994, U.S.) and *The Truman Show* (1998, U.S.).
34. Haneke (2000), p. 172.
35. See Appendix Two.
36. In July 2006 a DVD box set of the trilogy was released in France, shortly followed by similar releases in the U.S. and the U.K., undoubtedly on the back of the success of *Caché*.
37. Paul Farren, 'Breaking the Code', *Film Ireland* 80 (April-May 2001): 22–23, p. 23.
38. See Appendix Two.
39. Angus Finney, *The State of European Cinema* (London: Cassell, 1996), p. 41.
40. Farren (2001), p. 23.
41. Hans Eisler, *Composing for the Films* (New York: Oxford University Press, 1947), pp. 120–121. Co-authored by Theodor W. Adorno, who is not cited in this edition.
42. Eisler (1947), p. 121.
43. Bertholt Brecht, 'Der Dreigroschenprozeß', in *Versuche 1–12* (Berlin: Suhrkamp, 1948), pp. 280–281.
44. Haneke (2000), p. 172.
45. Walter Benjamin, 'One Way Street', trans. Edmond Jephcott, in *Selected Writings, Vol.1: 1913–1926*, eds Marcus Bruloca and Michael W. Jennings (Cambridge: Cambridge University Press, 1996), p. 460.
46. Robert Horton, *'Code inconnu'*, *Film Comment* 36(6) (November 2000): 18.
47. Peter Matthews, *'The Time of The Wolf'*, *Sight & Sound* 13(11) (November 2003): 98.
48. Paul Arthur, 'Endgame', *Film Comment* 41(6) (November-December 2005): 25–28, p. 26.

49. Arthur (2005), p. 26.
50. Patricia Thompson, 'Secret Lives, Hard Lessons', *American Cinematographer* 83(5) (1 May 2002): 22, 24, 26, 28.
51. Tony Rayns, 'The Piano Teacher', *Sight & Sound* 11(11) (November 2001): 54.
52. Fiona Morrow, 'All Pain and No Gain', *Independent*, (2 November 2001): 11.
53. Bronwyn Jones, 'More than a Master of Everyday Horror: The Films of Michael Haneke', *The High Hat* (website) http://www.thehighhat.com/Nitrate/004/haneke.html (last accessed 26 July 2006).
54. Jonathan Romney, 'If You Can Survive This Film Without Walking Out, You Must Be Seriously Disturbed', *The Guardian*, Section 2 (23 October 1998): 6.
55. Mark Kermode, 'Funny Games', *Sight & Sound* 8(12) (December 1998): 44.
56. J. Hoberman, 'Head Trips', *Village Voice* (17 March 1998): 89.
57. David Bordwell, *Making Meaning: Inference and Rhetoric in the Interpretation of Cinema*, (Cambridge, MA: Harvard University Press, 1989), p. 102.
58. Sharrett (2003), p. 29.
59. Nick James, 'Code Uncracked', *Sight & Sound* 11(6) (June 2001): 8.
60. Morrow (2001), p. 11.
61. Cieutat (2000), p. 26.
62. Haneke (2000), pp. 169–70.
63. Amos Vogel, 'Of Non-existing Continents: The Cinema of Michael Haneke', *Film Comment* 32(4) (July-August 1996): 73–75, p. 74.
64. Vogel (1996), p. 75.
65. For more on this, see, for example, Sergei Eisenstein, *Film Form, and The Film Sense*, trans. Jay Leyda (London: Meridian Books, 1957[1949]), *What Is Cinema? Volume 1*, ed. and trans. Hugh Gray (Berkeley: University of California Press, 1967), *Volume 2*, ed. and trans. Hugh Gray (Berkeley: University of California Press, 1971); Jean-Louis Baudry (1974–5); and Christian Metz (1974). Dudley Andrew's *The Major Film Theories* (Oxford: Oxford University Press, 1976) also offers an articulate introduction to the concepts raised here.
66. Baudry (1974–5); Metz (1974).
67. Noël Carroll, *Mystifying Movies: Fads and Fallacies in Contemporary Film Theory* (New York: Columbia University Press, 1983).
68. Richard Allen, *Projecting Illusion: Film Spectatorship and the Impression of Reality* (Cambridge: Cambridge University Press, 1995), p. 114.
69. Gregory Currie, 'Film, Reality, and Illusion', in *Post-Theory: Reconstructing Film Studies*, eds David Bordwell and Noël Carroll (Madison: University of Wisconsin Press, 1996).
70. The first use of the term 'dream screen' to refer to the cinema is generally attributed to B.D. Lewin, who used it in his 1946 essay 'Sleep, the Mouth, and the Dream Screen', *Psychoanalytic Quarterly* 15 (Winter): 419–434. However, a vast amount of literature has been devoted to the subject of dream and film, much of it concerned with psycho-semiotic accounts of subliminal desire. For the purposes of this study I intend to focus only on the similarity between the modes of perception that one experiences when dreaming and when watching films. For a more general overview of the subject, one particularly useful website is: www.kinema.uwaterloo.ca/rasc022.htm
71. Carroll (1983), p. 73. One can only wonder whether this desire to deny that one's thinking is 'corrupted' by the outside influence of the cinema is perhaps a motivating factor in Carroll's vehement rejection of apparatus theory.
72. Joan Copjec, 'The Delirium of Clinical Perfection', *Oxford Literary Review* 8(1–2) (1986): 57–65, p. 61. The comment is made in reference to the following passage from Baudry: 'No doubt the darkened room and the screen bordered with black like a letter of condolence already present privileged conditions of effectiveness [for the performance of 'ideological effects'] – no exchange, no circulation, no communication

with any outside. Projection and reflection take place in a closed space, and those who remain there, whether they know it or not (*but they do not*) find themselves *chained, captured, or captivated'* (1974–5: 44).

73. Baudry (1974–75).
74. Richard Allen and Murray Smith (eds), *Film Theory and Philosophy* (Oxford: Clarendon Press, 1997), p. 19.
75. Wollen (1982a), p. 88.
76. Wollen (1982a), p. 88.
77. Haneke (2000), p. 172.
78. Immanuel Kant, *Foundations of the Metaphysics of Morals*, trans. Lewis White Beck (New York: Macmillan, 2nd edn, 1990), p. 24.
79. See, for example, Leslie Brill, *The Hitchcock Romance: Love and Romance in Hitchcock's Films* (Princeton, NJ: Princeton University Press, 1989) and Raymond Carney, *American Vision: the Films of Frank Capra* (New York: Cambridge University Press, 1986).
80. Stanley Cavell, *Pursuits of Happiness: The Hollywood Comedy of Remarriage* (Cambridge, MA: Harvard University Press, 1981) and *Contesting Tears: The Melodrama of the Unknown Woman* (Chicago: Chicago University Press, 1997).
81. Stanley Cavell, *The Claim to Reason* (New York: Oxford University Press, 1979).
82. Christian Metz, 'History/discourse: a note on two voyeurisms' in *Theories of Authorship: A Reader*, ed. by John Caughie (London: Routledge, 1986), 225–231, p. 229.
83. Stanley Cavell, *The World Viewed* (New York: Viking Press, 1971), p. 40.
84. Cavell (1971), p. 40.
85. Louis Althusser, 'Ideology and Ideological State Apparatuses', in *Lenin and Philosophy and Other Essays*, trans. Ben Brewster (New York: Monthly Review Press, 2001), p. 171. My emphasis.
86. See Thomas Schatz, *The Genius of the System: Hollywood Filmmaking In The Studio Era* (New York: Pantheon, 1998).
87. Kant (1990).
88. Kant (1990), p. 397.
89. Kant (1990), p. 397.
90. Kant (1990), p. 398.
91. Kant (1990), p. 399.
92. This kind of modernist art has been described by Michael Fried as one in which an art leaves no room, or holds no promise, for the minor artist: it is a situation in which the work of the major artist condemns the work of others to artistic non-existence, and in which their own work is condemned to seriousness, to further radical success or to complete failure. For elaboration see Cavell (1971), pp. 13–14.
93. Wollen (1982a), p. 88.
94. Rodowick (1994), p. 61. My emphasis.
95. The plot of *The Reckless Moment* bears some similarity to that of *Benny's Video*, in that it involves a mother (Lucia Harper, played by Joan Bennett) who, after discovering the dead body of her daughter's lover, hides the body under the assumption that it was her daughter who killed the man.
96. Haneke (2000), p. 172.
97. See Stéphane Goudet '*Code inconnu* – La main tendue', *Positif* 478 (December 2000): 22–29, pp. 23–24.
98. See Kermode (1998), pp. 44–45.

# Chapter 2

# NEGOTIATING MODERNISM
*Der Siebente Kontinent, Benny's Video,*
*71 Fragmente einer Chronologie des Zufalls*

The theory of film spectatorship up to the present day is a historical dialectic where André Bazin's realism emphasises a range of possibilities in cinema that are not foregrounded by Eisenstein's formalism; and apparatus theory, along with political modernist theory, brings together aspects of the two earlier positions so that realism now becomes ideology and the alternative to ideology lies at the extremes of cinema, in the extremes of realist principles or in the kind of disruption produced by the formalist school, used not for the sake of propaganda but as a way of breaking the realist illusion, as we see in the films of Jean-Luc Godard, for example. Post-Godard, cinema always faces this problem of how to reconcile the realist legacy with the modernist self-awareness of form. The place of the spectator in contemporary cinema is determined by this dialectic and, as such, Michael Haneke is just one among many finding a way through this dilemma.

Haneke is working in a different time to the film-makers most commonly associated with counter-cinema. It is a time in which, he believes, people have become inured to the experience of real life through the medium of television (and film), which divides brute reality into neat segments and packages it between commercials, insinuating it into the daily routines of consumer life. His remarks on this point reveal a film-maker with a distinct social agenda, one that is very much linked to questions of cinematic perception. The modernist techniques propounded by the political modernist critics and practiced by the makers of counter-cinema serve Haneke's didactic intentions precisely because they offer so decisive a rupture with the current screen tradition of rapid, MTV-style editing. Haneke insists that his visual approach at this point is a reaction against the existing cine-televisual conventions that he considers to be pernicious. He believes that the traumatic impact of events taking place around the world is misaligned with the tradition of fast-paced, inconsequential cinematic events.

But this misalignment is never seen, since so many 'real' events are only made known to us as they are glimpsed on our TV sets. To Haneke, then, conventional film-making and television news seem to be performing a narcotic function, insulating people from the events around them (as we saw in our introduction, Haneke's belief in this function is consistent with the radical critique of the Debordian 'Society of the Spectacle' currently taking place in theoretical writings by Slavoj Žižek, amongst others).[1] By breaking with established representational conventions, Haneke aims to rupture this indistinction between the virtual and the real, revealing the virtual to be precisely that, and destroying its capacity to function as a place of refuge by shielding us from our complicity in the world.

Haneke's later works in particular are not, in the classic Hollywood tradition of John Ford or William Wyler, objects of entertainment whose psychological content will only be analysed by critics; but nor are they purely intellectual, abstract works of art, which wear their theoretical aspirations on their sleeves, as are some of the films of counter-cinema, such as Jean-Luc Godard's *Le Vent d'est* and Laura Mulvey's and Peter Wollen's *Riddles of the Sphinx* (1977). Rather, within his later films, Haneke resolves these two extremes of cinema into a form which takes the narrative as its basis, but which uses key concepts in political modernist theory to alter the standard spectator's perception of the act of viewing. Haneke's films bring the two into direct conflict so as to create a juxtaposition between two film forms: a moment of impact, as we will see in subsequent chapters.

The director's individual works can be viewed as constituent parts of a process of negotiation on Haneke's part on the way to reaching this endpoint. They move back and forth between the two overarching forms of film-making outlined above: on the one hand mainstream narrative cinema, relying on genre structures, linear narrative and the prompting of the pleasure drive into action; and on the other the counter-cinema which sets itself up in binary opposition to this first form, deliberately dispensing with narrative convention and frustrating the pleasure drive. Over the course of the next three chapters I will discuss the dialectical process that Haneke's early films are part of, examining the process of 'working out' of a number of aesthetic and moral concerns that Haneke enacts by way of his early oeuvre, partly in response to the reception of his films by critics and audiences. By examining the aesthetic relationship of the films to one another, these chapters will elucidate the changing nature of Haneke's approach to the spectator and of his conception of what makes a 'moral cinema'. With the description of Haneke's overall project which we gave in the previous chapter in mind, we can examine his distinctive use of modernist techniques, their operations and their effects, in order to measure the presence of this aesthetic framework against other frameworks in the later chapters and to evaluate his objectives in relation to his style. This will allow us to trace the development and evolution of these techniques, and of Haneke's overall project of using film to position the spectator morally, since the early films, taken as a whole, constitute the first stage in the process of 'working out' that Haneke's films enact, and in them we can already see a refinement of his methods for moral spectatorship.

In order to do so, we need first of all to situate Haneke's modernist aesthetic in relation to the cinematic traditions and film-makers that have influenced his work – and that we have touched upon within the previous chapter – in a more detailed manner, so that we might see how it grows from these traditions and develops them.

## First- and Second-generation Modernism

*Der Siebente Kontinent, Benny's Video* and *71 Fragmente einer Chronologie des Zufalls* draw upon some of the cinematic techniques established during the counter-cinema movement and, to an extent, the motivations that lie behind them are also reflective of this movement's ideological stance. As we discussed in Chapter One, counter-cinema set itself up in confrontation with Hollywood cinema, on the basis that, since Hollywood provided the dominant codes with which films could be read, this was the only way in which anything new could be produced. As opposed to the cinema of the 'avant-garde' – a phrase which implies being in advance of, and independent from, mainstream cinema in its narrative structures and forms – counter-cinema took these existing structures and forms and negated them. Counter-cinematic film-makers such as Jean-Luc Godard, Chantal Akerman, and the partnership of Jean-Marie Straub and Danièle Huillet therefore challenged illusionism with strategies that were the opposite of each of its major codes, disrupting linear causal relations, denying narrative closure, fracturing spatial and temporal verisimilitude, undermining identification and putting pleasure into question.

In his 1972 article 'Godard and Counter Cinema: *Vent d'est*', Peter Wollen tabulates the strategies that counter-cinema draws on to negate mainstream conventions, describing the binary oppositions which structure the counter-cinematic project as the seven deadly sins of Hollywood mainstream film and the seven cardinal virtues of counter-cinema.[2]

| Deadly Sin (Hollywood) | Cardinal Virtue (Counter-cinema) |
|---|---|
| Narrative transitivity | Narrative intransivity |
| Identification | Estrangement |
| Transparency | Foregrounding [of the signifier] |
| Single diegesis | Multiple diegesis |
| Closure | Aperture |
| Pleasure | Un-pleasure |
| Fiction | Reality |

In the analyses that follow, I shall use Wollen's table as a grid through which to filter my examination of how Haneke's project of positioning the spectator evolves. This will allow us to see the extent to which Haneke shifts between the two sets of principles over the course of his oeuvre, starting from a rigorously counter-cinematic position and moving towards one which encompasses some of the 'deadly sins' of Hollywood, but puts them to radically different use.

However, we should first note that, while there is a tendency amongst film historians to discuss counter-cinema as a formal monolith, characterised by the principles that Wollen lays out in his essay on *Le Vent d'est*, the actual films that counter-cinema consists of are in fact extremely varied in their approach to repositioning the spectator as ideologically aware. For our purposes, we can divide these films into two categories, exemplified by, on the one hand, Akerman's *Jeanne Dielman* and, on the other, Godard's *Le Vent d'est*. While both categories of film-making have been associated with the political modernist agenda of placing the spectator in a position where he is rationally aware of the film as construct, they operate in very different ways, and can in many ways be seen as extending the formalist/realist disjunction, albeit in a mitigated form, into counter-cinema.

The first category of counter-cinematic films is characterised primarily by a simplification of the filmic medium and an extension of Bazinian principles. Films such as *Jeanne Dielman* are aimed at restoring realism to the cinematic experience, maintaining continuity editing but doing so in such a way that the spectator is forced to engage rationally with the minutiae of the filmic image. They rely on what I shall term a 'benign' form of reflexivity, which allows the spectator an extended period of time to reflect upon the image and thus distances them from the action on screen. And they echo Bazinian theory in their reliance on ambiguity within the image and their fidelity to reality itself. So Akerman's film, for example, forces us to sit through the tedium of a housewife's routine, prompting us to experience each of her chores as she performs them. There is more often than not a political agenda underlying these films – in this case a feminist one – but there is also a 'message' which has to do with the nature of cinematic perception and interpellation. By distancing the spectator from the narrative and by reducing narrative and meaning to mere schema, the first-generation modernist film thus serves as a total negation of mainstream Hollywood's techniques for absorbing the spectator, based as they are on absorption and passivity.

The second group of films, exemplified by Jean-Luc Godard's 1970s counter-cinema and in particular *Le Vent d'est*, takes a radically different approach to the spectator. Retaining first generation techniques, such films extend them into a more direct, 'aggressive' approach to the spectator, which is explicitly metatextual. These works can be seen as building on Eisensteinian montage techniques, rupturing continuity to jar the spectator into critical awareness. This second group of 'aggressively' reflexive films is not concerned with distancing the spectator from the cinematic action, but with emphasising their proximity to it. That is, where first-generation modernism only calls the spectator's attention to the film, second-generation modernism calls their attention to *themself*.

So, if first-generation modernism attempts to place the spectator in a more objective relationship to the image, second-generation modernism emphasises the subjectivity of the spectator and makes it count for something. Each has an essential part to play in Haneke's critical aesthetic, and the distinction between the two will, we shall see, assume an increasing importance throughout its development. What happens is that they come to be indicative not of different categories of film-makers, but of film-making. For it is pivotal to Haneke's project, and our understanding of it, that he comes to combine and contrast the two modes within any one film. For the most part, the early Austrian films are characterised predominantly by benign reflexivity, although moments of aggressive reflexivity do appear within these films as well. However, it is in subsequent chapters that we will come to understand the real significance of the conjunction of the two forms of reflexivity.

## *Der Siebente Kontinent*

As I have stated above, the distinction between first- and second-generation modernist techniques will come to play an important role in how we understand Haneke's developing approach to the spectator. Although it is not as clearly defined in the early films, we must nonetheless bear it in mind as we turn to look in some detail at Haneke's three early works, moving through them in chronological order so that we can understand how the director's treatment of the spectator evolves throughout his oeuvre.

Let us begin, then, with Haneke's first cinematic release, *Der Siebente Kontinent*. As we will see, Haneke's debut feature establishes the director as working firmly within the modernist tradition, drawing on cinematic structures familiar to us from counter-cinema, but using in particular the techniques of first-generation modernism, based as it is on principles of fragmentation and distanciation, and aimed at restoring the spectator to the conditions of perception with which they confront reality.

As Adam Bingham underlines in his short but insightful article on Haneke's film, its opening scenes set up the style and theme of the film in a wordless, synecdochic manner.[3] After several extreme close-ups of a saloon car in a car-wash, the film cuts inside and holds a long take (under the credits) from the back seat looking out of the front window as a family of three – who we will later learn are father George, mother Anna and daughter Eva – sit in silence; when the credits have rolled and the wash has finished, the car drives away past an oversized, exotic tourist advert for Australia which will recur in attenuated forms throughout the film. Based on a news story about a family opting for collective suicide rather than continuing in the present alienated world, the film takes numerous deceptive turns as we expect the members of the Schöber family, who go through daily life in a set of rote behaviours, to leave for the promised utopia of rural Australia, since this advert, shot in much brighter colours than the body of the film and transformed into a moving landscape, appears at regular intervals throughout the film. However, the film's climax, which lasts some thirty minutes, sees the family systematically destroy their home and possessions before taking their own lives. It is divided into three sections, of which the first two chronicle a series of episodes, or moments, in the family's life, and this opening segment sketches in notions of automatism and alienation whilst simultaneously laying out both the dialectical style of the film's intrinsic norms – long-take master shots and more rapidly cut close-ups – and its particular manner of usage to convey both fragmentation and stasis, the disjointed aimlessness of contemporary, lived reality. It also provides, as Bingham puts it, 'a microcosmic metaphor for the family: trapped in a car/cage [if not of their own design, then at least of their own purchasing], moving slowly, silently and mechanically through their lives'.[4]

Themes of modernity, commodification and emptiness – present in the work of many counter-cinematic film-makers – are prominent throughout the film. At the very beginning of the second 'chapter', just before the daily routines witnessed in the first are repeated, Haneke shows George and Anna having sex. For a minute nothing seems out of the ordinary but, as they draw to a close, the alarm clock goes off for them to get up, and their act is revealed for what it is. This is not love, or even functional procreation, but a way to pass the time between waking and starting their day. Their intercourse is reduced to a meaningless exercise in a series of meaningless exercises. For this episode is followed by a series of very brief images or snapshots of the family performing their morning routine: brushing teeth, pouring cereal, tying laces.[5]

In addition to reframing the sexual act, re-emphasising its status as routine, automated, the series of condensed images points to the presence of a binary image system operating within the film, a system linked to questions of time. On the one hand Haneke offers us what we can term 'episodes' from the Schöbers's lives – such as the parents' perfunctory sex scene – in which a sequence is developed that is, to some extent, complete in itself. On the other hand we have what I shall refer to as the film's 'moments', in which we see only a brief glimpse of an action. So, for example, in one episode, the daughter of the family, Eva, feigns blindness; we see her carried out of the classroom by her teacher and questioned until eventually her deception is revealed. The ensuing confrontation between Eva and her mother Anna possesses a similarly hermetic structure. Elsewhere, meanwhile, we see brief shots, held for only a few seconds (although long enough for their content to clearly register), of Anna or her husband George paying at supermarket tills, performing work or household tasks, climbing out of bed: these are the film's 'moments', which are without explanation, often without dialogue, and which seemingly have no internal narrative structure. The more extensive 'episodes' (and I use the adjective loosely here, for none are fully developed or psychologically explicable) form a contrast with the briefer moments: while the episodes combine to convey the family's disaffection through their internal narratives (a couple has sex for the sake of it; a young girl feigns blindness for attention), the moments have a cumulative effect arrived at only through montage (a hand, a dish, a cloth, water). Combined, these shots reveal the washing up as a rote activity, human beings as the mechanisms that perform it.

It is through the combination of the episodic and momentary that *Der Siebente Kontinent* paints a picture of bourgeois life as mundane and alienated. What little action there is takes place in a strangely anonymous Linz, the city 'rendered as a wasteland of industry, *Autobahn* and terraced houses'.[6] With its many silences, its elliptical structure, its interest in the alienating features of contemporary urban life, and its notable sense of architecture as signifier of alienation, the film recalls Antonioni's *Il Deserto rosso*, full of deadening, stifling examples of technological progress: from the car wash (teasingly juxtaposed with the tourist ad) to the television, to the machines Anna

**Figure 2.1** *Der Siebente Kontinent* (1989): For Anna (Birgit Doll) and George
(Dieter Berner) existence is reduced to a series of daily rituals.
*Courtesy of the BFI stills department. Permission graciously supplied by WEGAfilm.*

(an optician) works with. More striking still are several long and
extreme-long shots of George, an engineer, walking through the
industrial environment of his workplace in total isolation, conjuring a
powerful image of humans as modern automatons. Likewise, the
climactic scene of annihilation, which runs for nearly half an hour,
cannot help but invite comparisons with *Zabriskie Point*, albeit as a kind
of inverted depiction of that film's scene of ultimate destruction: where
Antonioni presented a cathartic and chaotic explosion, Haneke's family
triad undergoes a sterile and systematic implosion, carrying out the
destruction with the same constriction and painstaking care with which
they live their lives.

The meticulous attention to detail and the oppressiveness of the day-
to-day life that the film's style conveys also calls to mind Chantal
Akerman's *Jeanne Dielman*. For both films, the overall effect or impression
arises through a combination of real-time filming and cumulative
imagery. Slow intercutting and tightly framed close-ups force the viewer
to consider the features of banal activities; the rhythm of family life
echoes the automatic car wash that we watch the family roll through not
once, but twice. Both follow a directive of obsessive compulsion, in which

balance is construed through the guise of an overly ritualised presentation of quotidian routines shot in real time. They are structured by a combination of display (of household chores) and elision (of 'events'). Where Akerman's film takes place over three days, Haneke's takes place over three years, but in each film a sense of stasis is built up by the repetition of key anecdotal moments and episodes.

However, while Akerman's film is relentless in its chronology, which devotes the appropriate or 'realistic' amount of time to each household chore that her protagonist performs, Haneke's fragmented narrative chops activities into synecdochal pieces, a fact highlighted by the director's use of the close-up to alienate action from actor. Indeed, we do not see any of the three main characters' faces flush-on for the first fifteen minutes of the film. The disembodied hands that pick up a toothbrush, colour a picture or tie shoelaces, effectively state how mechanically such tasks, the everyday tasks that make up these characters lives, are performed. The cutting within the cumulative sequences of moments constitutes an effective form of condensation, an effect simultaneously balanced and reinforced through the use of blank spacers of varying length at the cut from one scene to the next (although not each shot) which further fragments the images, reinforcing the sense of disparity. The spacers break with the continuity and seamlessness of classical narrative cinema, but more than creating a mimetic reproduction of perception, they afford the spectator time to contemplate the images they have just seen, time to engage actively and rationally with the film's themes and motifs.

Haneke also refuses any psychological elucidation or insight into the characters' particular states of mind. Anna's sudden breakdown into tears in the car wash in part two is left unexplained. And Eva's feigning of blindness, though explained in part later in the film by the newspaper article Anna finds in her bedroom about a young blind girl who overcame loneliness, is presented anecdotally, never explored. The epistemological restraints that Haneke places on the film create a dynamic whereby, as Adam Bingham underlines, the spectator is, on the one hand, kept at a marked distance from the characters, and on the other is presented with the diegesis and thematic of the film in a much more direct, immediate way: 'What is achieved is an extra-textual underlining of the theme of modern alienation ... of the essential *unknowability* of anyone in the modern world. Just as there is a barrier between the characters within the film, so one exists between those characters and the audience'.[7] Haneke echoes this sentiment when he remarks of his films that: 'I can lead a character in a story in such a way that the sum of his behaviour does not give sufficient explanation for his decisions. The audience will have to find one'.[8] It is a strategy exemplary of Wollen's description of a cinema that replaces identification with estrangement, and transparency with foregrounding of the signifier. The film's explicitly elliptical narration makes it comparable with Robert Bresson's *Pickpocket*, of which Richard Roud has written: 'We must make the connections; we participate in the final meaning of the film'.[9] This sense of incompletion prompts a search for completeness, prompts reflection in the search for an answer that would offer the whole. As we have seen, Haneke has stated that, 'the more radically answers are withheld, the sooner [the spectators] will have to find their own'.[10]

It is evident from the above analysis that the fragmentation of form and narrative that operates within *Der Siebente Kontinent* imitates the counter-cinematic practices that we see in films such as Akerman's *Jeanne Dielman* and the modernist strategies that we see in, for example, Bresson's *Pickpocket*. *Der Siebente Kontinent* demonstrates the same reflexive foregrounding of the signifier and the suppression of the signified that Peter Wollen sees as characterising modernist filmmaking,[11] and functions as a systematic challenge to the illusionism of mainstream cinema just as Wollen calls for counter-cinema to do.[12] Formally, the process of reflexivity that Haneke operates is mirrored by the film's central motif: just as in a car wash, lacking anything else to do we turn our attention to the surrounding mechanics; so, when watching the film, we similarly become aware of the mechanisms of cinema itself.

## Benny's Video

We can see, then, that within *Der Siebente Kontinent*, the search for a radical formal style that will break with the mainstream conventions of classic realist cinema and allow for a repositioning of the spectator as an active participant in the construction of meaning fundamentally aligns Haneke's film with modernist film-making and the political modernist project in particular. But the problem that this alignment presents is that the position that *Der Siebente Kontinent* offers the spectator is not particularly different from that offered by the majority of counter-cinematic, modernist films: its consistency with Wollen's cardinal virtues underlines this point. For his part, Haneke explains the precision of the film's aesthetic as 'the appropriate format for the concept of individual objectification,' drawing 'a clear relationship between the content and the form' of the film.[13] But he is yet to suggest that the source of this objectification of the individual could be the cinema itself, to connect the disjointed aimlessness of contemporary, lived reality with the rapid flow of cine-televisual imagery which constantly surrounds us. The film offers the spectator an alternative form of perception from that which dominant contemporary conventions offer, yet at the same time it offers little by way of critique of the cinematic medium, negating dominant cinematic practices, but failing to connect them to moral concerns.

Haneke's next film, *Benny's Video* – billed as the second instalment of a trilogy – turns however towards an aesthetic which is not simply a negation of dominant film forms, but also a critique of them. The film opens with an image that clearly references the cine-televisual medium: the end of a television broadcast, the screen of 'snow'. This foregrounding of the cinematic medium follows a scene of destruction: the televisual 'snow' and white noise signals the end of a videotape showing the slaughter of a pig. Not only visually but also aurally violent, the screen image is extremely disturbing to the spectator, placing them in a very immediate, visceral relationship with the film's content, not least because it is initially presented to us as part of the film's diegesis. But telltale white lines across the screen soon signal to us that this is an intra-diegetic image sequence, now in the process of being rewound: what we have been watching is a film within the film, Benny's video rather than *Benny's Video*.[14] We are thus critically distanced from the images that had previously been so visceral as we become aware of the film as construct.

Looking back to *Der Siebente Kontinent*, we note that the film in fact closed with a similar image sequence to that which opens *Benny's Video*. We might revise our conclusion then, and say that rather than making no comment on the relationship between cine-televisual and the alienated experience of contemporary life, it makes a very subtle one. The only item to remain intact at the end of the destructive process we witness within *Der Siebente Kontinent* is the family television, which is switched on, although relegated to the background or off-screen space, throughout. At the end of the film, the 'snow' that signals the end of the television broadcast is mirrored by the eyes that can no longer see, while the white noise that substitutes for sound falls on deaf ears: the TV programme and the family of three have met their end, leaving the spectator of the film to watch the final, empty images that signal the film's end. This sequence of visual and aural effects, which briefly calls the spectator's attention to the cinematic medium, serves as a precursor for Haneke's subsequent introduction of the theme of cine-visual perception into the narratives of his films.

In both *Der Siebente Kontinent* and *Benny's Video*, then, the presence of snow on the screen is both a sign of the termination of the image chain and a visual correspondent to a 'real' death: that of the Schöber family in the earlier film, the slaughtered pig in the later one. But the scene of destruction in *Der Siebente Kontinent* was calm and aestheticised; here, it 'assaults' the spectator from the film's outset. In the context of *Benny's Video*, the snowy screen functions as an aggressively reflexive device, highlighting the relationship between the spectator and the screen image, between emotional or affective response and intellectual response, in a much more transparent manner than in the earlier film. The image that functioned as an oblique reference to the relationship between the on-screen characters, the spectator, and the cine-televisual medium in the first film signals the commencement of an explicit attack on the same medium and its consumers in the later film. As in *Der Siebente Kontinent*, Haneke's theme is the emotional glaciation of society, but while in the earlier film, as Brigitte Peucker puts it, 'social commentary lies within Haneke's purview', in this instance, she notes, 'the media in particular come in for a share of the blame'.[15]

The eponymous anti-hero is a fifteen-year-old boy who murders a young girl and videotapes the killing, playing and replaying it in his bedroom. Unlike *Der Siebente Kontinent*, *Benny's Video* offers some explanation for the protagonist's actions: although Haneke once more eschews psychological realism and character subjectivity, the film provides us with a wealth of sociological detail to suggest how, for Benny, perception comes to be mediated by the technology with which he is surrounded. Visual discernment takes place chiefly through a video camera, and the sounds of television and rock CDs form an aural space that envelops him. Benny spends his time watching the choreographed violence of action movies and the restrained, 'normalising' television reportage of scenes of death in Bosnia. In these news programs, images of carnage are accompanied by voices of commentators carefully trained to exclude all emotion, thus rendering a sanitised version of the real precisely where the spectator has come to believe he has access to its immediacy.

Television reportage, Haneke's film therefore suggests, has anaesthetised our capacity to respond to scenes of suffering. If the realism of film is conceptualised in spatial terms, Mary Ann Doane has argued, the realness of television lies in its relation to temporality, to its sense of 'liveness'. The temporal dimension of television would seem to be 'an insistent "present-ness" – a "This-is-going-on" rather than a "That-has-been"'. Television, she claims, deals 'not with the weight of the dead past but with the potential trauma and explosiveness of the present'.[16] But while Doane connects the liveness of television to trauma, to Haneke's mind the medium works hard to keep the shock of catastrophe at bay. Benny reflects the calm detachment of a news commentator. Perhaps what is more important than the liveness of the instant of filming is the way in which the very fact of filming automatically consigns its subject matter to the past, packaging it up neatly and sealing it away. For as Doane continues: 'Insofar as a commercial precedes news coverage of a disaster which in its own turn is interrupted by a preview of tonight's made-for-TV movie, television is the pre-eminent machine of decontextualisation'.[17] The very sense of liveness that characterises televisual information as part of the present means that it effaces the past. Television, as she puts it, inhabits a moment in time and then is lost to memory: it 'thrives on its own forgettability'.[18] Urgency, enslavement to the instant and hence forgettability are the attributes of televised information and catastrophe. By filming his murder of the young girl, Benny captures it in a constant present, a present without history or consequence, as demonstrated by his replaying and rewinding of the video cassette, reducing and deflating through its overpresence, the murder's shock value.

At a narrative level, then, the film functions as a critique of how the cinematic conventions of mainstream film and television can contribute to the Debordian 'Society of the Spectacle'. This point is echoed on a formal level through Haneke's use of varying levels of cine-televisual 'reality', which render the film extremely reflexive. As the film's title and opening scenes suggest, the boundary between the ongoing diegetic video and the so-called 'reality' of the film narrative is repeatedly called into question, and at various junctures the spectator is only retrospectively made aware that the footage he has been watching is actually part of Benny's video (as opposed to Haneke's film), a technique that will be reprised to even greater effect in the later *Caché*. One of the most effective of such moments within the film occurs at its end, when we see footage shot from the darkness of Benny's bed into the brightly lit room beyond. The spectator does not recognise the image, but the soundtrack is familiar: it is a conversation in which his parents discuss how best to dispose of the body of the young girl that Benny has killed. This sequence, out of temporal order, is momentarily confusing: although the image is unfamiliar, the spectator has heard the dialogue before. The spectator gradually realises that Benny had asked his parents on that occasion to leave the door of his room open because he had meant to videotape (or rather, as it is dark, to record) their conversation. It is not long before the spectator becomes aware that Benny's video is once again being viewed within the diegesis of Haneke's film. This time the soundtrack consists in a voiceover conversation about the footage, a conversation that Benny holds with the policeman with whom he is viewing it. We are well aware that, deprived of a context and without the image of his parents' suffering to which he had initially been privy, their dialogue on tape will, in all likelihood, serve to indict Benny's parents for the murder that their son has committed. Hence the videotape functions not only as a document of violence, but as its instrument as well, as Brigitte Peucker astutely points out.[19]

The contribution of *Benny's Video* to Haneke's developing project of ethical spectatorship lies with this explicit critique of the cinematic medium that is introduced therein. Whereas *Der Siebente Kontinent* serves as an alternative to the dominant forms of cine-televisual representation and presentation – that is, as a negation of these forms – *Benny's Video* integrates aspects of mainstream cinema and television into its structure and content in order to explicitly criticise them. In terms of counter-cinema and political modernist film theory, Haneke's debut feature seems more concerned with the suppression of any clear 'meaning' and the creation of a more authentic form of perception, in which film is as fundamentally unreadable as everyday life. It is characterised entirely by the aesthetics of first-generation modernism. His second film, on the other hand, functions as a critique of the cinematic medium itself, introducing in a protean form some of the techniques of second-generation modernism that will come to bear heavily upon Haneke's later films: the diegetic screen, the rewind/pause, and the shock moment of violence which opens the film will all recur within subsequent works, albeit within a much altered context. Nonetheless, *Benny's Video* is also heavily dependent on benign modernist devices, and its purpose is not to look to past forms of representation nor to propose new ones, but to expose the present mainstream conventions of meaning production. In this regard, its allegiances to counter-cinema's binary system of opposition are clear.

For all the inroads that it makes into the development of Haneke's critical aesthetic, there is, moreover, a troubling paradox operating at the level of form within *Benny's Video*. The film opens with Benny's video images presented directly to the spectatorial view, and its middle section repeatedly sets up situations in which the nature of its images is at first ambiguous. But finally, Peucker remarks, Haneke's film subsumes Benny's video.[20] The closing frames of *Benny's Video* represent the scene in the police station through the distancing device of multiple images on the monitors of video surveillance equipment. As Benny's parents are brought in to the police station and meet him being taken out, Haneke cuts to the impersonal video image of a security camera recording this encounter. As Maximilian Le Cain suggests, in one cut the subtle nuances of the characters' situations and resultant choices disappear. 'What is left is the simple fact of their crime'.[21]

This fact finally imprisons them thanks to the coldly judgmental camera gaze that they are caught in. It is a gaze that denies the possibility of varying degrees of guilt and blame, a black and white image in every sense. It is not neatly packaged and voice-overed for television, nor edited for cinema. After an hour and a half of moral exploration and debate carried out through comparative visual strategies that remain constantly sensitive towards the characters, the instant brutalisation of the security camera image is deeply troubling. Peucker argues that, doubly mediated by technology, these cold, impersonal images are offered up to the anonymous spectator representing the Law, as well as to the audience itself.[22] But, she goes on to hypothesise, the final images of the scene, images that view the scene from above in long shot, are clearly cinematic images, neither part of Benny's video nor of the police surveillance tapes.[23] They are images that now frame and control the images that they contain. The film's conclusion thus suggests to Peucker that Haneke's modernist cinema has managed to contain and master the more problematic images that it introduces.[24]

Peucker's is a persuasive argument, but while the film's open-ended narrative conforms, on the level of content at least, to political modernism's call for aperture, its formal properties negate this effect. The final images, which offer a clear comment on what has gone before, shut down the previous open-endedness of the narrative. The film offers a sense of closure to the troubling of fiction and reality via its form, compromising its otherwise rigorous critique of the spectatorial experience.

## 71 Fragmente einer Chronologie des Zufalls

The final frames of Haneke's second film notwithstanding, both *Der Siebente Kontinent* and *Benny's Video* adhere for the most part to Peter Wollen's vision of an alternative cinema. They also illustrate the ethical imperative at the heart of ideology critique, for the films negate the illusion-making strategies of classic realist cinema, allowing the spectator a position of rational awareness and so 'freeing' them from the state of suspended awareness that Hollywood cinema would usually place them in. In Kantian terms, *Der Siebente Kontinent* and *Benny's Video* each position the spectator as a rational agent, granting them the potential to be autonomous and therefore responsible for their actions and their beliefs. As we have seen, the spectator cannot become a moral agent, (or rather a 'moral spectator' since their capacity for action while in the cinema is limited) unless they have the capability for rational engagement. The two films offer them precisely this capacity.

For all its ethical implications, however, the act of awakening the spectator and restoring them to human dignity remains an act fundamentally concerned with questions of awareness and ideology, questions raised in the numerous examples of counter-cinema that call the cinema's status as construct to the spectator's attention. For Haneke to move beyond purely ideological concerns, he must bring other facts to the spectator's attention, most importantly the moral aspect of the act of spectatorship. And in his two earliest feature films, he fails to complete this half of the equation: the spectator of *Der Siebente Kontinent* and *Benny's Video* is rationally aware but not morally aware. Therefore, although the spectator has the potential for autonomy, this potential is not realised, and the spectator is not autonomous, at least not in the

Kantian sense. Rather, the spectator is positioned as passive, their response to the film over-determined by Haneke's reliance on reflexive devices which do not provoke self-reflection. Or, put otherwise, the two films do not prompt the spectator to consider their own responsibilities, their own position vis-à-vis the action on screen and the act of film-viewing itself.

So at this point in Haneke's oeuvre, responsibility for the spectator's 'freedom' from the cinematic apparatus rests with the omnipotent director, not with the spectator themself, as is best evidenced by the paradoxical closing scene of *Benny's Video* in which the director re-establishes control over the cinematic spectacle, hermetically sealing the previously threatening series of rogue images, which blurred the boundaries between different levels of reality. It is perhaps no coincidence then that the closure and specific kind of formal control that characterises *Benny's Video* is the object of Haneke's formal attention in *71 Fragmente einer Chronologie des Zufalls*, a film that attempts – to some extent at least – to provide an alternative to these strategies. Indeed, Haneke's third feature film offers a reversal of the paradigm we see in *Benny's Video*: now, the framework is explicitly metatextual, whereas the main body of the film is more closely aligned with first-generation modernist techniques. *71 Fragmente* does not, however, mark a radical departure for Haneke since within it, he develops the counter-cinematic techniques that operated within *Der Siebente Kontinent*, once again relying on counter-cinematic convention to produce a position of rational awareness for the spectator.

Narrative in *71 Fragmente* is multiple: instead of giving us a 'longitudinal' section by means of a family history, Haneke here presents the action within the context of a cross section through the structure of society. The film's formal structure is nonetheless an extension of that of *Der Siebente Kontinent*, depicting moments and episodes in the lives of a myriad of characters who in various ways will be affected by the massacre of a number of bank customers by a nineteen-year-old student. The ultimately interconnecting narrative strands represent contrasting strata of modern urban existence, each with their own ethical problems to confront, from an illegal immigrant boy to an angst-ridden security guard to a middle-class couple trying to adopt a child and the gun-toting student who finally brings about the film's climactic crisis.[25]

With this multiple narrative comes a concomitant reduction of character development: the spectator is not introduced to these 'characters' in any conventional sense; exposition is restrained even more than in the preceding films; the spectator does not even learn the names of many of the characters. And by relegating the character who commits the film's ultimate act of violence to the ensemble cast, Haneke minimises any empathetic engagement with him, foreclosing the possibility of a psychological explanation for the film's climax, which is unannounced and unexpected: no sense of tension presupposes it.

The fragmented and divergent narrative is thrown into relief by the similarly fragmented cast of characters and their disparate comings and goings, further reinforcing the theme of alienation and communication breakdown inherent to the various personal stories by alienating them from one another not only as individuals, but also as a society. To Maximilian Le Cain, 'there is no sense of community whatsoever in the film, each group of characters – arguably each individual – exists in isolation'.[26] Formally, black spacers once more separate the fragments of image sequences and the bits of narrative of which the film is comprised. They become a stylistic correlative to the fragmented action; that is, each scene, and later each shot, exists with no obvious connection to any of those preceding or following it. Context is not even provided by the continuity of characters that we see in *Der Siebente Kontinent*. It is worth noting furthermore that where the spacers in *Der Siebente Kontinent* were cut in proportto the length of each 'scene' – so the spacer is longer at the end of a longer episode, very short at the end of a brief moment – the spacers in *71 Fragmente* are all the same length. An equalising effect, the difference between the use of spacers here and in *Der Siebente Kontinent* is that here it affords the spectator no more time to think about one scene than another. Every scene we are presented with strikes us as just as (un)important as all the others.

In *71 Fragmente*, Le Cain states, society is fragmented, and each fragment cuts off the characters it contains, preventing them from communicating with others. He points out that even when an attempt is made to bridge this gap, as in the couple's decision to adopt the independent immigrant boy instead of a mentally disturbed little girl, the motives for this decision remain opaque. Interaction between the characters occurs with no real understanding of the emotional reasoning behind the others' actions. One key scene sees the bank's security guard and his wife at dinner, filmed in a single-take medium shot and punctuated with drawn-out silences. Shyly, he tells her that he loves her. She first asks if he is drunk and then, apparently suspicious, demands to know what he wants. His reaction is to quite suddenly slap her. After a pause, his wife reaches out and touches him gently. The scene ends with the couple continuing their meal in silence.[27]

Both Le Cain and Adam Bingham have both ventured intelligent readings of this episode,[28] but I would argue that what is truly remarkable about it is its opacity, its inability to be 'read'. It notably bears comparison with a dinner scene in *Der Siebente Kontinent* at which Anna's brother abruptly breaks down in tears over the death of a relative, only to be met with a stunned silence. But lacking the wider context of that film, it is impossible to attach any clear 'meaning' to such a scene in the later film. While vague narratives gradually emerge from the film's fragments and even merge loosely in the act of violence in which the film culminates, each subplot struggles against our attempts to read it as a unified whole, in a way which does not occur in either *Benny's Video* or *Der Siebente Kontinent*. The 'episodes' of *71 Fragmente* are thus reduced to the status of what we referred to as 'moments' in the earlier film, contributing to meaning only through their cumulative montage with other scenes and images. Viewed in isolation, they are open to endless interpretation: which is to say, they are not open to interpretation at all.

However, if we are alert, we can see that Haneke does in fact impose an interpretation of sorts upon the fragmented narrative as a whole. Each scene can be compared to the pieces of a puzzle. Indeed, a puzzle of sorts recurs as a motif throughout the film: a collection of individual pieces of paper, scattered disparately across a table top, are just a collection of shapes; but when rearranged in the correct manner they form a cruciform. In her discussion of the film, in which she claims that there is no overarching sense to be made from the narrative, Brigitte Peucker argues that 'the image of the cross that these pieces are repeatedly made to form is an interpretive red herring'.[29] But quite to the contrary, the piecing together of the component parts in order to see the whole lies, I believe, at the centre of Haneke's project for *71 Fragmente*. Its relevance perhaps emerges most clearly when we note the similarities with the motif of the puzzle and his method of conceiving the film: transcribing each idea or scene on a separate piece of paper, the director assembled all his ideas on a large board, (re)arranging them until he had found a suitable overall structure.[30] As with the cruciform puzzle, there is only one way of putting the pieces together. And this method of arrangement has been predetermined by Haneke through his structuring of the film along the basis of a linear, forward-moving chronology that culminates with the tying together of the various narrative strands. Each of the various episodes and moments – although unresolved – clearly takes place before the bank robbery. They build up to a coherent, albeit extremely understated, climax. Their positions within the film are then determined by the film's linear narrative, which proceeds from beginning to end, rather than in a more haphazard manner.

So although the director describes the film as being 'open on all sides',[31] then, we can perceive the ambiguity of the claim by comparing *71 Fragmente* to a film such as Alain Resnais' *L'Année dernière à Marienbad* (1961), in which the narrative is fragmented to the point where it is impossible to distinguish spatial or temporal coherence. Or we might equally measure it against one of Haneke's earlier television works, *Wer war Edgar Allen?* A twice-told story 'about' an identity crisis,

*Wer war Edgar Allen?* sees its narrator try to make sense of events that happened to him long ago by piecing together journal entries, diverse notes and papers, as well as fragments of his literary attempts from that earlier time. Here, as in Resnais's film, the film's fragmented narrative is held together by a dream logic which makes no coherent sense. In Willy Riemer's words, it is a filmic 'jigsaw puzzle in which most pieces are overprinted with several patterns'.[32]

Overlaid with different pictures, these jigsaw pieces (or fragments) are thus amenable to numerous arrangements. And indeed, Haneke introduces iterations of images, as well as employing association and repetition as structural principles, most evidently at the beginning of *Wer war Edgar Allen?* The eponymous character himself might be a Freudian symbol or the projection of a drugged mind; the viewer is systematically disorientated and challenged to keep reality and illusion apart. But while markers are sometimes provided to indicate the narrator's hallucinatory realm, at other times they are not. Riemer states that as a result of these techniques, the viewer of Haneke's film, like the reader of Peter Rosei's novel upon which it is based, 'does not so much extract a singular meaning from Rosei's narrative as participate in the intricacies of its iterative design'.[33] He continues, 'Neither Rosei's novel nor Haneke's film engage in the representation of a realistic world'. According to Riemer, Haneke and Rosei are both 'more concerned with the artistic possibilities of their medium than with the telling of a story that explains events and encounters. Using iterative fragments, they oblige the reader or spectator to participate in a creative process that involves both reason and fantasy'.[34] Comparing the formal structure of *71 Fragmente* with the more radically fragmented narratives of *L'Année dernière à Marienbad* or *Wer war Edgar Allen?* it becomes clear that the fragmentation that operates within *71 Fragmente* is subordinated to the film's linear chronology, allowing us to 'make sense', to some extent, of the various fragmentary images and stories (if only in retrospect). There is a logic to the film's structure, even if it does not automatically call for a decipherment. So Haneke does not totally throw off narrative convention even in what is perhaps the most conventionally counter-cinematic of his feature films.

And yet there is another way of looking at this problem. The film becomes 'open on all sides' if we place it within the context of the film's overarching framework: a matched pair of opening and closing scenes that bookend the narrative, and which offer both a resolution of the various fragmentary narratives and a method of avoiding the closure that characterised *Benny's Video*. Each of these scenes shows a news bulletin, covering a series of contemporary news stories that specifically locate the film in the moment of its creation and which are repeated in the television footage which repeatedly crops up on monitors in scenes

**Figure 2.2** Gabriel Cosmin Urdes as a homeless Romanian boy
in 71 *Fragmente einer Chronologie des Zufalls* (1994). The film's fragmentary
narrative cuts off the characters it contains, preventing them from
communicating with others.
*Courtesy of the BFI stills department. Permission graciously supplied by WEGAfilm.*

during the main body of the film.[35] In the film's final sequence, after the
student has carried out the massacre in a bank that involves most of the
film's characters and ends in his suicide, the film switches to a simulated
news report of the killing in which witnesses express their horror and
incomprehension. The report then moves on to real news stories such as
the war in Sarajevo and Michael Jackson's alleged child abuse.

A content-based interpretation of this framework and its relation to
the main body of the film is suggested by Maximilian Le Cain: that real
lives and real people so easily become just another news story in a
parade of media images, the actual state of their lives becoming lost as
they – like the family at the end of *Benny's Video* – become subject to a
relentlessly impersonal image system. In a world already saturated
with images, they become just another image. A conclusion that echoes
Doane's thoughts on television's lack of a past, of a significance aside
from its liveness, this reading is certainly consistent with Haneke's
social concerns of alienation and the mediatisation of perception.[36]

However, looking at the scene's place in the film's structure, we
might offer an alternative explanation of it as a device for re-opening

the film after the apparent closure that the coincidence of the various narratives has offered. In the bank massacre the smallest units of the narrative cohere into one large unit, as with the cruciform. But by bringing in the news footage, Haneke effects an interesting reversal. Having trained the viewer to engage with small units and brought him or her to understand their ultimate agglomeration, by inserting the large unit into the context of the news programme, the director edits it down, turning it into a small unit within a larger framework. The process begins once again with the news programme as the new large, encompassing narrative unit. The 'narrative', made up of 'fragments of chance', becomes a fragment itself, this time a short bulletin in a news programme, made up of many short bulletins, all of which are distillations of much wider-reaching, fragmented narratives. So just as we think that the puzzle is complete, the film reveals that it is in fact just a smaller part of an even larger puzzle, capable of expanding in all directions, encompassing all the narrative fragments that make up all the lives in the world. These bookends thus give the disconnected narrative an overarching sense, but at the same time, they open it out, placing it within a much wider situation of fragmentation.

So the cruciform puzzle *is* a red herring, but not in the way that Peucker understands it: by bookending the narrative of *71 Fragmente* with the news bulletins, Haneke transforms the film into a kind of *mise-en-abyme*, in which television and 'real life' continuously consume and reflect one another. It thereby avoids the apparent closure that *Benny's Video* offers, and indeed reverses it. For if the main body of the film is resolutely modernist, or counter-cinematic – once more offering an alternative form of perception but failing to comment (except by negation) on existing ones – by offering a reflection on the cinematic medium as its parting shot, the film suddenly undermines Haneke's position as omnipotent director. His work is subsumed by its cultural antagonist: the rapidly-edited news bulletins that dull our perception and foreclose any visceral engagement with the real traumas that take place around the world on a daily basis. What the film 'says' then, with this final gesture, is that it has offered us a 'realistic' perception of an event, as opposed to the conventional manner in which the televised news would distil this information into a thirty-second newsbite: easily consumable, but ultimately meaningless. As Doane explains it, 'the tendency of television to banalize all events through a kind of levelling process would seem to preclude the possibility of specifying any event as catastrophic'.[37] Or, as Walter Benjamin points out in a statement which seems to best capture television's effect here, 'The concept of progress is to be grounded in the idea of catastrophe. That things "just go on" *is* the catastrophe'.[38]

# The Trilogy, Modernism and Morality

Taken as a trilogy, Haneke's three earliest films can be seen to establish a number of formal and thematic concerns that recur throughout Haneke's body of work: on the one hand, notions of alienation and 'emotional glaciation' reflected in a Brechtian distanciation from the image which offers a negation of – and therefore an alternative to – dominant cinematic conventions; and on the other, the real/virtual (in)distinction and the critique of the cine-televisual medium, reflected in a layering of cinematic styles, which offers a comment (by comparison) on dominant mainstream conventions. In *71 Fragmente* Haneke goes some way to resolving these two approaches, which operate in *Der Siebente Kontinent* and *Benny's Video* respectively, with regard to the visual image, both as a theme and as the medium within which he is operating. For there is a 'disconnect' of sorts between the provision of an alternative cinema and a comment on the existing one in each of Haneke's two earliest works. *Der Siebente Kontinent* foregrounds the alienated nature of modern day life through its form, but fails to link this comment on contemporary society to the cine-televisual medium except in the most oblique of ways. Its structure is in itself a comment on our nature of perception, as Haneke explains:

> Contemporary film editing is most commonly determined by the practices of TV-timing, by the expectation of a rapid flow of information. Apart from its visual attractiveness, a picture is to provide linear information which can be quickly consumed and checked off. Video clips and commercials have established the benchmark for timing. They offer the most persuasive guarantee for sanitised emotions, that is, for sterility.[39]

And yet, discussing the same film with Christopher Sharrett, the director acknowledges that, 'the audience does not have to concern itself with structure,' which is only necessary, 'so that the story I'm narrating produces the desired effect'.[40] In the case of *Der Siebente Kontinent*, this 'effect' may well be too subtle to prompt the spectator to consider the relationship of the alienated characters on screen to the very fact of their on-screen-ness. The critique of the cine-televisual medium is certainly not foregrounded within the film's diegesis in the way that it is in *Benny's Video*. The latter meanwhile makes its criticism of the medium clear, while portraying a disaffected and alienated society as effectively as its predecessor, but it offers a form of closure through the authorial stamp of counter-cinema which positions the spectator as passive – by forcing them to follow an argument through to a predetermined conclusion – and thereby revokes some of their responsibility. The reflection on the medium offered throughout the film is safely contained by its ending. (It is indeed perhaps *too* aggressive in the reflexive devices that it uses, prompting spectators to reject the position it offers through them. But we shall discuss this possibility further in subsequent chapters.)

Although the link between the two remains somewhat inexplicit, *71 Fragmente* retains, and indeed expands, the fragmented structure of *Der Siebente Kontinent* whilst simultaneously incorporating elements of the more explicit reflexivity that characterises *Benny's Video*. In this respect it is the first step for Haneke towards bridging a gap between the negation of Hollywood technique that the former presents and the more explicit cine-televisual critique offered by the latter, bringing the critique of the medium to bear on the fragmented portrayal of a disaffected society. Moreover, *71 Fragmente* prefigures later attempts that Haneke makes to find a balance between aperture and closure. Its semiotic sophistication has an experimental importance for Haneke, and the investigation into meaning-making that takes place here is subsequently transformed by being placed within a different context within Haneke's next film, *Funny Games*. However, as did *Der Siebente Kontinent*, the film retains a preoccupation with ideological and formal concerns, with placing the spectator in a position of rational awareness without necessarily prompting them to become morally aware. Despite the radical rupture with the dominant visual conventions of its time, Haneke's aesthetic paradigm does not really represent an original or unique application of stylistic principles, and it is only in the films that follow that various reflexive strategies introduced within the trilogy are developed in a more productive manner.

The fact that Haneke does not yet radicalise the spectator's position is perhaps reflected in the reception of the trilogy. What is remarkable about almost all the critical appraisals of the three films is that they read the films as social critiques, rather than as cinematic critiques. For the most part, analyses of *Der Siebente Kontinent* and *71 Fragmente* confine themselves to an examination of how the films' forms reflect the perceived problem of emotional glaciation in Austria.[41] *Benny's Video*, with its explicit critique of the cinematic medium, has produced a wider variety of responses. However, these still tend to be content-based: assuming that the film enacts on a narrative level the story of a boy who, inured to the violent spectacle, commits a murder with seemingly no sense of reality or remorse. These readings, then, revolve primarily around questions of violence and censorship, and a surprising number simply use Haneke's film as a springboard for discussion of wider issues, overlooking the rich texture of Haneke's own portrayal of cinematic violence. British critics such as Geoff Brown connected the film (which was released in 1993) with the Jamie Bulger killing that dominated that year's news.[42] Austrian Claus Wecker similarly compares the film's events to contemporary news stories in his own country.[43] The fact that Haneke's film was almost banned in Switzerland may have contributed to this tendency for metatextual readings of the film. Certainly, the timing of the film's release – at a period when the controversy surrounding virtual violence and its effects on young people was at a peak – will have done so. But even the more sophisticated readings of the film, such as those offered by Karl Suppan and Mattias Frey – who draw on postmodernist theory by Baudrillard and Žižek to analyse the film – are purely concerned with Haneke's intradiegetic troubling of levels of reality.[44] At no point do any of these critics connect Benny's position with their own position as spectators; at no point in either Suppan's or Frey's articles is awareness of the film medium connected to *self*-awareness. Like the rest of Haneke's trilogy, then, *Benny's Video* seems to offer a cinematic experience that is based on the negation of existing cinematic forms: it places the spectator in an extremely distanced, 'objective' relationship to the narrative.

Again, we might speculate that it is for this reason that the trilogy has been the subject of so much more academic criticism than Haneke's later, better known films (with the notable exception of *Caché*). The three films invite academic study since they resemble academic study: rational, analytical, making claims to objectivity. Only the two diegetic killings within *Benny's Video* connect with the spectator on anything other than a purely rational level, and this emotional connection to the film is then immediately undermined and kept at bay, unlike in the later films, which operate a dialectic between reason and emotion. The spectator's scopophilic pleasure is never mobilised in any of the three films that make up the trilogy. In this respect, as we have seen, they are resolutely counter-cinematic pieces of work.

Which leads us on to another problem with the trilogy. In the forms they take and the manner in which they are marketed, the three films might be said to be preaching to the converted: *Der Siebente Kontinent*, *Benny's Video* and *71 Fragmente* are 'art films' for 'art audiences'. Consider Jonathan Romney's review of *Benny's Video* for *The New Statesman* in 1993, in which he refers to it as a European art film of the most austere tradition.

> The film is without real impact. That's partly because it occupies such familiar territory. … But it also disappoints because there's no ambivalence, no sense that the film, despite its loathing of video, might be susceptible to some of the form's seductions. Instead, its disdainfully moralistic view is delivered strictly from the high ground, not least aesthetically, in its long takes from a static camera and absolute refusal of spectacle.[45]

Recognising the shortcomings of Haneke's early modernist aesthetic brings us to an important point. If the counter-cinematic modernist aesthetic that operates within *Der Siebente Kontinent*, *Benny's Video* and

*71 Fragmente* was to characterise Haneke's later work to this extent, then his films would offer little new perspective on how we think about spectatorship.

The early modernist aesthetic, by itself, is grossly insufficient as a means for analysing Haneke's unfolding project of positioning the spectator morally. It is insufficient because it treats the films as purely intellectual objects of epistemological enquiry, and fails to take into account other elements that Haneke introduces into his subsequent films. For counter-cinematic strategies of modernism, both first- and second-generation, are not the only frameworks deployed in Haneke's later films. By superimposing an additional framework onto the modernist aesthetic in *Funny Games*, Haneke's films go some way to attaining the Kantian moral orientation that their use of purely modernist techniques had not yet attained, and they become part of an enduring humanistic project of allowing the spectator to engage morally with their content. This other framework develops on techniques introduced but left undeveloped in the early films, most prominently in *Benny's Video*. The filmic strategies that this film introduces and that Haneke extends into *Funny Games* include the metatextual troubling of levels of reality, and the use of sound and static cameras. In the later film, these devices are mobilised not only in service of pleasure negation, but also to create an active sensation of unpleasure for the spectator.

Most important of all may be the fact that, like *Benny's Video*, *Funny Games* not only takes a linear narrative, but it also draws (albeit very loosely) on the generic structures of the thriller and the horror film. *Benny's Video* may have its flaws, as Jonathan Romney rightly points out, but, as we saw Amos Vogel explain, it is also the most 'accessible' of the three of films.[46] This accessibility is pivotal to Haneke's project of positioning the spectator morally, and a generic framework – both within the text and surrounding it – introduces an element of seduction into the project not available to pure modernism. So it is to this generic framework that we will now turn.

## Notes

1. Guy Debord, *La Société du spectacle* (Paris: Editions champ libre, 1967). Žižek references Debord in numerous works, including, as just one example, *Welcome to the Desert of the Real* (London: Verso, 2002).
2. Wollen (1982a), p. 79.
3. Adam Bingham, 'Life, or Something Like It', *Kinoeye Online Film Journal*, http://www.kinoeye.org/04/01/bingham01_no2.php (last accessed 18 August 2006). My emphasis.
4. Bingham, 'Life, or Something Like It'.
5. Bingham, 'Life, or Something Like It'.

6.  Frey, 'A Cinema of Disturbance'.
7.  Bingham, 'Life, or Something Like It'.
8.  Achim Engleberg, 'Nine Fragments about the Films of Michael Haneke', *Filmwaves* 6 (Winter 1999): 31–33, p. 31.
9.  Richard Roud, 'Robert Bresson', in *Cinema: A Critical Dictionary*, ed. Richard Roud (London: Secker & Warburg, 1980), p. 148. Cited in Bingham, 'Life, or Something Like It'.
10. Haneke (2000), p. 172.
11. Peter Wollen, 'The Two Avant-Gardes', in *Readings and Writings* (London: Verso, 1982).
12. Wollen, 1982a.
13. Cieutat (2000), p. 27.
14. Peucker (2000), p. 179.
15. Peucker (2000), p. 179.
16. Mary Ann Doane, 'Information, Crisis, Catastrophe,' in *Logics of Television: Essays in Cultural Criticism*, ed. Patricia Mellencamp (Indianapolis: Indiana University Press, 1990), pp. 222, 225.
17. Doane (1990), p. 225.
18. Doane (1990), p. 226.
19. Peucker (2000), p. 184.
20. Peucker (2000), p. 185.
21. Maximilian Le Cain, 'Do The Right Thing: The Films of Michael Haneke', *Senses of Cinema Online Film Journal*, http://www.sensesofcinema.com/com/contents/03/26/haneke.html (last accessed 18 August 2006).
22. Peucker (2000), p. 185.
23. Peucker (2000), p. 185.
24. Peucker (2000), p. 185.
25. Le Cain, 'Do The Right Thing.
26. Le Cain, 'Do The Right Thing'.
27. Le Cain, 'Do The Right Thing'.
28. See Le Cain, 'Do The Right Thing', and Adam Bingham, 'Modern Times: Notes towards a Reading of Michael Haneke's *71 Fragments of A Chronology of Chance'*, *Senses of Cinema Online Film Journal*, http://www.sensesofcinema.com/contents/cteq/05/34/71_fragments.html (last accessed 18 August 2006).
29. Peucker (2000), p. 186.
30. This information comes from an interview with Haneke aired at the same time as the film on Austrian television. Footage was generously supplied by Thomas Ballhausen at the Film Archiv Österreich.
31. Haneke (2000), p. 175.
32. Willy Riemer 'Iterative Texts: Haneke/Rosei, *Wer war Edgar Allen?'*, in *After Postmodernism: Austrian Film and Literature in Transition*, ed. Willy Riemer (Riverside, CA: Ariadne Press). p. 192.
33. Riemer (2000b), pp. 191–2.
34. Riemer (2000b), p. 197.
35. In fact, Haneke toys once more with intra-diegetic cine-televisual imagery within these scenes: for example, the young couple who are looking to adopt see one of their potential adoptees – a young Romanian refugee – in a news story on television. However, the intra-diegetic footage does not lead to any slippage between levels of 'reality' here, since it is consistent with the narrative scenario and is always clearly presented as part of the diegetic world.
36. Le Cain, 'Do The Right Thing'.
37. Doane (1990), p. 229.

38. Walter Benjamin, 'Central Park', trans. Lloyd Spencer, *New German Critique* 24 (Winter 1985), p. 50. Quoted in Doane (1990), p. 229.
39. Haneke (2000), p. 173.
40. Haneke (2000), p. 162.
41. See, for example, Raphael Busson, 'Glaciation des Sentiments', *Le Mensuel du cinéma* 5 (April 1993), pp. 33–6; and Bert Rebhandl, 'Kein Ort. Nirgends: *71 Fragmente einer Chronologie des Zufalls* von Michael Haneke', in *Der Neue Osterreichische Film*, ed. Gottfried Schlemmer (Wien: Der Deutsche Bibliothek, 1996).
42. Geoff Brown, '*Benny's Video*' (review), *Times* (26 August 1993), p. 31.
43. Claus Wecker, '*Benny's Video*', *Filmfaust Internationale Filmzeitschrift* 88 (18 January 1993): 46–49.
44. Karl Suppan, 'Die Asthetik der Gewalt in Hanekes *Benny's Video*', in *Visible Violence: Sichtbare und verschleierte Gewalt im Film*, eds Franz Grabner, Gerhard Larcher and Christian Wessley (Münster: Lit,1998); and Mattias Frey, 'Supermodernity, Capital and Narcissus: The French Connection to *Benny's Video*', in *Cinetext Online Film Journal*, http://cinetext.philo.at/magazine/frey/bennysvideo.html (last accessed 18 August 2006).
45. Jonathan Romney, '*Benny's Video*' (review), *New Statesman* (20 August 1993): 36.
46. Vogel (1996), p. 75.

*Chapter 3*

# THE ETHICS OF AGGRESSION:
## *Funny Games*

Michael Haneke's critical aesthetic is strongly grounded in political modernist thought and counter-cinematic practice, his early films in particular drawing on modernist models of distanciation and reflexivity in order to forestall the pleasure drive and thereby allow the spectator to engage rationally with the filmic text. These modernist structures allow the spectator an enhanced position of knowledge about the cinematic medium, but they remain concerned with the medium itself, and do not force the spectator to consider their own position in relation to the image. That is, the spectator becomes aware of the film as a product, but they are not necessarily aware of themselves as a consumer.

*Funny Games* extends Haneke's modernist project of alienation, for the most part characterised by a 'benign' form of first-generation reflexivity, to a more direct and 'aggressive' approach towards the spectator, which Haneke expresses as a drive to 'rape the viewer into autonomy' by confronting them directly with their complicity in the cinematic production of desire and illusion.[1] While the film adheres to many of the precepts of the alternative counter-cinema as defined by Laura Mulvey and Peter Wollen, it also involves the production of 'cinematic unpleasure': a term which signifies not only the frustration of the pleasure drive, but also the mobilisation of a range of 'negative' emotions on the spectator's part, among them discomfort, embarrassment, anger and guilt. As unpleasure calls attention to itself in a way that pleasure does not, it prompts the viewer to question what it is in the film that causes this feeling, and hence forces them to engage rationally with the image on screen. The film thereby employs spectatorial 'unpleasure' as a device for mobilising a tension between reason and emotion, creating a moment of 'impact' for the viewer. This notion of impact looks back to an Eisensteinian moment in film theory, in which a dialectical relationship between emotion and reason was used to create a shock effect on the spectator. However, as we will discuss, Haneke's use of impact differs from Eisenstein's in its solicitation of an individuated spectator response. In Haneke's films, impact is not the point at which content is produced but the point at which the spectator is invited to engage morally with the film. *Funny Games* can therefore be considered a 'breakthrough' not only in terms of its propulsion of Haneke from a national to an international film forum, but also in terms of the radicalisation of the response it prompts.

## A Generic Structure

*Funny Games* opens with an overhead tracking shot (taken from a helicopter) of a family saloon driving along a country road, set to classical music. A series of close-ups taken from within the car introduces us to a middle-class family of three – who we will later learn are Anna and George Schöber and their son Georgie – playing a game in which they have to name the classical pieces and their composers. Quite abruptly the diegetic classical music is replaced by the roars of a John Zorn thrash punk score and the film's title superimposes itself on the screen in blood-red letters. Just as suddenly Zorn's music cuts out, and we return to the diegetic soundtrack. This opening sequence nicely encapsulates Haneke's modus operandi within *Funny Games*. Here, what initially appears as unthreatening and knowable soon transforms into something strange and unsettling. So it is that *Funny Games* sees Haneke draw heavily on the generic conventions of the suspense thriller, introducing a new paradigm into his critical aesthetic.

Before we examine Haneke's use of the generic structure in *Funny Games*, some background on genre theory is useful. There is an ongoing debate, led by Judith Hess and Jean-Loup Bourget, regarding the ideological implications for any film-maker working within a genre format. On the one hand, the Hess school of thought believes that genre films are, in their nature, conservative propositions grounded in the predictability of convention (it is for precisely this reason that counter-cinema has, for the main part, avoided genre films).[2] Bourget and his supporters, on the other hand, argue that, for this very reason, a genre film can gain the power to become a subversive statement.[3] The Hess/Bourget debate centres on the ability (or lack thereof) of individual directors to undermine the ideology embodied in a genre format; what both critics agree on is the fact that the Hollywood genre system is based on a fundamentally conservative, capitalist ideology, which to some extent inflects all of the films produced under it. But it is difficult to say whether – in the Hess model in particular – it is the genre forms themselves that are ideologically conservative, or the fact that all the genre films analysed are the products of the Hollywood studio system.

One seemingly obvious way in which to approach this problem would be to consider the European appropriation of genre. And yet this remains an area of genre production that is frequently overlooked in critical studies of the topic. For example, whilst they acknowledge that the genre film is not the exclusive territory of Hollywood directors, genre theorists such as Rick Altman, Steve Neale and Thomas Schatz focus almost exclusively on the question of whether it is possible to consider genre specialists – such as Howard Hawks, Douglas Sirk or Vincente Minnelli – to be *auteurs* if they are working within the Hollywood system. In doing so, they overlook the question of what happens when an established *auteur* makes a genre film outside the Hollywood system. Only Robin Wood, in his seminal article 'Ideology, Genre, Auteur', in which he examines a number of genres in terms of ideological oppositions, has pointed, albeit briefly, to the ability of the European director to trouble dominant capitalist ideology through the transgression of genre conventions, citing Rainer Werner Fassbinder's melodramas and Wim Wenders' film noirs as examples of this practice.[4] Yet, after *Funny Games*, the majority of Haneke's films draw on generic conventions to highly subversive effect (*Code inconnu* being the only exception in Haneke's body of French-language films). Haneke's genre-based films, like those of Rainer Werner Fassbinder and Wim Wenders before them, ironise generic conventions, but at the same time they use these conventions to place the spectator in a more immediately responsive position than the counter-cinematic principles of pure negation of mainstream convention allow, as we will see.

Although *Funny Games* announces a clearly resolved concern with generic strategies, a concern that will come to play a part in the later films, it is not in fact Haneke's first experiment with generic convention. A generic framework is also present, in a mitigated form, within *Benny's Video*, in which the film's narrative produces an engagement with the film based on its use of a 'paradigm scenario'. As Thomas Schatz underlines in his 1981 book, *Hollywood Genres*, the genre film is essentially predicated on the familiar: at its most basic, he writes, 'a genre film involves essentially one dimensional characters acting out a predictable story pattern within a familiar setting'.[5] Both *Funny Games* and *Benny's Video* make use of our familiarity with similar generic conventions in order to prompt certain responses. In the case of *Benny's Video*, response primarily takes the form of an engagement with the narrative based on our desire to know 'what will happen next'. As we mentioned in Chapter Two, the film has plot similarities with Max Ophüls's *The Reckless Moment* (1949) amongst other films: a murder is committed, a cover-up is instigated, the audience waits to find out whether or not the conspirators will be caught.[6] The spectator's essential empathy with the protagonists – based on the fact that it is their point of view that the narrative aligns itself to – thus encourages occasional moments of suspense. This is why, when we watch *Benny's Video*, our dawning awareness that Benny has framed his parents for the murder causes a vague sense of discomfort. However, as we saw in the previous chapter, the generic narrative is undermined by the film's extreme counter-cinematic style, which distances us from the film as a narrative-led genre piece and precludes a strong emotional engagement with the film's characters or events.

In *Funny Games*, Haneke draws on another paradigm scenario familiar from the suspense thriller. Arriving at their lakeside house, the Schöbers are besieged by two young men calling themselves Peter and Paul, who challenge them to a bet which the family will win if they can survive the next twelve hours. The basic narrative premise – the family under threat from an outside force – is a standard trope within Hollywood cinema, associated as much with the melodrama (in which the threatening other takes the shape of the tempting seductress or seductor) as it is with suspense thrillers such as *The Hand that Rocks The Cradle* (1992), *Fatal Attraction* (1987) and both the 1962 and 1991 versions of *Cape Fear*.[7]

*Funny Games*, however, extends its use of generic convention to encompass not only familiar plots and settings, but also the *formal* conventions associated with the suspense thriller. Here, the narrative scenario combines with the film's formal structure to situate the film as a suspense thriller, and to encourage the expectation that its narrative structure and form will conform to the conventions of the genre. For the majority of the film's running time the director employs classical suspense strategies that echo Hitchcockian technique.[8] Although these suspense strategies are not based, as in Hitchcock's *Vertigo* for example, upon an epistemic disjunction which places the spectator in a privileged position of knowledge exceeding that of the characters,[9] the film is instantly recognisable as part of the suspense thriller genre: cutting is moderately paced, speeding up at points of high tension; shot/reverse-shots, point-of-view shots and lingering close-ups of various objects (a knife left on a boat, a set of golf clubs, the family dog, all of which will play an important role later in the narrative) function as generic signposts.[10]

The way in which Haneke presupposes the audience here is key. As we have seen, film theory up to the 1970s tended to place emphasis on what happens *inside* the movie theatre between spectator and screen, and to analyse the components of cinematic signification without fully considering how that situation arose in the first place. It therefore overlooks one crucial aspect of the spectator's agency. For the spectator may indeed collude by deferring to the requirements of the text, but apparatus theory falls short of completing the other half of this equation: the film may bend the viewer to expect certain qualities, but it exists first and foremost to fulfil a desire on the viewer's part. As Steve Neale points out, genre does not just refer to film type but to spectator expectation and hypothesis (speculation as to how the film will end).[11] It also refers to the roles of specific extra-cinematic discourses that feed into and form generic structures. In other words, genre must also be seen as part of a tripartite process of production, marketing (including distribution and exhibition), and consumption. In relation to marketing, publicity also contributes to the exercise of situating the film as part of a genre. The promotion of *Funny Games* sets up generic expectations, through marketing and distribution right down to the fact that when the film premiered at the 1997 Cannes Film Festival, advance information about the film was kept to an absolute minimum, tickets to the film were issued with a red warning sticker (a measure previously only taken with one film – Quentin Tarantino's *Reservoir Dogs*, of which more later), and the film was billed in the catalogue as a 'thriller', priming audiences to expect, as Jonathan Romney puts it, 'a blood-soaked nail-biter'.[12]

In the opening thirty minutes of the film, Haneke deliberately heightens these expectations. He establishes *Funny Games* as part of the suspense thriller genre in order to lull the spectator into a false feeling of security, stating that: 'Elements from the history of the suspense thriller appear as quotes – the classical opening, the scene when the boy escapes to the villa – very classical, like Hitchcock. And the audience only engages with the film when they don't know what's going to happen, when they allow themselves hope'.[13] This statement underlines a key motivation for drawing on generic conventions, both narrative and formal. For while the use of generic conventions within a film indicates to the audience the course that they can expect its narrative to take, it also serves as a guideline for what emotional response the spectator will take to that film.[14] By establishing Anna, George and Georgie as a family group who are under threat from two outsiders, Haneke places us 'on their side'. We may draw a sadistic pleasure in watching their struggle, but we are positioned in such a way that we want them to triumph over their captors, at the time and in the manner that conforms to the spectator's expectations of the suspense thriller's narrative trajectory.[15]

There is a dual shift here from *Benny's Video*: firstly, from a narrative that aligns our point of view with the 'villain' of the piece to one which aligns us with the 'victims'; and secondly, from one in which this alignment is based purely on plot structures to one in which the formal construction of the film deliberately encourages emotional engagement. This engagement is not attached to characterisation, for 'characterisation' here is nothing more than schematic. Both protagonists and antagonists retain the one-dimensionality that Schatz sees as the basic situation of

**Figure 3.1** The opening scenes of *Funny Games* (1997) see the Schöber family
(Stefan Clapczynski, Ulrich Mühe, Susanne Lothar) come under threat from
two anonymous intruders (Frank Giering and Arno Frisch).
*Courtesy of the BFI stills department. Permission graciously supplied by WEGAfilm.*

generic characters. From the film's opening shots, the family are
recognisable as the identikit family of fable and fairytale (father bear,
mummy bear, baby bear) and are initially framed as such through the car
windshield, with Georgie between and to the rear of his parents. After
this initial shot we very rarely see the three of them in the frame together,
and even as individuals they are reduced to discrete body parts; it is very
difficult to judge their relationships, both psychological and
geographical, to one another.[16] Likewise, the spectator is never given a
psychological explanation for the actions of the film's antagonists. The
characters are deliberately reduced to the status of ciphers: they function
as generic markers, in much the same way as certain shots or editing
techniques do.

   This one-dimensionality of characterisation is a pronounced feature
of most suspense thrillers. Suspense maximises audience involvement
with the narrative's characters, not on the basis of emotional
exploration but rather on that of situational positioning. Writing about
Hitchcock, Susan Smith elaborates upon this, stating that when
watching a suspense thriller, we are more likely to 'associate' our
emotions with the character(s) than to 'identify' with their ordeal.[17] Or,

as V.F. Perkins puts it: 'We become involved in the action of a picture in a way which precludes a specific loyalty, a direct emotional commitment to particular characters ... The spectator's involvement is a hopeful dread, both wishing and fearing to be brought face to face with the worst thing in the world'.[18] For evidence of this, we might consider the concept of consequence in the suspense thriller: so often the genre ends with the defeat of the villain, with no indication of how the surviving protagonist will be affected by the events they have endured, which may include losing loved ones and committing murder, albeit a murder (or murders) justified by narrative events. Moments such as the end of *Shadow of a Doubt* (1943), in which Teresa Wright finds herself so suddenly a melancholy adult whose naïveté is but a distant memory, are all too rare.

The suspense thriller is nonetheless a genre that depends heavily on emotional response, albeit a response circumscribed by the film's narrative and formal structures. Like horror and comedy, its label refers to a particular audience response that it provokes: one of feeling, of experiencing a 'thrill', a word that the *Oxford English Dictionary* defines as 'a wave or nervous tremor of emotion or sensation', with a 'suspense thriller' being 'an exciting or sensational story'.[19] Such definitions reveal something about the nature of our emotional responses to the genre.[20] Spectatorial emotions such as fear and frustration, which echo those of the protagonists, are emotions that we have come to associate with a film that markets itself as a suspense thriller, and we may indeed feel 'cheated' or 'disappointed' if such a film did not provoke these sentiments. These feelings, which might be considered 'negative' emotions in any other context, are part of the pleasurable trajectory of the suspense thriller. They must be established and enhanced to such a point that we can better enjoy the suspense thriller's cathartic climax.[21]

In *Caché*, a film which also draws on the generic conventions of the suspense thriller in order to subvert it, the director presents us with an intra-diegetic model of how the genre affects us emotionally. At a dinner party, one of the guests, Yvon, holds the assembled guests – and the cinematic audience – spellbound with a tale of an eerie encounter with an elderly lady, who believes him to be the reincarnation of her pet dog. As hostess Anne leans over to touch the scar that he offers as proof of his story, Yvon barks, causing her and the other guests to jump, and then to burst into laughter. The scene illustrates how the cathartic moment in the suspense thriller generally provides relief and amusement.

In this respect, the thriller is a particularly apposite genre for Haneke to use in order to examine the tension between reason and emotion. One of the ways in which *Funny Games* provokes an alternative emotional response to that arising from the use of generic conventions is by subverting the pleasure of thrill, by frustrating the moment of catharsis and replacing it with an aesthetic of consequence and a concomitant experience of unpleasure, making the spectator aware of the suffering that results from the violence that the suspense thriller inevitably displays.

## Unpleasure

In order to fully understand the experience of unpleasure that *Funny Games* provides for the spectator, it is worth briefly surveying some key points in thinking about cinematic pleasure and 'unpleasure'. Let us begin by looking to *Psychoanalysis and Cinema*, in which Metz discusses the film as a 'bad object': 'The good object relation is more basic from the standpoint of a socio-historical critique of the cinema, for it is this relation and not the opposite one that *constitutes the aim of the cinematic institution* and that the latter is constantly attempting to maintain or to re-establish'.[22] Yet, he states, certain films and spectator combinations induce reactions in which effective irritation or fantasmic allergy appear. These films provoke hostile reactions: they either frustrate the spectator by disappointing them or alternatively repulse them by overwhelming them. The classic response to the negative set of emotions that the films produce is then aggression, and this aggression is directed towards the frustrating agent: the film.

Using a psychoanalytic model, Metz states that filmic unpleasure can arise from one or both of two distinct sources. It can arise on the side of the id when the id is insufficiently nourished by the diegesis of the film. Instinctual satisfaction is stingily dealt out, and then we have a case of frustration in the proper sense: films that seem to us dull, empty and so forth. It can also result from an intervention of the superego and the defences of the ego, which are frightened and which counter-attack when the satisfaction of the id has, on the contrary, been too intense, as sometimes happens with films in 'bad taste', or films that go too far, or are childish, or sentimental, or sometimes pornographic; that is, films against which we defend ourselves by smiling or laughing, by an allegation of stupidity, grotesqueness or lack of verisimilitude. Film must apparently please conscious and unconscious fantasies enough to permit instinctual satisfaction, *within a certain limit*. Metz explains: 'In short, every time a fiction film has not been liked, it is because it has been liked too much, or not enough, or both ... One goes to the cinema because one wants to and not because one has to force oneself, in the hope that the film will please and not that it will displease'.[23] Thus for Metz filmic pleasure and filmic unpleasure are not arranged in a position of antithetic symmetry, since he believes that the institution as a whole has filmic pleasure alone as its aim.

The discourse of political modernism provides an alternative to the Metzian view of pleasure as the sole aim of the cinematic institution, and attempts to reinstate the antithetical symmetry that Metz dismisses, by calling for a cinema based on unpleasure. In her seminal essay on visual pleasure, Laura Mulvey pointed to pleasure-production as mainstream cinema's most effective mode of interpellating the subject, and called for the 'destruction of pleasure as a radical weapon'.[24] Likewise, in his tabulation of Hollywood's deadly sins and the cardinal virtues that counter-cinema must offer as a response, Peter Wollen opposes 'Pleasure' to 'Un-pleasure' (entertainment, aiming to satisfy the spectator, versus provocation, aiming to dissatisfy, and hence change, the spectator).[25] This concern with the unpleasurable was reflected in counter-cinema which, in its social and political concerns with the how and the why of film-making, was very formalist and materialist and therefore very difficult to watch. Feminist film-makers such as Chantal Akerman, for example, responded to Mulvey's call to arms by making some determinedly unpleasurable films that operated, as film-maker Eric de Kuyper puts it, on a principle of 'boredom'.[26]

But while it allows for a critical relationship to the film, this principle of pleasure-negation has two crucial flaws. Firstly, as we have seen, counter-cinematic films seek to determine the spectator's responses: in creating a cinema that works on a purely rational level, they set out to place the spectator in a fixed relationship to the spectacle. Secondly, it sees that it is the responsibility of the director to 'liberate' the spectator from the grip of Hollywood illusionism by providing an alternative cinema that does not draw on the former's interpellative structures. Such a position overlooks the spectator's own role as a consumer of mainstream cinema. As a result, counter-cinema was addressed to a relatively limited audience, who believed in its principles and aspirations, concurring with counter-cinema's premises and actively seeking out an 'alternative cinema' which would be 'radical in both a political and an aesthetic sense', challenging 'the basic assumptions of the mainstream film'.[27] The movement's film-makers, then, can be seen to an extent to be preaching to the converted: Akerman's film was doubtless seen mainly by the intellectual, feminist demographic for whom it was intended, who found a cerebral satisfaction in the film's 'difficult' form and content.

Haneke's films, on the other hand, attract wider audiences. In fact, we have seen that he goes so far as to claim that the spectators that he has in mind for his films are 'the willing consumers of movies that operate with an aesthetics of distraction'.[28] *Funny Games* was marketed to emphasise the film's generic qualities and thus lure in these spectators. The director can then go on to trouble these conventions to varying extents, to reveal their inherent flaws. The film uses the tools of the industry, namely its genre models, in order to deconstruct the system (including its promotional aspects) and, by creating distinctly unpleasurable films, it is able to confront spectators with their own participation in the scopic act, rather than to simply negate the scopophilic situation.

In addition to relating to issues of emotion and rational awareness, Haneke's use of unpleasure also relates to the opposition of realism to constructedness, as exemplified by the conflict between Bazinian and Eisenteinian theory. For we discover something about film's relationship to reality by watching *Funny Games*, and inasmuch Haneke's film stands within a 'realist' tradition. But what we discover is not reality in the sense of spatial relations and bodily gestures revealing the movement of life as in Bazin's spectatorship theory. Rather, it lies with the reality addressed within the construction of the film, a construction that draws on both classical narrative editing and Eisensteinian montage. Unlike Eisenstein, however, Haneke does not mobilise montage techniques with the sole aim of manipulation: their significance instead lies in Haneke's *exposure* of them as devices for manipulation. This revelation of the mechanics of manipulation is a critical strategy born out of a long tradition of modernist film.

There is clearly an analogy to be made between a film-maker like Jean-Luc Godard's project of counter-cinema and *Funny Games*, a work that demonstrates a continuing preoccupation with film thought, with the language of cinema, and with the circulation of images in society, much like many of Godard's films. Haneke, like the makers of counter-cinema, uses film as a tool to reveal the medium's inherent falsity; his films are aimed at bringing about a confrontation with the dominant mainstream image system in order to challenge the system of representation and perception that it perpetuates, and which he sees as pernicious. He brings about the confrontation with dominant forms of perception and representation through the denial of pleasure. But Haneke employs this tool in service of a different cause to that which preoccupied his modernist predecessors. While Godard, for example, started from the assertion that the illusionist conventions of mainstream cinema function to obscure the real conditions of film production, Haneke takes as his basis the belief that its pleasure-driven conventions obscure the ethical void at the heart of its narrative structures and forms. There is a purism in the work of Godard and his contemporaries relating to the creation of an experience which aims to radicalise the medium. This purism is absent from Haneke's critical aesthetic: while Haneke builds upon modernist techniques in order to take film in a different direction, he is clearly not an anti-narrative film-maker in the sense that Akerman and Godard were.

For rather than eschew what we might call 'Hollywood technique' entirely, Haneke's films enter into dialogue with and draw upon existing narrative forms and genre conventions in order to generate a new spectatorial experience which focuses on the spectator's ethical position in relation to the film. Instead of simply undermining the generic mechanisms for involving the spectator, he situates them within a larger framework of representation within the film. In contrast with counter-cinema, Haneke's cinema does not eschew plot in order to create an atmosphere of extreme detachment; indeed plotting is mobilised in the service of providing a response to the film that is both somatic and rational. Haneke extends counter-cinema's denial of pleasure to a distinct confrontation with the inverse of pleasure – unpleasure – by drawing on structures that put pleasure into motion, and then blocking them with structures that suddenly rupture the pleasure drive.

Unpleasure is experienced differently in Haneke to how it is experienced in Godard's *Le Vent d'est*, for example, or indeed to how it is experienced in counter-cinema more widely. That 'unpleasure' can refer to a number of different spectatorial experiences points to a confusion in the semantics of counter-cinema. The 'destruction of pleasure' has been equated, variously, with the negation of pleasure, the frustration of pleasure (or dissatisfaction), and/or the production of 'unpleasure'. But there are distinctive differences between these three phenomena. Mulvey's oversight – reiterating Wollen's – is to conflate 'not enjoying' a film, which is in effect the negation of emotion, with blocking an emotion already operating (the frustration of pleasure) and actively experiencing an unpleasant negative emotion (unpleasure). The difference is that between a film that we assess on a purely intellectual level, since it simply refuses us the pleasures of scopophilia; a film that disappoints or bores us, because we had previously been enjoying it, or had at least been expecting to enjoy it; and a film which causes us such discomfort as to make us tangibly unhappy or sickened. For example, *Der Siebente Kontinent* negated cinematic pleasure through the use of Wollen's cardinal virtues, thereby engaging the spectator on a purely intellectual level. The opening scene of *Benny's Video* on the other hand creates an active sensation of unpleasure through a very visceral attack on the spectator's senses. Here, unpleasure is experienced as discomfort (resulting from the loud squeals of the pig), revulsion (at the graphic depiction of slaughter), and shock (at the brutality of these opening scenes). Both of these techniques come into play in *Funny Games*. But we shall now see how the generic structure within which the film operates radicalises them.

## The 'Modernist Episode'

To recount, Haneke uses genre forms and classical narrative conventions – as well as stylistic techniques such as classical editing and Eisensteinian montage – in order to mobilise the spectator's desire for a familiar form of cinematic pleasure. The unpleasure we often experience whilst watching Haneke's films arises from the blocking or mitigating of this pleasure. It is therefore not only linked to the way in which the film mobilises desire, but also to the way in which it constructs a scenario that operates directly on the emotions, in a manner very similar to how Hitchcock's suspense operates directly on certain, minimal emotions. Unpleasure is then intensified, as we will see, by Haneke's ability to draw out these emotions, and allow us time to reflect on their sources. In this space for reflection on their own emotional experience of the film, the viewer must consider not only the film itself but also their relationship to it. They can thereby gain insights into their own engagement in the act of film spectatorship.

In *Funny Games*, unpleasure arises from two distinct sources, both of which work in tension with the film's generic framework. The first of these I shall refer to as the 'modernist episode', as it draws on the 'benign' modernist structure demonstrated in the cinema of Bresson, for example. This 'episode' forms a coda to one of the film's central sequences, which sees Georgie escape from his captors and flee to a neighbouring villa – with Paul in pursuit – before being recaptured and killed. Involving a long shot, taken with an almost static camera (movement is severely restricted) and held for approximately ten minutes, it provides a stark contrast to the ten minutes of rapid editing and close-ups that lead up to it. Viewed in conjunction with the preceding sequence, the 'modernist episode' thus highlights a juxtaposition of stylistic modes that Haneke operates within the film: the 'modernist episode' throws the classic generic conventions of the chase and murder sequences which precede it into relief.

We can divide this twenty-minute section of *Funny Games* into three acts, or segments: the chase, the murder, and the aftermath.

1. **The chase:** Rapid cuts show Georgie and Paul alternately crossing the bayou that divides the Schöbers house from that of their neighbours and entering the latter. The (anti)climatic moment, in which Georgie confronts Paul with a gun, is thrown into sudden light as the latter flicks a switch. A medium-long shot showing Paul approaching Georgie establishes the set-up; then there is a graphic match between a close-up of Paul and a close-up of Georgie. An extreme close-up of the trigger as it snaps (but the gun fails to go off) closes the sequence.

2. **The murder:** A medium-distance shot of the living room in Anna and George's house (re)establishes the cinematic space: Anna and George sit on a couch at the right-hand edge of the frame; Peter is at the left-hand edge. The television, showing a motor race, is in the centre of the frame. The camera cuts to Georgie running back into the frame and

joining his mother on the couch, then to Paul entering the room carrying the gun. A sequence of medium-paced cuts ensues, central to which is a matched pair of close-ups of Paul and Peter each loading one bullet into the gun. A shot/reverse-shot of the two facing couches introduces a counting game in which the person counted out will be shot. As Peter begins to count, the camera follows Paul through the hallway and into the kitchen. The camera remains on Paul, and we hear a gunshot and the noise of sobbing on the soundtrack.

3. **The aftermath:** The sequence opens with a close-up of the television. As the camera lingers, blood spattered over its screen becomes perceptible. On the soundtrack, the killers' conversation makes it clear that they have killed Georgie and that they are leaving. Cut to a medium distance shot of the room: there is no movement, the soundtrack is dominated by the sound of car engines coming from the television. The room is darkened, lit only by the flickering television, a lamp in the corner illuminating Anna, and the hall light which spills into the room. The shot lasts for ten minutes in total, two of which pass before any movement of camera or character occurs, four before anyone speaks. Some eight minutes into the scene George starts to sob. After he calms himself there is another minute's silence before Anna announces 'We've got to get out of here', reintroducing the narrative drive for action. Following Anna's excruciating efforts to lift her husband, the action (and cutting) recommences.

The first segment, the chase, constitutes the most obviously Hitchcockian sequence of *Funny Games*. A long shot of the house's darkened exterior held for several moments lends it the sinister aspect of the Bates Motel. The chase is punctuated by rapid cuts that match Georgie (the pursued) with Paul (the pursuer). In the house, the suspense is heightened by the *mise-en-scène*: darkened rooms prevent Georgie and the audience from seeing Paul. The soundtrack emphasises every heavy breath and creaking door until Zorn's score comes in (from a diegetic source), creating a sense of irritation and excess: the screams on the tape pre-echoing the potential screams we expect to hear.[29] The scene thus builds in tension to the anticlimactic moment, with cuts increasing in frequency and close-ups tightening the viewer's focus on to the characters' faces and the gun's trigger. Cutting away at this point to the family living room, Haneke leaves his spectators in a position of suspended tension, anxious as to whether Paul will kill Georgie.

Throughout the chase segment, the action is cross-cut with another scene in the living room, where Anna and George remain with Peter (parallel action being one of the classic formal tropes of the suspense thriller). The second segment, the murder, begins with a cut back to the living room, in which the television is central within the frame, the characters relegated to the sidelines. The noise of motor racing on-screen provides a backdrop to the dialogue throughout the scene, steadily increasing in volume as the scene progresses, echoing the Zorn soundtrack in its irritating, tuneless noise. As Paul and Georgie enter the frame the latter announces to his mother, 'They've killed Sissi'. This signals, in case we had any doubt, that their captors are capable of murder (and more significantly, the murder of a child: it is established in an earlier conversation between Georgie and his father that Sissi is a little girl of around Georgie's age). The close-ups of Peter and Paul loading the gun bestow an ominous significance on their actions, and the gun's presence in the frame (cutting into and across the screen both vertically and horizontally at different moments) contributes to the build-up of tension. As Paul leaves the room and the camera follows him into the kitchen, his footsteps, which are paced in time with Peter's counting, encourage the spectator to keep marking time mentally as we wait for Haneke to cut back to the living room. Once more, tension is built up to an anticlimactic moment, but in this case it is not an anticlimax of narrative, but one of form: we do not see the killing, but hear the gun go off and the screams that follow, while the camera remains in the kitchen with Paul.

The anticlimactic moment that marks the end of the chase is one familiar from the suspense genre: the director builds up to a climactic moment, creating a false hope of catharsis, and then frustrates this hope in order to reignite the viewer's sense of tension. In this case, the climactic moment is literally suspended. The end of the second segment, on the other hand, creates an opposite effect. Here, the climactic moment that the spectator has been waiting for (a gun to be shot, a murder to take place) does indeed occur, but the spectator is denied the pleasure of catharsis by the anticlimactic manner in which it is presented. This moment of anticlimax leads us into the following segment, the aftermath, which functions as an extended enactment of the same principle. In the run up to the modernist episode, Haneke is uninterested in showing the assault itself: sound conveys the fact that it is occurring. He concentrates, instead, on the consequences of this bloodshed. The spectator, both seduced by the classical suspense structure that Haneke employs and suddenly removed from the safety of the familiar, is confronted with a close-up of the television. It is only as Haneke holds the shot that the blood splattered across the screen becomes visible. For the first time in the film, the spectator is forced to examine the image before them, rather than passively accept it.[30]

As Paul and Peter's dialogue is layered over the sound of the television, we learn that Georgie is dead and that the villains are now leaving. Not only does the villains' departure remove the sense of threat, but the death of Georgie unsettles the viewer, as it breaks one of the

suspense thriller's unwritten rules: as Hitchcock's *Sabotage* (1936)
established, the murder of a child is generally too emotionally unsettling
for an audience to absorb within the limits of the pleasure drive. The
'rules' of the suspense thriller are thus simultaneously ruptured on a
narrative and a formal level: with the driving force of the film's narrative
gone, the spectator is confronted with a void, the pleasure drive
suddenly forestalled. Unpleasure arises as a result of the obstruction of
the pleasure drive which, having been mobilised, is suddenly thwarted.
It also arises from the spectator's emotional reorientation. With the
selfish emotional drive for pleasure blocked, the spectator engages with
the events on screen in a different manner: discomfort comes from being
forced to witness the aftermath of Georgie's death and engage with a set
of emotions unfamiliar to the genre. For the presentation of consequence
does not mobilise an epistemic concern with what *will* happen, but
rather it forces the spectator to consider the implications of what *has*
happened. At this moment in the narrative there is no immediate
imperative for the characters to act, and so we are put into contact with
how they *re*act. As Haneke explains (in a somewhat biased, but
nonetheless persuasive, example):

> In general, a stationary picture shows the result of an action, whereas a film
> shows the action itself. A stationary picture mostly appeals to an observer's
> empathy with the victim, whereas generally in film the viewer is placed in
> the role of the perpetrator. When looking at Picasso's *Guernica*, for instance,
> we see the victims' pain for the eternity of viewing: solidarity with the
> victims, without moral stumbling blocks. But in the massacre in Coppola's
> *Apocalypse Now* (with Wagner's 'Ride of the Valkyries' playing in the
> background) we are in the helicopter, firing at the stampeding Vietnamese
> below us, and we do this all without a bad conscience, because – at least in
> the moment of action – we are not aware that we are adopting this role.[31]

So while this 'modernist episode' in the film adheres to many of the
precepts of the alternative cinema as defined by Mulvey and Wollen, its
juxtaposition with a classical cinematic narrative gives rise to the
production of cinematic unpleasure; a term which here signifies not
only the frustration of the pleasure drive, but also the mobilisation of a
range of 'negative' emotions on the spectator's part. Apparatus theory
states that the spectator is positioned by classical-realist structures to
believe that they have control over the cinematic image. This illusion of
control is troubled as the spectator gradually becomes aware of the
image frame, and hence of the fact that the fictional space is, after all,
narrowly circumscribed. The realisation stimulates the desire to see and
find out more, and the former illusion of the image as offering a
'window on the world' yields to an unpleasant perception of the film as
artefact, a system of signs and codes that lie outside the spectator's

control. The unpleasure that springs from this recognition is only overcome by the advent of the next shot, which apparently restores the previous condition of the spectator's imaginary unity with the images and starts the cycle off again.[32]

Haneke operates in accordance with this principle throughout the film's generic framework, editing the film at a rapid pace so that the spectator's imaginary unity with the image is secured. But in the 'modernist episode' he delays the advent of the next shot, which would maintain the spectator's illusion of control, and extends the moment of realisation of the film as construct that Baudry sees as characteristic of the apparatus effect. In this way he extends the spectator's awareness of the film as artifice. For when the image does not abruptly change (when, in fact, it lingers on the screen for many minutes at a time, with only minor variations in framing and/or movement within the frame) the spectator is forced to do that which they do when confronted with a painting in a museum or a gallery: they must scrutinise the image, deconstruct it, consider the margins and borders of the frame, and 'contemplate' the structure of representational strategies that informed the creation of this image.

The formal reflexivity of Haneke's *Funny Games* is thus distinguished by its context: its combination with other stylistic modes is what separates it from similar scenes in *Der Siebente Kontinent* and *71 Fragmente einer Chronologie des Zufalls*. So, in its juxtaposition with the generic suspense structures that Haneke operates, the 'modernist episode' allows for a binary reorientation of spectatorial reflection. On a primary level this relates to how the spectator perceives the image itself: the practically static ten-minute take leads the spectator to examine the image visually on an aesthetic and intellectual level, rather than to 'scan' the image mentally in order to place it within the context of the narrative. But on a secondary level, the extended duration of the image, coupled with the lack of narrative drive, creates an awareness in the spectator of themselves *as a spectator*. As the director puts it, 'the reduction of montage to a minimum tends to shift responsibility back to the viewer in that more contemplation is required'.[33] He elaborates:

> As soon as time becomes manifest in a film, it disturbs the spectators who are used to a fast pace, especially if the pictures concern matters which they have learned to suppress. At first they react with irritation, then they are bored and finally annoyed – the classic sequence of a defensive reaction. If one has the courage to put them through this ordeal, they will in the end come to face the condition with which they are confronted in picture and in sound. As a result, the contents *once again will become felt*, instead of being merely registered as information to be checked off.[34]

While the 'modernist episode' allows the spectator time to become rationally aware of the cinematic image as construct, it also gives rise to an emotional or 'felt' reaction. This reaction stems from two sources: the awareness that Baudry links to the spectator's awareness of the film as a construct, and the extended exposure to the depiction of Anna and George's grief (the consequence of their son's death), which brings these one-dimensional ciphers into focus as more psychologically-rounded characters for whom we feel empathy. Both are experienced as unpleasurable.

## 'Aggressive' Reflexivity

The 'modernist episode' thus develops what Susan Smith terms the feeling of 'discomfort' which the spectator of Hitchcock's suspense thrillers often experiences as a result of 'tension between conflicting responses' as we are made aware of 'our own involvement in desires and emotions that are the reverse of admirable'. Smith states that this 'is one of the means whereby we participate in Hitchcock's films rather than merely watch them' so that we come to sense 'the complex moral implications of the experiences we share or which are communicated to us'.[35] By the film's end, this discomfort is subordinated to the pleasure drive as a result of the intensity of Hitchcock's suspense strategies: the ludic tone that returns the spectator to an experience of the film as pleasurable, and the narrative closure that he offers. Haneke, however, reinforces the unpleasurable effect of the 'modernist episode' through the introduction of a second mode of reflexivity that contrasts with the film's generic conventions as well as with the 'modernist episode'. This second mode of reflexivity is used to confront directly the cathartic effect of the generic suspense thriller in order to expose these features as parts of its conventional construction, thus heightening the unpleasurable experience.

Because they operate in different manners, it is important to distinguish clearly between the two predominant modes of reflexivity that operate within *Funny Games*. In order to do so, we shall have recourse to the concepts of first-generation and second-generation modernism, as introduced in Chapter Three. To recap, the 'modernist episode' demonstrates a first generation reflexivity, which shares common ground with the self-conscious style of Robert Bresson or Chantal Akerman, for example, and which we saw characterised *Der Siebente Kontinent*. This is a 'benign' form of reflexivity, which allows the spectator time to reflect on the image and thus distances them from the action on-screen. The second mode of reflexivity is not postmodernist, but meditates on first-generation reflexivity, and is demonstrated by the later films of Jean-Luc Godard, for example, which, retaining first-generation techniques, extend them into a more direct, 'aggressive' approach to the spectator, which is explicitly metatextual. While both modes of reflexivity have been associated with the political-modernist agenda of placing the spectator in a position where they are rationally aware of the film as a construct, they operate in very different ways. For the second set of techniques, 'aggressively' reflexive, are not concerned with distancing the spectator from the cinematic action, but with emphasising their proximity to it. That is, where first-generation modernism only calls the spectator's attention to the film, second-generation modernism calls their attention to *themselves*, as a consumer of that film. If first-generation modernism attempts to place the spectator in a more objective relationship to the image, then second-generation modernism emphasises the subjectivity of the spectator, and makes it count for something.

Haneke thus installs a third aesthetic frame around and within his work, hinted at but far from actualised in his earlier works. This is composed of a second-generation reflexivity used to control and contextualise the messages viewers should extract from his work, making them directly relevant to their own situation as complicit in the cinematic spectacle. In the case of *Funny Games*, Haneke employs 'aggressive' reflexivity in order to call attention to the spectator's consumption of the (violent) spectacle as commodity and his emotional investment in the generic structures of the suspense thriller. The film's antagonists, who hold the family members hostage (proceeding to torture and kill them), acknowledge the audience's presence directly at various moments in the film's narrative (or at least one of them does). Beginning some twenty minutes into the film with a wink to the camera, Paul addresses the audience at a number of points over the course of the film.[36] When George pleads with his torturers to put an end to his family's suffering, Paul replies, 'We are still under feature length.' Turning to address the audience directly, he continues: 'Is it enough already? You want a proper ending with plausible development, don't you?'

Such moments occur at regular intervals throughout the film. However, they are not frequent (occurring only five times throughout the film's 108 minutes) and they do not constitute a sustained overture to the spectator as is the case in Rémy Belvaux, André Bonzel and Benoît Poelvoorde's *C'est arrivé près de chez vous/Man Bites Dog* (1992), in which the killer is the subject of a documentary, constantly commenting on his actions to the camera; or Kubrick's *A Clockwork Orange* (1971), in which protagonist Alex's asides harmonise with the film's surreal aesthetic and stylised *mise-en-scène*. There is apparently no narrative grounding within the generic structure of *Funny Games* for the characters to break with the film's diegetic universe.

Moreover Paul is the only character who acknowledges the presence of the camera/audience, a fact which leads Mark Kermode, in his review of the film for *Sight & Sound*, to claim that the killers and their victims 'seem to be in different movies, with [Arno] Frisch [playing Paul] nipping merrily back and forth between the film's world and ours, while [Suzanne] Lothar [as Anna] remains resolutely locked ... within Haneke's narrative'.[37] Kermode's comment implies a tacit understanding of Haneke's use of two – or three, if we consider the 'modernist episode' as separate from this 'aggressive' reflexivity – different stylistic modes which operate within *Funny Games*: and in effect, Paul and Anna *are* in different films. In *Benny's Video*, Haneke switches between various filmic realities, between *Benny's Video* and Benny's video, troubling the divide between 'real' and 'virtual'. In much the same way, the generic framework of *Funny Games* reveals itself to be a façade of sorts for the 'real' film that Haneke is making, although the distinction between the two is heavily blurred.

The use of aggressively reflexive devices such as audience address is by no means an original technique, and Haneke has acknowledged his debt to films such as Richardson's *Tom Jones* (1963), in which the eponymous hero, a third of the way through the film, turns to the camera and comments on the difficulty of his predicament.[38] However, Haneke's deployment of a similar device in *Funny Games* differs from Richardson's in two aspects: firstly, it is the *antagonist*, rather than the protagonist, who addresses the audience; and secondly, the address to the audience constantly refers to the fact that the antagonists are 'performing' for the audience as part of a film. Paul does not merely acknowledge the audience as spectators, but he also accuses them of being his very *raison d'être*: the cinematic violence in *Funny Games* exists only because the audience expects it.

This technique of 'aggressive', second-generation reflexivity finds its culmination towards the end of Haneke's film, in a scene in which Anna shoots one of her captors, Peter, only for his accomplice, Paul, to seize a diegetic remote control and rewind the film's action from within the diegetic universe and then 'replay' events to his advantage. Not only does Anna's murder of Peter occur at the climactic point of another Hitchcockian build-up of tension, but it also includes the only instance in the film of violence occurring on screen. As Anna seizes the gun, the camera rapidly follows her lunge for the weapon and then cuts to her swinging it around to point at Peter. A cut to a reverse shot of Peter follows, as his stomach bursts open and he is thrown back by the force of the blast, and then a medium shot of Paul's reaction, which features the film's only verbal obscenity ('Where's the fucking remote?'/'Wo ist die Scheiß-Fernbedienung?')[39]

The sequence is clichéd in the extreme, mimicking the 'guts and gore' sequences of numerous Hollywood actions films. Indeed, it may be construed as representing a fourth stylistic mode: the Hitchcockian suspense thriller becomes the all-action 'shoot 'em up', a cinematic tradition that we can say starts with 'New Hollywood' film-making, a term that is used to refer to the cinema of Dennis Hopper, Martin Scorsese and Francis Ford Coppola, amongst others. This cinema, Pam Cook points out, 'plays' with stylised violence,[40] producing a violent spectacle that is perhaps best exemplified by Sam Peckinpah's 'ultraviolent movies',[41] from *The Wild Bunch* (1969) to *Bring Me the Head of Alfredo Garcia* (1974),[42] in which a combination of slow motion footage of violent encounters, detonating squibs and exploding blood bags is used to portray violent death, much to the delight of many spectators.[43] Several directors of violent films have been heavily influenced by Peckinpah's visual signature. But while upon their release Peckinpah's films reinscribed the cultural depiction of violence and lent it a new power to shock – and thus connected it to a set of moral concerns – in its contemporary incarnations, what seems like excess has, Linda Williams claims, become a routine element.[44] Directors such as Quentin Tarantino use explicit portrayals of violence for both aesthetic and dramatic effect, but the critical response to their techniques is ambivalent: some critics decry their works as too realistic and graphic, while others dismiss the violence as unrealistic and cartoonish.[45] Like many of his peers (such as Kathryn Bigelow, Oliver Stone and Tony Scott), Tarantino's rendition of screen violence is thoroughly postmodern.[46] This might extend to his entire aesthetic: Tarantino's images are pastiches, inflected by the movie and TV culture he imbibed in his youth, and their emotional and moral content is second-hand, derived from, and mediated by, the pop-cultural material that is their immediate referent. As Stephen Prince puts it, 'the style itself is the subject and form of [Tarantino's] work'.[47]

What films such as *Natural Born Killers* (1994), *Strange Days* (1995) and *Reservoir Dogs* (1992) are mainly concerned with, in their postmodern style, is the imagery of violence, violence as pop-culture iconography. The films are preoccupied with a derivative, second-order movie and media-based iconography. In this postmodern style, the film-maker's images comment on other images, other films, or television shows because the possibility of the image having a referentially real relationship with a representable world is mistrusted by the film-maker (Tarantino) or else she or he is simply uninterested in that relationship (Stone with *Natural Born Killers*). When Oliver Stone, therefore, attempts to put a high moral gloss on *Natural Born Killers* by recycling the terms by which a director such as Sam Peckinpah spoke of his work on violence, the attempt seems not merely hollow and imitative, but strangely anti-historical, as if the intervening decades of movie violence had not demonstrated the limitations of that effort.

Haneke's attack is aimed not at the stylised violence that Peckinpah's films demonstrate: clichéd as it has now become, it was at the time both well meant and effective. However, Peckinpah's praxis – using montage style to give a new degree of realism to cinematic violence, which had the power to shock the audience – became the practico-inert of these techniques' frequent adoption, first by film and then by television, so that they have now become commonplace, and the montage style actually *complements* the violence represented and presents it largely in a positive light. Haneke's attack, then, is directed against the postmodern films that mimic Peckinpah's style, without attempting to restore it to its original power to horrify. Haneke makes his targets clear, explaining the film as a 'counterprogram' [sic] to Stone's *Natural Born Killers*, and introducing it at Cannes as an 'anti-Tarantino film'.[48] These directors, he states, 'make the violent image alluring while allowing no space for the viewer'.[49] His counter-project aims to accord the spectator this space, and to prompt them to use it to consider their own part in the production and consumption of these violent images.

By drawing on another set of 'generic' clichés – in this instance those associated with the 'ultraviolent' movie – Haneke again deliberately aims to provoke a suspension of critical awareness by using cinematic signposts associated with the pursuit of cinematic pleasure. In this short sequence, the spectator experiences not the tension associated with a building up of suspense but a cathartic release provided by the moment of the victim's revenge. The switch in generic convention points can perhaps be attributed to Haneke's desire to draw on the most extreme instance of violence functioning as catharsis: the more satisfying the release of tension, the more powerful the effect of its rescindment. The spectator, caught up in the violent fantasy of retribution and escape, is at their most vulnerable for the ensuing rewind sequence.[50]

To frame it once more in terms of apparatus theory, Haneke creates for the spectator a secure, imaginary relationship to the film. He encourages the desire for catharsis and narrative closure and satisfies it so that the spectator might maintain the illusion of privileged control over, and unmediated access to, the fictional world. The effect of the rewind is to shatter this illusion, seizing control from the spectator and situating it firmly in the hands of the director. Once again, the impact of this technique is intensified by the contrast with the preceding scenes, and heightened by the bathos of George's ensuing death: in an elliptical montage, Haneke shows Paul aiming the gun at the position we know George to be in, then cuts to the killers leaving the house as the sound of a gunshot extends across the cut between the two scenes. The spectator, divested of the illusion of themselves as the omnipotent subject

– somehow in control of the narrative – by the preceding rewind, is left with the quick and unseen death of a character whose salvation they had witnessed only minutes before.

The rewind scene thus provides us with an alternative, but no less effective, example of how Haneke mobilises emotion and judgement simultaneously within his films. Let us use an analogy here. If we think of the pleasure drive as a train, travelling with a forward (e)motion, then we might say that when the pleasure drive is very strong, the train is travelling very fast, so fast that we can't see anything out of the windows and are oblivious to everything but the hermetically sealed world in front of us. The effect of benign reflexivity that distances the audience from the image is to slow down the pleasure drive so that we can see more clearly. A modernist film that does not mobilise the pleasure drive at all can be said to be driving slowly or not driving at all, whereas the 'modernist episode' in *Funny Games* puts the brakes on a train that had previously been driving at very high speed. The effect of 'aggressive' reflexivity, on the other hand, when coupled with an operating pleasure drive, is to place an object directly in the train's path, causing a sudden and jarring shock. The size of the object determines the effect that it will have on the train's forward momentum. If the object is too small, the train will push it out of its way and continue en route. On the other hand, if it is too large, the object will derail the train altogether (and it may be that this is precisely Haneke's aim if, as he claims, the correct response for a spectator of *Funny Games* is to leave the cinema – ceasing altogether the forward momentum of the pleasure drive).[51] But it is possible that the train may continue en route, if the object is of a certain size, its effect not too overwhelming, only now it will be somewhat less stable than before.

In the case of both the 'modernist episode' in *Funny Games*, which has the effect of slamming the brakes on the pleasure drive, and the film's 'aggressive' reflexivity, which causes a collision, an impact occurs. The point of impact is the moment at which the spectatorial pleasure drive (attached to the narrative) and the spectator's conscious reflexivity about the status of the film as a film coincide. It is the result of reason and feeling conflicting. The spectator's comfortable position as the unseen viewer, caught up in the narrative developments on-screen, is very abruptly destabilised.

## Eisensteinian Impact

This notion of impact as a collision between reason and emotion looks back to an Eisensteinian moment in film theory. Eisenstein emphasised the spectator's status as a real person (rather than a theoretical or

**Figure 3.2**  Paul (Arno Frisch) holds Georgie (Stefan Clapczynski)
hostage on the sofa in *Funny Games*.
*Courtesy of the BFI stills department. Permission graciously supplied by WEGAfilm.*

commercial concept), establishing a model of the cinematic experience as a transaction between the screen image (and soundtrack) and the spectator in the cinema. According to Eisenstein, meaning in the cinema was not inherent in any filmed object, but was created by the *collision* of two signifying elements, one coming after the other, their juxtaposition producing 'specific emotional shocks in the spectator in their proper order within the whole'.[52] There is here a clear convergence with the way in which impact works in Haneke's films.

However, a key difference between the two models of spectatorship centres upon their approach to emotion. Like many film theorists (including, as we have discussed, the proponents of political modernism), Eisenstein displays a clear mistrust of emotional manipulation, perceiving a danger in what he called 'psychological retrogression', in which cinema becomes subordinated to the automaton of sensual, prelogical thinking.[53] This sensual thought can suddenly become dominant, even in the most complex of social constructions, because the margins between the higher phases of intellectual order and the primitive and baser instincts are extremely mobile and volatile, and they often undergo sudden shifts at each stage of development. Eisenstein writes that:

> This continual sliding from level to level, forwards and backwards, now to
> the higher forms of an intellectual order, now to the earlier forms of sensual

thinking, occurs at each ... phase in development. ... The margin between the types is mobile and it suffices a not even extraordinarily sharp affective impulse to cause an extremely, it may be, logically deliberate person suddenly to react in obedience to the never dormant inner armory of sensual thinking [sic] and the norms of behavior [sic] deriving thence.[54]

Nonetheless, rather than recoiling in fear and thereby avoiding further research into the use of emotional manipulation, Eisenstein perceived in the cinema the potential for a dialectical progression that would maintain the pursuit of highly complex intellectual forms and processes and, at the same time, the 'analysis' of the early forms of sensual thinking. He makes what Gregg Lambert, in his article 'Cinema and the Outside', terms 'Eisenstein's wager': to invent not a merely rhetorical cinema, but an analytic cinema, a cinematographic science of thinking.[55] By means of technical montage, cinema has to achieve neither a purely emotional engagement with the image nor an aesthetic-intellectual engagement which negates the former and is now exemplified by 1970s counter-cinema, but rather a 'dynamic perception of phenomena', which dialectically absorbs the first two. Eisenstein's theory of cinema, like Haneke's, is thus founded on a dynamic principle of interaction between these two manners of connecting with the cinematic image. Film, according to Eisenstein, had to avoid becoming too sensual on the one hand, and too formal and abstract on the other, always seeking as the principle of its development *a certain balance,* so that the total process achieves the figure of a dialectical 'spiral', following a dual unity in which the highest form of art has as its correlate the deepest form of subconscious: 'The effectiveness of a work of art is built upon the fact that there takes place within it a dual process: an impetuous progressive rise along the lines of the highest explicit steps of consciousness and a simultaneous penetration by means of the structure of the form into the layers of profoundest sensual thinking'.[56]

## Emotion and Feeling

Haneke revisits the Eisensteinian model of impact as a visceral force upon the viewer, but there is a crucial difference between how Eisenstein conceived of and employed the tension between reason and instinct and how Haneke views and uses it. This difference needs some attention if we are to understand why impact in *Funny Games* is related to questions of ethics.

To distinguish Eisensteinian impact from the impact that arises from Haneke's films, there is a need for some clarification here about how we understand one of the key terms of the spectatorship debate; that is, how we understand the term 'emotion'. Up until this point in the book, the word 'emotion' has been used as the prototypical term within a broader category of phenomena including feelings, affects and drives. We need now to be more specific in how we deploy each of these terms. This is no easy task: efforts to make strict definitions of emotion words have as yet failed. Sometimes the distinction between the terms is one of intensity: emotions are stronger than feelings. Sometimes the terms are used to distinguish between object-directed and non-object-directed qualities. Following for the most part psychologist C.E. Izard's definitions as a guideline, we will say here that feelings are often non-object directed (I feel sad, I feel happy and so on), whereas emotions often have an object-directed quality; strong emotions like love, hate or jealousy are often object-directed, but romantic feelings are often non-object-directed. When we love, we love *someone*; when we feel romantic, these romantic feelings might be directed towards someone, but they are equally likely to be the result of a general ambience, unattached to any one person in particular.[57]

We can now use these revised definitions of emotion and feeling to clarify our understanding of impact in Eisenstein and in Haneke, beginning with the former. In his 1935 lecture 'Film Form: New Problems', Eisenstein discusses the concept of 'inner speech', which occurs 'at the stage of the inner-sensual structure, not yet having attained that logical formulation with which speech clothes itself before stepping out into the open'.[58] The example that he gives is the pince-nez of the drowned surgeon in *Battleship Potemkin* (1925), which not only transcends the simple *pars pro toto*, but also supplants the necessity of representing the bloated corpse of the surgeon himself, and 'does so with a *sensual-emotional* increase in the intensity of the impression'.[59] The spectator's somatic response to the image sequence of which the pince-nez is part might be one of dread, sorrow or fear, but this response arises from a general synthesis of the whole sequence. It is not attached to a particular character within the film, since the principle of inner speech in montage privileges images over narrative and characterisation. Indeed, these images often remain meaningless until the mind creates the links between them through its metaphoric capability. What inner speech offers the spectator then, in terms of somatic response, is a response of feeling: a generalised experience rather than an object-directed emotion. The somatic experience thus has its place within Eisensteinian impact. But for Eisenstein, the experience is one of physiological sensations (expressed by Eisenstein as 'I feel'). Art requires conflict, and conflict produces vibrations.

Now, the sensual effect of montage leads, according to Eisenstein, to thought, by bringing body and mind together. The effect of impact produces an intelligence of the senses. The fact that the spectator experiences a generalised feeling rather than an object-directed emotion is pivotal to how Eisenstein conveys meaning within his films. As a director he was not interested in depicting the unfolding of events or in clarifying a narrative action, believing that such elucidations 'dilute the impact that metaphor and fragmentation can have'.[60] A first interpretation of this notion of dilution might lead us to believe that the term simply implies the weakening of a metaphor's impact, which seems to conflict with Izard's explanation of emotion as a much stronger sensation than feeling. But 'dilution' takes on new connotations when we view it in the light of Eisenstein's belief in cinema as an 'art of the masses'. His desire to make the masses a 'true subject' necessarily involves the treatment of the masses as a united subject: in a sense, the spectator of Eisenstein's films is not an individual but a collective consciousness. The spectator, by sensual thinking, becomes identical with every other spectator, a proxy for this collective consciousness, deprived of the capacity for individual response. Impact occurs at a prelogical level, but is expressed as thought, tied to a concatenation of meanings. It is thus linked to a desire to control the spectator's response: as such, the coercive aspect of Eisenstein's film gives rise to propaganda and the impact of film is effectively the bearer of the content or 'meaning' of Eisenstein's films.

Whereas Eisenstein saw felt response as being vibratory with, that is to say harmonious with, intellectual response, Haneke sees them as directly opposed. This is not to say that one should be sacrificed at the expense of the other (as we see happening in counter-cinema and in Hollywood cinema), but that this opposition should be used productively. Haneke's film, unlike Eisenstein's, is not a film of purely mental leaps, but a cinema of emotion and reason arising out of narrative concerns. But more importantly, it is also a cinema of emotion and reason *occurring in tension.* The spectator is prompted to respond both emotionally *and* intellectually to the film, and when these two different forms of response occur simultaneously, a productive conflict results: a conflict which forces the spectator to reflect rationally upon their own emotional response. Haneke mobilises emotion in the form of the pleasure drive by using narrative structures that we associate with Hollywood films. The difference, then, between his notion of impact and Eisenstein's is the difference between an impact that is immediate and which may be associated with an idea independent of narrative development – for this is one of the premises for Eisensteinian montage – and a much more complex cognitive involvement with a temporal development of narrative. Thus, while we can refer to the sentiments arising from Eisensteinian impact as 'feelings', the sentiments that are part of this involvement in Haneke's films we must call – by Izard's definition – 'emotions', in order to indicate that these affective states are oriented towards individual characters in narrative. They are concrete, externally directed and have clear sources, which Haneke intentionally puts before us.

## The Individuated Spectator

So, while Haneke, like Eisenstein and like the political modernists, is somewhat mistrustful of emotion, seeing it as the enemy of reason, it is nonetheless the emotions that Haneke manipulates in *Funny Games*. Of course, as Amos Vogel has underlined, cinema is to some extent always a manipulative medium. Hollywood cinema, montage cinema and counter-cinema all position the spectator as passive in their various ways – the receptacle of a set of fixed conclusions – but they also rely on a prior contract by which the spectator accepts this passive positioning. To some extent, the audiences for a film by Eisenstein, Capra or Akerman all know what to expect of the film they have paid to see, and they are rarely disappointed. The question of expectation, however, becomes problematic when applied to *Funny Games*: both those spectators expecting a genre film and those expecting a counter-cinematic work of 'art' cinema have their expectations troubled by the overlapping frameworks within which the film operates.

The setting up of certain expectations is, then, the first step for *Funny Games* in manipulating its spectator by various means. Through its generic structures, *Funny Games* enacts the 'hidden' manipulation of suturing the spectator into the cinematic spectacle, constructing them as the all-knowing, all-powerful subject. Suspense is a minimal way of engaging emotion, while the genre of melodrama connects emotion with moral character properties. On this spectrum between suspense and melodrama (and we will discuss melodrama in more detail in the following chapter), the central technical element is the concentration of *mise-en-scène* and cinematography around individual characters and their place in a plot. This framework is aimed foremost at drawing the spectator into the film.

However, Haneke's film also reveals this process of manipulation via the impact of its 'aggressive' reflexivity. This reflexivity enacts another mode of emotional manipulation, but the unpleasurable experience to which *Funny Games* subjects the spectator calls immediate attention to itself in a way that the pleasurable experience does not. For as Izard points out, unpleasurable emotions are object-directed: they have a source or a focal point. The spectator's desire to regain the narrative momentum which stimulates the pleasure drive and to avoid the unpleasure that arises from these moments of juxtaposition prompts them to look for the source of this unpleasure, to find the object to which this emotional reaction is attached. In order to do this they must engage rationally with the film as a construct, they must analyse and unpick it. Emotion thus gives rise to rational awareness. This is an awareness of our emotional state (unpleasure), and its relatedness to the cinematic spectacle (the thing we are watching that is causing us unpleasure). But it is also an awareness of the act of spectatorship that the viewer is engaging in (the fact that by watching the film we are experiencing unpleasure; if we should walk out, the unpleasurable experience would cease).

Only by creating a close relationship between film and film-viewer can Haneke prompt the spectator to think about that relationship, to assess it and to wonder why and how they came to form an attachment to the cinematic spectacle. The impact on the spectator that occurs at the junctions between the differing stylistic and narrative modes results in an emotional experience of unpleasure, the source of which the spectator seeks within the film. It occurs at the point when emotion (in the form of unpleasure) and reason (in the form of self-awareness) are both operating: it takes place beyond the sensual, prelogical moment that Eisenstein discusses but before the position of total rational awareness that counter-cinema argues for. The spectator is engaged emotionally with the film, so that when this engagement is ruptured it becomes the focus of the spectator's reflections.

Haneke thus controls the spectator's response to the film. But he does not control the nature of this response; rather, he causes the spectator to reflect on their relationship to the film. And Haneke does not determine what the outcome of this reflection will be. The spectator's thought process is not programmed in the same definite way as it is when watching *Potemkin*, for example. So although within Haneke's cinema the spectator is manipulated, they nonetheless remain active in a way that does not have a determinate content or context. Whereas in the case of Eisenstein, the relationship of emotion to reason is not causal and does not create a fixed position of judgement, here the spectator forms an individuated response.

This is why *Funny Games*, although polemical, is not propagandist. Eisenstein's cinema is aimed at leading the spectator to the 'right' response to his films. Haneke, however, might seek to preclude the 'wrong' responses, but that does not equate to a desire to instil the 'right' response. 'I am not a forger of *"opinions"'*, Haneke states, explaining that 'the film should not come to an end on the screen, but engage the spectators and find its place in their cognitive and emotive framework'.[61] This is where Haneke diverges not only from Eisenstein, but also from political film-makers whose formal concerns are dominated by a desire to convey a predetermined content, the endgame of the film-viewing process. Reflexivity in political modernism is aimed at causing the spectator to reflect on the film's content and to reach a conclusion desired by the film-maker. For Haneke, the goal is moral reflection in and of itself, not reflection upon a set of political themes. His films ask the spectator to consider certain moral questions but do not lead to any answers. As the director states: 'Art is the only thing which can console us. But every spectator must seek his own responses to it. It is pointless for him to find responses which aren't his own. That cannot lead to a clear conscience'.[62]

## The Invitation to Moral Engagement

Haneke's technique of moving between engagement and reflexivity is then opposed not only to Eisenstein's fixed positioning of the spectator, but also to the more radical 'modernism' that we find in the films of the counter-cinema movement, where the filmic language objectifies the character and creates such a distance between the character and viewer that the spectator is denied all emotional involvement with the film. Haneke's films create an emotional impact as well as allowing the spectator time to reflect. And in the conflict between the two, they invite the spectator to enter a thought space.

The space for reflection, arising from the conflict between emotional engagement and rational awareness, becomes concerned with morality when a moral problem is presented to the spectator for consideration. In *Funny Games* the moral problem centres on the spectator's realisation of themselves as a scopophilic subject. Again, this realisation involves both an intellectual response and an emotional response. The 'modernist episode' in *Funny Games* forces the character to consider a scenario unfamiliar to the suspense thriller genre: parental grief not as a motivation for revenge, but as a pure state of being.[63] The ten-minute scene, during which camera movement is minimised to only slight pans, functions as a gruelling exposé of consequence. The abrupt change in style from stylised montage techniques to what we might term 'hyperrealism' is jarring, but coupled with the content of the scene it becomes an almost unbearable experience for the viewer. Haneke's camera refuses to cut away from the immediate physical and emotional aftermath of Georgie's death, forcing us into a position of empathy with characters that had previously been psychologically one-dimensional. Exposure to such suffering gives rise to the desire to avert our eyes, but short of leaving the cinema this is not an option. The spectator might, if they were so inclined, shut their eyes, but the scene is perfectly harmonised on the level of image and sound, such that the effects of viewing and hearing the scene would not differ. The lack of movement forces our eyes to wander across the screen, picking out such details as Georgie's corpse lying on the floor and the hunched silhouette of

George, whilst Anna's laborious attempt to shut off the television and free herself are exposed as painful and grotesque.[64] This visual stillness corresponds to the droning roar of cars, and then to a resounding silence in which every noise becomes magnified: Anna's effort is expressed in her grunts and the rustling of duct tape, George's grief begins as a series of small snorts before developing into racking sobs.

The effectiveness of the scene in moral terms becomes clearer when we compare it to a much-commented-upon scene in *71 Fragmente*, in which the mechanically emitted ping-pong balls of a practice device are repeatedly smashed by the player from the deep space of the shot towards the screen, and towards the cinematic spectator. The repetitive, cacophonous sound that dominates the scene is intensified by its duration – it lasts a full three minutes – thus creating a painful sense of 'real time' that heightens the spectator's awareness of the cinematic viewing situation and, within that, of themselves. Repetition and duration are both involved in this sequence which functions as a precursor to the 'modernist episode' in *Funny Games*; the spectator becomes uncomfortable and may seek out the source of this discomfort. However, since the scene from *71 Fragmente* lacks any moral content (we do not engage with a character's suffering, for example), it does not place the spectator in a moral position: the source of my discomfort is the image on-screen, I am aware of that, but I do not consider my own relationship to that image, I am not implicated in it. And so I do not recognise myself as a voyeur, a consumer of the cinematic spectacle, since the scopic urge was never really operating: no scenario or spectacle is presented to my attention. The onscreen image fails to engage me emotionally, and reflexive devices have nothing with which to conflict. There is no point at which impact occurs, and a moral thought space fails to open itself up.

Elsewhere in *Funny Games*, the 'aggressive' reflexivity which Haneke employs calls the spectator's rational attention to themselves both as a spectator, that is, as someone who is watching events; and as a voyeur, that is, someone who takes pleasure from watching. In doing so, it effectively short-circuits any voyeuristic pleasure that comes from the spectator's belief that they are 'unseen' by the diegetic characters. But by having only one character acknowledge the audience's presence, Haneke ensures that the victims of Peter and Paul's 'games' remain the victims of the spectator's gaze. Paul's question – 'Is it enough already? You want a proper ending with plausible plot development, don't you?' – prompts us to ask what it is we really want from the film, what exactly the nature of the spectator's relationship to the screen is. Haneke reveals the spectator's appetite for on-screen violence to them, intensifying their unpleasurable emotional response to being 'caught out'. Each of Paul's asides functions as an accusation of moral guilt, from which the spectator must defend themself; they are like the Sartrean 'footsteps in the hallway', which induce the emotion of shame, an emotion which we shall analyse at greater length in Chapter Five.

As we have seen, the Kantian model of morality depends on the subject's assertion of their reason over their desire to seek pleasure and their instinct to avoid pain. It is through stimulating the desire for pleasure that Haneke can then bring the reason into conflict with it. But it is only by making the spectator aware of this desire, and of its moral implications, that Haneke can invite them to assert *their own* power of rational awareness over this desire, and engage with the cinematic image in a radically different way.

To recount, unpleasure in *Funny Games* arises from the rupturing of the pleasure drive and from the spectator's ensuing realisation that they are not in control of the cinematic image. The instinctive discomfort this produces might be overridden by the pleasure drive should it be strong enough – as is the case in Hitchcock's films – but use of first- and second-generation modernist reflexivity prevents the pleasure drive from becoming sufficiently stable as to re-establish itself over the feeling of discomfort. So the spectator becomes aware of their discomfort and, in a second moment, they become aware of the reason for this discomfort as their instinct to avoid pain leads them to seek its source in order that they might best diffuse it. In this second moment, unpleasure arises again, this time from the spectator's sense of shame at their realisation of themself as voyeur. By calling attention to the spectator's expectations through devices such as the diegetic rewind, Haneke prompts the spectator to question the morality of such desires. One of the questions that dominates ethical inquiry, and particularly Kantian ethics, is 'What *ought* I to do?' In *Funny Games* the spectator finds themself watching scenes that prompt the question, 'Ought I to be watching this?' In considering this problem, the spectator finds themself engaged in a process of moral deliberation.

# Notes

1. Morrow (2001), p. 11.
2. See, for example, Judith Hess, 'Genre Film and the Status Quo', in *Film Genre: Theory and Criticism*, ed. Barry Keith Grant (Metchuen, NJ: The Scarecrow Press, 1977).
3. See Jean-Loup Bourget, 'Social Implications in Hollywood Genres', in *Film Genre: Theory and Criticism*, ed. Barry Keith Grant (Metchuen, NJ: The Scarecrow Press, 1977).
4. Robin Wood, 'Ideology, Genre, Auteur', in *Film Theory and Criticism*, eds Leo Braudy, Marshall Cohen and Gerald Mast (New York: Oxford University Press, 1992).
5. Thomas Schatz, *Hollywood Genres* (New York: McGraw-Hill, 1981), p. 5.
6. In which a mother (Lucia Harper, played by Joan Bennett), after discovering the dead body of her daughter's lover, hides the body under the assumption that it was her daughter who killed the man.

7. As an interesting side-note, in all of these films the family group is composed of a three person family and their pet, which inevitably meets a sticky end. While there is no real evidence that Haneke deliberately references these specific films, it is some indication of (a) how formulaic the sub-genres of the suspense thriller can be; and (b) how thoroughly Haneke's film absorbs and reproduces the conventions of the genre, at least superficially (see later comments about the death of Georgie and on how Haneke successfully subverts them).

8. And indeed, the family under attack from an outside force (usually in their own home) is a recurring trope within Hitchcock's own work, as seen in *Shadow of a Doubt* (1943), *The Birds* (1963) and *The Man Who Knew Too Much* (both 1934 and 1956 versions).

9. Susan Smith, *Hitchcock: Suspense, Humour and Tone* (London: BFI, 2000), pp. 15–18.

10. Richard Falcon, 'The Discreet Harm of the Bourgeoisie', *Sight & Sound* 8(5) (May 1998): 10–12, p. 12.

11. Steve Neale, *Genre* (London: BFI, 1980), pp. 46, 48.

12. Romney, notes to *Funny Games*, *Artificial Eye* VHS release (1999).

13. Richard Falcon, 'Code Unknown', *Sight & Sound* 11(5) (May 2001): 46.

14. Torben Grodal, *Moving Pictures: A New Theory of Film Genres, Feelings and Cognition* (Oxford: Clarendon Press, 2000[1997]), p. 161.

15. It is pertinent to note here that Haneke stresses that the film draws on the conventions of the suspense genre, rather than that of horror; see Falcon (2001), p. 46. The strategies of identification that apply to horror, where the spectator identifies with both victim and monster, are therefore not explicitly mobilised within the generic structure of the film, although the spectator is encouraged to be complicit with the torturers (and to recognise this complicity) through their desire for narrative momentum.

16. Perhaps the most striking example of this comes in the middle of the film, when victims and killers line up on facing sofas. The family are never shown in one shot. Headshots and extreme close-ups prevent us from ascertaining even their positions on the couch. They remain alienated and alienating, an effect only exacerbated by the blank, inscrutable looks on their faces throughout their ordeal. Even at the end of the film, Anna's face is physically ravaged, but it is strangely devoid of emotion.

17. Smith (2000), p. 22.

18. Victor Perkins, *Film as Film* (Harmondsworth: Penguin, 1972), p. 40.

19. Online Edition: www.oedonline.com.

20. Charles Derry's rigorous analysis of the suspense thriller genre, *The Suspense Thriller: Films in The Shadow of Alfred Hitchcock* (Jefferson, NC: MacFarland, 1998), argues that the genre of the suspense thriller can be perceived not so much as a group of films which thrill their audiences but as a group of films whose content consists essentially of thrills, using Michael Balint's psychoanalytic definition of the concept 'thrill' as its basis.

21. Derry (1988), p. 7.

22. Christian Metz, *The Imaginary Signifier: Psychoanalysis and Cinema*, trans. Celia Britton, Annwyl Williams, Ben Brewster and Alfred Guzzetti (London: Macmillan, 1982), p. 7, my emphasis. Metz develops the idea of the 'bad object' on pp. 111–112.

23. Metz (1982), p. 7.

24. Mulvey (1989), p. 15.

25. Wollen (1982a), pp. 87–89.

26. See Ivone Margulies, *Nothing Happens: Chantal Akerman's Hyperrealist Everyday* (Durham, NC: Duke University Press, 1996), p. 211. Akerman's *Jeanne Dielman, 23 Quai du Commerce, 1080 Bruxelles* (1976), has been received by many as an exemplar of Mulvey's writings. Using a minimalist form comprising long takes, static camerawork and no analytical editing or reverse shot, Akerman presents the daily

existence of a widowed Belgian housewife whose routine chores include prostituting herself to support herself and her son. The three-and-a-half hour film observes the tiny lapses in control building up to Jeanne's loss of self-control with a client, whom she murders. Most of the film's action consists of domestic chores, and this has led feminist critics to see it as a discourse of woman's looks. In her book, Margulies cites filmmaker Eric de Kuyper's description of the film's aesthetic as suggestive of 'a melopée [a long, recitative chant], a slow and diffuse boredom, a white neutrality' (p. 211).

27. Mulvey (1989), p. 15.

28. Haneke, in Anon., 'Beyond Mainstream Film: An interview with Michael Haneke', in *After Postmodernism: Austrian Film and Literature in Transition*, ed. Willy Riemer (Riverside, CA: Ariadne Press, 2000), p. 161.

29. Haneke says of the Zorn score: 'I see in John Zorn a kind of *über*-heavy metal, an extreme and ironic accentuation of that form just as the film is an extreme inflection of the suspense thriller. I think Zorn's style tends to alienate the listener in a sense that heightens awareness, which was effective to the points I wanted to address'. Quoted in Sharrett (2003), p. 29.

30. Note that when I use the term 'passive' here I do not mean to (re)open the debate as to whether the spectator is active or not in the creation of meaning, but rather to suggest that there is a difference in the way in which we look at a set of rapidly shifting moving images, and at one that is static with little or no movement. Rather than making sense of the narrative by linking each image to the next one in order to absorb the narrative thrust, the spectator is made to examine one image for an extended time, and so begins consciously to perceive its detail.

31. Michael Haneke, 'Believing not Seeing', *Sight & Sound London Film Festival Supplement* (November 1997), p. 22.

32. See Jean-Pierre Oudart, 'Cinema and Suture,' in *Cahiers du cinema: The Politics of Representation*, ed. Nick Browne (Cambridge, MA: Harvard University Press, 1990).

33. Sharrett (2003), p. 29.

34. Haneke (2000), p. 174. My emphasis.

35. Smith (2000), p. viii.

36. The two characters are represented as having very distinct personalities or personas, and for this reason I deem it necessary to refer to them as individuals, rather than seeing them as interchangeable. They refer to themselves by various sets of names throughout the course of the narrative, ('Tom and Jerry', 'Beavis and Butthead', 'Fatty and Skinny' ...) none of which are any more fixed (or any more likely to be attached to them as their 'real' names) than any other. Indeed, it is striking that personal and family names are reused/recycled from one film to another, as if even this aspect of a character's individuality could detract from Haneke's aims and render the spectator overly engaged with the character at the expense of moral engagement. For the purposes of this study, I shall refer to the antagonist's of *Funny Games* by the names which they use first and most frequently (and which they are given in the pressnotes): Paul and Peter.

37. Kermode (1998), p. 44.

38. 'In my last year at the *Gymnasium* I saw Tony Richardson's screen adaptation of Fielding's *Tom Jones*. The film relates the eventful story of an orphan boy growing to maturity in eighteenth-century England; it was directed with a sure sense of pace, and succeeded in its efforts to make the viewer into an accomplice of Richardson's fun-loving hero. Suddenly, perhaps a third of the way into the film, in the middle of a hair-raising chase sequence, the protagonist stopped in his tracks, looked into the camera, and commented on the difficulty of his predicament, thereby making me aware of mine.

The shock of recognition of this moment was in every way equal to the terror of my childhood movie experiences. Naturally I had long since grasped that movies were not real, naturally I had long since distanced myself physically and probably mentally by ironic observations from the unnerving immediacy of a suspense thriller, but never before this shocking discovery of my constant complicity with film protagonists had I experienced the dizzying immediacy that separates fiction and reality; never before had I physically experienced to what extent I and my fellow humans – that is, the audience – were largely victims and not partners of those whom we paid to "entertain" us.' Haneke (1998), p. 552.

39. While the prefix 'Scheiß-' is merely coarse rather than obscene, in English-language translation it becomes the much stronger 'fucking'. Considering Haneke's film is a comment on American cinema's predilection for sex, violence and obscenity there is some irony in the fact that the subtitler has 'Americanised' this phrasing.

40. Pam Cook and Mieke Berninck, *The Cinema Book* (London: BFI, 1999), p. 100.

41. Prince (1998).

42. I am aware that Peckinpah has made films – and violent films, at that – outside this period. However, the period between these two films is arguably the definitive portion of Peckinpah's output. Before 1968, the director was constrained by the MPAA Production Codes and could not explore (or exploit!) the violence issue as he did in the years that followed, and after 1974 his work becomes quite chequered.

43. In some ways, Peckinpah's use of slow motion foreshadows Haneke's use of the long take: they are two different ways of turning time into excess, slowing down the forward progression of action in order to encourage a more detailed perception of the onscreen image, and a concomitant reflection about the on-screen event. Where they diverge is in their subject matter: Peckinpah tends to use slow motion in his depictions of the violent event, forcing us to recognise what violence is; Haneke uses the long take in depicting the consequences of violence, forcing us to recognise what it does, what it means. A corresponding use of ellipsis frequently occurs, so that while Peckinpah elides consequence, Haneke elides the violent event itself.

44. Linda Williams, 'Sex and Sensation', in *The Oxford History of World Cinema*, ed. Geoffrey Nowell-Smith (Oxford: Oxford University Press, 1997), p. 194.

45. Sylvia Chong, 'From "Blood Auteurism" to the Violence of Pornography: Sam Peckinpah and Oliver Stone', in *New Hollywood Violence*, ed. Steven Jay Schneider (Manchester: Manchester University Press, 2004).

46. Prince (1998), p. 240.

47. Prince (1998), p. 241.

48. See Jonathan Romney's 1998 interview with the director in the *Guardian*. The director continues: 'it's totally exploitative, playing with the cheapest of emotions. It's this way of working on two levels that makes it revolting ... It's not a question of high art and popular culture'. Quoted in Romney (1998), p. 6.

49. Sharrett (2003), p. 29.

50. At some screenings that I have attended, I have witnessed spectators clap and cheer at the point where Anna shoots Peter, indicating the extent to which Haneke is successful in operating these structures of classical emotional manipulation.

51. See Falcon (1998).

52. Sergei Eisenstein, 'The Montage of Attractions', in *The Eisenstein Reader*, ed. and trans. Richard Taylor (London: BFI, 1998), p. 30.

53. Sergei Eisenstein, *Film Form, and The Film Sense*, trans. Jay Leyda (London: Meridian Books, 1957), p. 142.

54. Eisenstein (1957[1949]), p. 143.

55. Gregg Lambert, 'Cinema and the Outside', in *Deleuze and The Philosophy of Cinema*, ed. Gregory Flaxman (Minneapolis: University of Minnesota Press, 2000), p. 261.

56. Eisenstein (1957). pp. 144–5.

57. C.E. Izard, *The Psychology of Emotions* (New York: Plenum Press, 1991).

58. Eisenstein (1957), p. 130.

59. Eisenstein (1957), pp. 132–3.

60. Eisenstein (1957), p. 87.

61. Haneke, in Artificial Eye's pressnotes to the U.K. release of *Code Unknown*, 2000. Available at the British Film Institute Library.

62. Haneke, in Cieutat (2000), p. 25. My translation.

63. An interesting reversal of this scenario takes place in Todd Field's 2001 film *In The Bedroom*. The film starts out as a study in parental loss, before developing into a suspense thriller, in which a couple plot and enact the murder of their dead son's killer.

64. One might compare Haneke's portrayal of Anna hopping to the kitchen to free herself from her bonds to the ubiquitous intercutting between bound prisoner and returning captor which appears in countless suspense thrillers, usually incorporating numerous close-ups on the knotted ropes.

# Chapter 4

# EMOTIONAL ENGAGEMENT
# AND NARRATIVITY
*Code inconnu, La Pianiste, Le Temps du loup*

---

The reactions that arise from the spectator's awareness of being manipulated by Haneke's film have distinct implications for their moral response to *Funny Games*. What Haneke achieves through his aesthetics of aggression and the unpleasurable feelings that it gives rise to is to position the spectator as the film's real protagonist: the narrative content of the film becomes significant only in relation to the viewer's situation. In this respect, *Funny Games* does not prompt a purely intellectual response but a very personal, felt experience, making the action on screen relevant to the spectator in such a way that they cannot neatly consign it to the status of 'other'.

That *Funny Games* places the spectator in a very different position from any of the films in Haneke's Austrian-set trilogy is made clear by the extreme responses to the film. However, these responses also indicate that the very formal conventions that he sets out to criticise create a position whereby the film itself could be said to overmanipulate the spectator, just as in the trilogy Haneke's overdependence on the early modernist structures of distanciation and the ongoing negation of pleasure threatened to undermine his project of positioning the spectator morally by preventing them from engaging emotionally with the film. At the same time that the films are destined to make us more reflective, Haneke's authorial position within *Funny Games* seems to convey that the spectator is not autonomous. Many critics noted this paradox in 1997 when *Funny Games* was released. As we saw in the Introduction, perceptive reviewers, including *Sight & Sound*'s Mark Kermode and *The Village Voice*'s J. Hoberman, pointed to the contradiction between Haneke's stated aims and his cinematic aesthetic. The film's heavy dependence on the very generic structures it critiques led to accusations of hypocrisy on the director's part, begging the question of whether in *Funny Games* the director attempts to make a moral point through immoral, or at least amoral, means. Haneke's position, his critics argue, entails a potential loss of coherence within the film in terms of its ability to construct a coherent perspective on the violence it depicts, and it also threatens an inversion of Haneke's radical positioning of the spectator as autonomous whereby that position might seem to become its opposite: namely, a position of overdetermination and subjection, not unlike that which the spectator assumes when watching a mainstream Hollywood film.

This is the problem that occurs from wanting to make something that is fascinating but also repulsive. We saw in the previous chapter that *Funny Games* introduces an element of seduction to Haneke's filmic oeuvre, which calls to mind, for example, the opening scenes of John Crowley's *Intermission* (2003) in which a charming young man (played by Colin Farrell) blithely chats up a shop girl before quite suddenly punching her in the face, in order to steal the takings. It seems that Haneke's attitudes towards the brutal treatment of the spectator of *Funny Games* – as these attitudes arise both through the film and in public statements – are not always clear or coherent. We referred in the previous chapter to Haneke's comment that he wanted to 'rape his spectators into awareness'. Metaphor this may be; nonetheless, its (un)ethical implications cannot be overlooked, for it seems indicative of a brutality towards the audience, that may or may not be warranted, but that certainly problematises Haneke's own ethical standing. The rigorous systems of control and the patent audience manipulation that his films demonstrate work at cross-purposes with the film-maker's humanistic intentions to position the spectator morally and to force them to examine the systems of control and manipulation that they so willingly submit to when viewing a mainstream film. In this way, Haneke's brilliance as a manipulator of audiences' responses threatens to undermine the very freedom his film seeks to accord them.

## Code inconnu

Recognising this contradiction between Haneke's laudable moral intention of bringing his spectators to moral awareness and his somewhat dubious ethical approach brings us to a consideration of how this contradiction might be resolved while retaining a moral position for the spectator within the films. Apparently, this is the director's own concern in his later films. For he, too, recognises that while audience reactions to *Funny Games* included the ethical responses that he had hoped for, the film was also interpreted by some genre fans as a straightforward thriller, or rather a postmodernist work in the style of *C'est arrivé près de chez vous*, *Reservoir Dogs*, or John McNaughton's *Henry, Portrait of a Serial Killer* (1986). In interviews with Michel Cieutat and

Christopher Sharrett, Haneke acknowledges and understands the reasons why the film caused such strong and varied responses, and why many viewers felt antipathy towards it.[1] He admits that although *Funny Games* was successful commercially – bringing the film-maker and his polemic to the attention of international audiences and critics – responses to the film suggested that the director, in employing the structures of linear narrative, generic convention and extreme reflexivity, had not managed to produce a film that provided a satisfactory alternative to the 'violating closeness' of Hollywood cinema.

Haneke is thus led to reconsider his approach to the spectator. Before beginning *Code inconnu* (full title: *Code inconnu: Récit incomplet de divers voyages*) he drafted a set of questions (which he later released in a press statement alongside the film's release), which are concerned with form, content, ethics and perception:

Is truth the sum of what we see and hear?
Can reality be represented?
To the observer, what makes the represented object real, credible, or more precisely, worthy of being believed?
What is the responsibility of the puppet master if the puppet perfectly imitates real life?
In the world of moving pictures, are illusion and deception twins or merely closely related?
Are the answers lies?
Are the questions answers?
Is the fragment the aesthetic response to the incomplete nature of our perception?
Is editing the simulation of the whole?
Is precision an aesthetic or a moral category?
Can allusion replace description?
Is that which is off-camera more precise than that which is on?[2]

*Code inconnu* should not be seen as a thesis film, but it is undoubtedly the case that it is the most theoretical of Haneke's films. In this film the director sets out to produce a thorough filmic response to questions that have been raised in various forms throughout the history of modernist film-making and the critical theory that surrounds it, as well as to the questions that responses to his own, earlier, films raised. A precise formulation of the concerns that we can retrospectively see as constituting the basis of all of Haneke's early filmic experimentation, the questions that guide the film tackle the subjects of truth and deception, reality and illusion, aesthetics and morality. As Haneke admits, 'none of these questions are new'. Nonetheless, 'they are topical in the light of the prevailing media scene'.[3]

Perhaps it is because the aggressive reflexivity of *Funny Games* caused such diverse and frequently hostile responses that Haneke returns in *Code inconnu* to the style of his earlier productions in order to see how he can position the spectator morally without falling into the traps that *Funny Games* opened up. As in *Der Siebente Kontinent* and *71 Fragmente*, *Code inconnu*'s narrative is fragmented. It is closer in style and subject to the later part of the trilogy: once more Haneke takes a cross-section of society and interweaves various subnarratives, bookending them at the beginning and end with a pair of matched scenes in which deaf children mime words to each other, foregrounding the theme of (mis)communication and alienation.

These bookend scenes are classically shot and edited, the film intercutting between mid-distance shots of the mime and close-ups of the students as they try to guess the word in question. But outside this framing device, the film starts in earnest with an eight-minute tracking shot, the scatter device for the film's fragmented narratives. On Paris's Boulevard Saint Germain, a woman, Anne, steps out of her building, strides off-screen right, and is stopped by a young man, Jean, who it transpires is the brother of her boyfriend. He explains that he could not access the apartment building in which she lives because he doesn't know the code to her outer door. The two walk along the pavement, paralleled by the camera, before Anne stops to get some pastries, explaining that she is late for a meeting but that the teenager can stay at her apartment, if only for a while. She then bids him goodbye. Having travelled a little further along the busy street, the camera, which has been non-committally paralleling this conversation, now reverses with Jean as he heads back towards the apartment. Halfway there he pauses to listen to some street musicians. Crumpling up the paper bag from the pastries, he throws it into the lap of a middle-aged woman begging for coins on the corner of the alley. Moving on, Jean is accosted by a young black man, Amadou, of around his own age, who insists that Jean apologise for humiliating the woman. Anne returns to break up their fighting, the gendarmes intervene, and Amadou and the beggar are arrested.

The stories of the characters we are introduced to in this scene – Anne, Jean, Maria (the Romanian beggar) and Amadou – overlap and run parallel over the course of the film, but they are not arranged into any fixed pattern or order which allows the spectator to arrive at a definite interpretation. As Peter Bradshaw puts it in his review of the film for *The Guardian*: 'These scenes are not to be developed and interweaved in the manner of an Altman or a P.T. Anderson, neither do they form an ingenious construct of perspectives of the sort offered by Tarantino. … They have, through happenstance, and the nature of urban life which crunches lives and experiences together – often bruisingly – simply become entangled with one another'.[4] Leaving aside the framing device (the deaf-mute children trying to communicate), the film consists of forty-two sequences, each separated from the next by blank spacers of equal duration.[5] And as if to examine the truth of Luc Moullet's belief that 'morality is a question of tracking shots',[6] all but four of these are sequence shots without cuts, thus preventing the possibility of the fragments of narrative being further fragmented into several shots.

Haneke thus returns to but also develops on the formal style of the film that operated within *71 Fragmente*. *Code inconnu* is much more episodic than either that film or *Der Siebente Kontinent*; indeed, many of the scenes could work effectively in isolation as short films were it not for the fact that Haneke also introduces into the film Godardian sound-edits which overlap sequential scenes. We frequently arrive in the middle of an episode, even halfway through a sentence, and leave before its end, and so are 'cut off' from the information that we seek on a narrative level. The effect of this narrative style is exemplified by the scene of Maria's extradition from France, which opens with a static shot of the door of a plane that runs for a whole minute before Maria appears. As the spectator watches passengers boarding they try to discern what is happening, what is important about this scene. When Maria enters from the off-screen space, escorted by a policeman, the implications of her deportation dawn on the spectator. This scene draws on many of the principles behind Haneke's use of the 'modernist episode' within *Funny Games*, itself developed, as we saw, from the early films: time is made manifest, the spectator is forced to work to make sense of the image. The spectator is gradually – through boredom and sheer effort – forced into a position of self-awareness and of awareness of the image-as-construct. But they are also engaged with Maria's predicament, in much the same way that the drawn out suffering of the 'modernist episode' encourages an empathetic perspective on the parents' grief. However, lacking a generic format which the 'modernist episode' would then rupture, this filmic style would seem to reflect a largely Bazinian position, concerned with reflecting 'real' modes of perception and creating empathy for the character.

Bazin's basic position was a reaction against the principles of film-making that had prevailed, as critiqued in his essay 'The Evolution of the Language of Cinema'.[7] In this essay, Bazin placed the long take in opposition to two forms of editing. The first of these was Eisensteinian montage, which he saw as self-willed and, above all, manipulative in the extreme. The second was mainstream narrative editing, what Bazin refers to as *le découpage classique*. Both forms, Bazin claims, historically tended to favour editing as a technique which allowed them to impose an interpretation on the events they portrayed. But, he contended, while editing may superficially organise representations as we are in the habit of organising 'real life', it rules out the freedom that in 'real life' is at the base of our power to organise and the autonomy of the objects – real or represented – that exist for others as well. As he explains: 'Editing totally suppresses [the] reciprocal freedom between us and the object. It substitutes for a free organisation, a forced breaking down where the logic of shots controlled by the reporting of the action anaesthetises our freedom completely'.[8]

Bazin argued that it was the film-maker's responsibility to stand aside and reveal reality rather than impose their opinion on the viewer, thereby preserving the freedom of the spectator to choose their own interpretation of the object or event. He therefore upholds *mise-en-scène*, depth of field and the long take against editing because, to him, the former represented true continuity and reproduced situations more realistically, leaving the interpretation of a particular scene to the viewer rather than to the director's viewpoint through cutting. In other words, technique functions in this instance so as not to provide an encoded preferred reading, to offer the viewer precisely that element of choice that Eisensteinian montage deprives them of. Consider, for example, Bazin's description of Willam Wyler's early film-making technique: 'the depth of field [is] as *liberal and democratic* as the conscience of the American spectator and of the heroes of his films'.[9] While Bazin's optimistic view of American democracy might raise an ironic smile from some contemporary readers, his contention that Wyler grants the spectator a privileged position of control over their own interpretation – providing them with a vast amount of information and encouraging them to choose to a large degree their own perspective on what they saw – is nonetheless significant.

To Bazin, the very idea of cinema conveying a fixed message is antithetical to his belief in the value of film. Film's ambiguity is, to Bazin's mind, a value, and cinema should preserve it since it affords the spectator the opportunity to be active in the creation of meaning; that is, they interpret the film in their own manner. There should be no a priori meaning, only a series of objects which the spectator then accords meaning to in their own way. He explains that the realist cinema that he propounds,

> implies ... both a more active mental attitude on the part of the spectator and a more positive contribution on his part to the action in progress. While analytical montage only calls for him to follow his guide, to let his attention follow along smoothly with that of the director who will choose what he should see, here he is called upon to exercise at least a minimum of personal choice. It is from his attention and his will that the meaning of the image in part derives.[10]

And this implicit ethics of film form is redoubled by the humanist outlook that underpins Bazin's emphasis on the ambiguity of the image. To illustrate, let us take, for example, his description of a scene from Roberto Rossellini's *Paisà* (1946), in which a woman learns of her fiancé's death:   *see "Die Ehe der Maria Braun" in search scene.*

> Ultimately and by chance, the woman learns from a wounded partisan that the man she is looking for is dead. But the statement from which she learned the news was not aimed straight at her – but hit her like a stray bullet. The impeccable line followed by this recital owes nothing to classical forms that are standard for a story of this kind. Attention is never artificially focused on the heroine. The camera makes no pretense [sic] at being psychologically subjective. … The camera, as if making an impartial report, confines itself to following a woman searching for a man, leaving to us the task of being alone with her, of understanding her, of sharing her suffering.[11]

Here, the very ambiguity of aesthetic openness leads to the notion of the spectator as active, and this activity is itself a moral category. For we are involved with other people (the characters on-screen) in a way that makes us morally responsible: we engage with their moral dilemmas, the choices that are open to them, rather than simply following the moral drama of a narrative. Ambiguity and the concomitant activity on the spectator's part sensitises us to others and to the choices that they have to make, and we therefore engage morally with the film in the moment of activity. For Bazin, in the engagement with ambiguity, what we perceive is always a moral situation.

In this position are reflected the beginnings of Haneke's critical aesthetic for moral spectatorship, the principles which to some extent underpinned *Der Siebente Kontinent* and *71 Fragmente einer Chronologie des Zufalls*. Superficially, then, *Code inconnu* appears to mark a retrogressive move for Haneke, in which he looks back not only to the counter-cinematic structures of the trilogy, but even further back to this type of Bazinian realism. If *Funny Games* is situated at one extreme of a spectrum between linear narrative and aggressive reflexivity on the one hand, and fragmentation and distanciation on the other, *Code inconnu* is situated at the opposite pole. In an interview with Michel Cieutat, Haneke initially states: 'For me [fragmentation] is not a gimmick, but a necessity, because mainstream cinema [*le cinéma de distraction*] claims that it can show us reality in its totality, which is wrong. If the cinema wants to be responsible, if it wants to be a true art form, it must realise that our perception of the world is naturally fragmented'. So, he concludes, 'we need to find the aesthetic means to transfer this fragmented vision to the screen'.[12]

But Haneke continues: 'I used single takes in *Code inconnu* for several reasons. Firstly … it distinguished them from the scenes of the film within the film, which, themselves, are edited in a very standard fashion'. Another reason, he adds, 'was to let each scene unfold in real time: a way of not manipulating time'. This is itself a kind of manipulation; because it involves 'showing that the scenes from the film within the film are as artificial as the other sequences'.[13] What transpires from this statement, and is born out within the film, is that despite Haneke's use of deep focus photography, long takes and minimal editing, the film is not exactly an extension of Bazinian principles of realism – as Paul Arthur suggests in *Film Comment*[14] – for there is an underlying paradox here in the use of tracking and sequence shots. The implicit Bazinian idea – made explicit by Luc Moullet – that such shots have a moral implication refers us back to his resistance to classical editing. But Haneke's break with classical editing seems to achieve the opposite of Bazinian humanism, precisely to objectify the characters.

In fact, *Code inconnu*, and indeed the entire body of Haneke's work, can be understood as a filmic refutation of Bazin's renowned claim that, 'originality in photography as distinct from originality in painting lies in the essentially objective character of photography'.[15] What Haneke attempts to show through his films is that no matter how 'realistic' a film is, no matter how closely it attempts to follow real life, it is *always* manipulative, never 'objective', in a Bazinian sense. Even a security camera must be positioned by someone in a certain place, at a certain angle, and this positioning will determine the images we eventually see. His films take us back, then, to a political modernist position: Haneke wants the spectator of his films to be aware of their situation and therefore to be able to make conscious, and conscientious, judgements about the images on screen. Haneke's use of the fragmented narrative constitutes part of a formal critique of cinematic convention: *Code inconnu* is aimed not at the recreation of reality, but at the creation of a space between film and filmic interpellation in which the viewer can make a cognitive analysis of what they are seeing.

With *Code inconnu*, then, we have by far the most rigorous exploration of first-generation modernism and its possibilities in Haneke's films up to this point in his film-making career. And yet the film does not entirely sacrifice the media critique that is present to varying degrees in the earlier works. While the film is predominantly characterised by the benign reflexivity which encourages the spectator to engage rationally with the narrative, and thus is not, for the most part, aggressively reflexive in the way that *Funny Games* is, Haneke is nonetheless able through the occupations of Anne and Georges, her boyfriend – actress and photographer – to voice concerns with truth and manipulation in cinema. Aside from the static camera sequences, the remaining four edits are, crucially, ones in which the photographer/director is ostensibly not Haneke, but a film-maker inscribed within the diegesis of the film: two are the photomontages of Georges's work in foreign countries; the other two are the sequences from a film which Anne herself is starring in (apparently a version of John Fowles's novel *The Collector*, incidentally filmed in 1965 by William Wyler).[16] These four scenes recall the reflexivity and troubling of cinematic reality that is so prevalent in *Funny Games*. And all of the sequences put together by alternative directors occupy a privileged position within the film, definitive by negation of Haneke's stylistic choice and intention throughout the thirty-eight sequence shots.

The modernist concerns with the way in which even the most superficially 'honest' art can deceive are examined through Georges's work as a photographer. His surreptitious photographing of people on the Métro is a form of surveillance that leads to a marvellous montage of portraits (in fact the work of war photographer Luc Delahaye, who collaborated with Haneke on the film), augmenting the film's insistent thematic build-up around the relativity of truth, perception and film/photography. There is a remarkable disjunction between Georges's photographs of people on the tube and the process by which he takes them. The people on the Métro are blank and impersonal, refusing to make eye contact with each other or with Georges. But his photos show them looking directly into the camera, as if they know they are having their pictures taken. It is a subtle manoeuvre on Haneke's part, far more so than the aggressive reflexivity of his previous work (or even, to a lesser extent, *Benny's Video*), but if we consider it carefully, we realise it is yet another example of the way in which the truth slips somewhat when it passes through the camera lens. Even a photographer such as Georges – a photographer of 'reality', the equivalent of documentarist – manipulates the truth through his images. Indeed Georges might be understood as a less extreme, but no less alienated, variation on the character of Benny. Like the protagonist of Haneke's earlier film, Georges uses his camera as a tool to distance himself from the horrors of the world that he catalogues. The photographs he takes on the Métro illustrate his failure to engage with the world in any 'authentic' sense: they are a misguided method of simultaneously connecting to and distancing himself from the world.

Of even greater importance to Haneke's project of co-opting the spectator into a position of ethically engaged reflection is a sequence (presented without any narrative signal of a change in level) that is subsequently revealed to be taken from the film that Anne is shooting. Anne, in a rooftop swimming pool, becomes hysterical as she realises that a child is teetering on the edge of the roof's wall, trying to reach a balloon. After a tense moment, the child is seized from the wall just as he is on the verge of falling. Suddenly we hear a laugh from off-screen. A cut reveals the whole sequence was taking place at a sound studio where Anne was synchronising her voice for the soundtrack of a film she had appeared in: the woman we saw in the pool was not Anne herself, but a fictional character that she was playing. And if we are alert, we should recognize at once, on purely stylistic grounds, that the scene is an anomaly, an abrupt stylistic break. It uses all the standard devices of Hollywood film-making: shot/reverse shot, point of view shots, the zoom, some very dubious spatial relationships, deliberate deception of the spectator (the point of view zoom from the child's viewpoint clearly implies that he has fallen or is falling). All these devices typically involve us in the action as more than spectators, playing on strong basic emotions, depriving us of critical distance. They are rigorously rejected throughout the remainder of the film. Here, however, Haneke draws on generic strategies of suspense and identification once more, drawing out a tension between his own modernist methods and those of mainstream commercial cinema.

The scene looks back to *Benny's Video*, then, in its incorporation of films-within-films, and to *Funny Games*, with its superimposition of generic convention over modernist techniques, creating a sudden moment of impact which occurs at the point that we realise that this scene – the first within *Code inconnu* to engage us emotionally – is both manipulative and manipulated: we are jolted out of our engagement by the sudden reflexivity of the ensuing scene. In many ways, the sequence is a correlate of the rewind scene within *Funny Games*, only here its impact is mitigated by the fact that suspense is not built up over the course of an hour, but is restricted to a four-minute interlude.

The aggressive reflexivity of this scene is contrasted with Haneke's 'own' suspense scene in which Anne is harassed by an aggressive *Beur* on the Métro. This scene is filmed in a more classically modernist style. Haneke positions a deep focus, static camera at one end of a Métro carriage, with Anne seated at the opposite end in profile. She is approached by the young Arab who propositions her and then, when she ignores him, becomes aggressive. Anne moves to the foreground and sits facing the camera. The young Arab follows her. Their position directly opposite the camera/spectator recalls similar set-ups in *Funny Games* and a similar effect is achieved, whereby the spectator is implicated in the scene as the young man continues to harass Anne. The emotional response it elicits, as the spectator feels both fear on Anne's part and guilt for their complicity in the viewing situation (paralleled onscreen by the diegetic spectators who look on but do not act), is much more complex and disturbing than the pleasurable suspense that arises in the diegetic film. In this way, Haneke incorporates elements of the deliberate unpleasure that we see operating in *Funny Games* into a narrative which is much less directly accusatory. Once more, he draws on the principles of the 'modernist episode' in order to place the spectator in an unpleasurable relationship to the image, drawing out the experience such that, on the one hand, time becomes manifest and we are forced into a rational awareness of film as film, but, on the other, we are emotionally engaged with the scene's narrative content. Its effect is much more powerful than that of the aggressive rupture of the earlier suspense scene. One can conclude from our responses to it, therefore, that the creation of unpleasure through benign reflexivity is less reliant on the prior operation of the pleasure drive than its creation through aggressive reflexivity.

As a filmic investigation of the possibilities of first-generation modernism for creating an unpleasurable response for the spectator, *Code inconnu* is by far the most complete of Haneke's works. But how adequately does *Code inconnu* meet Haneke's moral intentions? Speaking of the film, the director professes to a hope that viewers will realise that they 'fall into all kinds of traps' and that they should struggle against these traps.[17] He insists that in making the film he aimed to 'unsettle the viewer and to take away consolation or self-satisfaction'.[18] Assuming that these were his genuine intentions, how successfully does the early modernist aesthetic convey them? If it was clear to Haneke that *Funny Games* drew too heavily on generic structures and aggressively reflexive devices, does *Code inconnu*'s modernist aesthetic manage to attenuate its more aggressive episodes such that the spectator is positioned morally without the director's own ethical intentions being compromised?

Far from it. In fact, Haneke's most successful attempt at relinquishing his own authority over the conclusions that the spectator should reach leaves perhaps too much room for interpretation. Despite the director's repeated insistence that the film cannot be reduced to a single 'theme', *Code inconnu*, like the trilogy, has been the subject of numerous cultural and socio-political readings, with almost no attention being paid to the reflexive structures that it employs. Critical reception of the film can loosely be divided into two camps. In the first camp, a small number of liberal left wing critics such as Robin Wood have read the film as a political comment on racism, social hierarchy and immigration laws, with Wood claiming its overriding 'message' is the need for empathy in today's disaffected and defensive society.[19] Such readings overlook the significance of Haneke's reflexive devices, and are perhaps too specific in their interpretation of a film which, like Haneke's earlier works, takes not specific social problems but rather a general climate of Western disaffection as its subject. More troubling for the director, however, was the film's appropriation by the the French right-wing press. The director himself noted that such reactions were at odds with the responses he intended viewers to have. In an interview with Nick James for *Sight & Sound*, the director, usually notoriously reticent when it comes to discussing interpretations of his work, expressed concern about responses to the film in France: 'I'm really very irked about the reaction because in the past it was always the same people who were for or against my films. This time, those who were for my other films [i.e. the French left] were against *Code inconnu* and vice versa. I just don't understand'.[20]

It is clear from this that *Code inconnu*'s success within Haneke's project of ethical spectatorship must be seen as limited. The reason for that limitation lies perhaps in its lack of a defining directorial authority coupled with a failure to cement the link between the disaffected climate of society and Haneke's critique of the cinematic medium. What is missing from the interpretations of both parties – left and right wing – is sufficient acknowledgement of the film's structures of reflexivity, which call into question everything that we see and hear, and which should foreclose the possibility of the film being 'read' as a clear statement. This might indicate that the reflexive devices in *Code inconnu* are not sufficiently prominent to induce self-appraisal on the spectator's part. The contrast between Haneke's film and the diegetic film (and photos) is the closest Haneke comes to a critique of mainstream media within the film. The conventions of classic realist cinema that Anne's version of *The Collector* draws upon are held up for comparison with the alternative method of film-making that Haneke's own film exemplifies, but they are not rigorously criticised in the same manner as in the case of *Funny Games*. Perhaps Haneke, having been accused of making a didactic and 'heavy-handed' film in *Funny Games*, veers too far here in the other direction. The spectator's reaction to *Code inconnu*, it seems, is often one of accusation, but not one of self-accusation.

## Stars and the Seduction of the Spectator

So far then, we have seen how Haneke's body of work up until *Code inconnu* can be characterised as a process of negotiation between different forms of cinematic modernism. On the one hand we see a benign, first-generation modernism that refutes pleasure and places the spectator at a distance from the cinematic image, forcing them to engage rationally with the film's content. This technique prevails in *Der Siebente Kontinent*, *71 Fragmente einer Chronologie des Zufalls* and *Code inconnu*. On the other hand there is an aggressive, second-generation modernism that gives rise to a feeling of active unpleasure on the spectator's part, thereby emphasising their proximity to the cinematic image. This is the dominant technique operating within *Funny Games*; to some extent it is also present within *Benny's Video*. These techniques are not, however, entirely discrete, and we have examined how Haneke combines and contrasts them within each film, mentioning the incorporation of one instance of 'aggressive' reflexivity into *Code inconnu*, and paying close attention to the insertion of the 'modernist moment' into the generic suspense strategies that operate within *Funny Games* in order to create a moment of 'impact'. The moment of impact opens up a space into which the spectator is invited to enter, a space for reflection on the film's content and its relationship to the spectator themself.

The key factor that distinguishes *Funny Games* from the films that precede it, as well as from *Code inconnu*, is its dependence on generic convention.[21] The film's generic structure – in this case, that of the suspense thriller – is pivotal to the way in which Haneke mobilises impact, for the reference allows him to minimally engage the spectator's emotions, and enables the bringing of these emotions into tension with the spectator's rational awareness – prompted by reflexive techniques – at the moment of impact. As we discussed in Chapter Three, this is one respect in which Haneke's films diverge from counter-cinema, where the filmic language objectifies the characters and creates such a distance between on-screen event and viewer that the spectator is denied all emotional involvement with the film.

The generic qualities of *Funny Games* do not simply encourage emotional engagement: they also prompt the spectator to expect certain qualities from the film. These expectations are prompted by the film itself, with its 'quoting' of classical elements from the suspense genre (paradigm scenario, formal composition and so forth). But they are also set up even before the spectator has entered the cinema by the film's promotion and marketing. The presentation of the film via posters and trailers, film magazines and festival catalogues, leads some film-goers to believe that it will be a constituent of a genre with which they were familiar: the suspense thriller. On this basis, some film-goers are led to purchase tickets, attend the screening, and thereby expose themselves to Haneke's manipulations.

That this technique was successful is testified to by the box office success of *Funny Games*.[22] The film propelled Haneke into the international critical limelight, and his subsequent decision to move production of his films from Austria to France has been widely speculated upon as primarily financially motivated, a view propagated by the Austrian press and supported in part by comments made by Haneke himself.[23] In fact, as mentioned in Chapter One, Haneke was wooed to France by producer Marin Karmitz (the producer famous for also bringing director Krzysztof Kiéslowski to France) and actress Juliette Binoche. Described by David Thomson as 'the art-house actress for a generation',[24] Binoche's presence within *Code inconnu* has been generally seen as part of the overarching project of making Haneke's films more commercially viable on an international stage. And with good reason: as Thomson puts it, Binoche, who has successfully bridged the gap between European art films and Hollywood blockbusters such as *The English Patient* (1996) and *Chocolat* (2000), has

**Figure 4.1** Juliette Binoche in *Code inconnu* (2000):
'The art-house actress for a generation'.
*Courtesy of the BFI stills department. Permission graciously supplied by WEGAfilm.*

become 'the smiling face that ought to be on the Euro coin with which film business is done'.[25]

However, the casting of Binoche in *Code inconnu* also signals a new development in Haneke's project of positioning the spectator morally, which is as important in many ways as the introduction of genre into his oeuvre with *Funny Games*. Binoche, as Thomson acknowledges, is a 'star', and her position as such carries with it implications for how the spectator engages with any film that she appears in. For using a star like Binoche within his film allows Haneke to operate certain strategies of seduction, strategies not unlike those which genre opens up to him, strategies that are both intra- and extra-cinematic.

Let's look briefly at how this might be the case, before moving on to an analysis of how star and genre both function within Haneke's next film, *La Pianiste*. At an extra-cinematic level, stars provide an attractive 'hook' for the spectator, and enable the film-maker to lure audiences into his films. The figure of the star can be deployed in marketing to achieve a similar effect as genre, drawing spectators in to see films that they might not otherwise have been interested in seeing, and it is remarkable that Binoche's face dominates the publicity material for *Code inconnu* and Isabelle Huppert's that for *La Pianiste*. In this way, the casting of stars in Haneke's films is part of the trap he sets for the spectator, a trap that extends beyond the screening itself, but into the institional structures surrounding each film: posters, magazines, TV ads and so forth.[26] This luring in of the spectator re-emphasises their own collusion with the cinematic institution, and as such it looks back to apparatus theory's unresolved concern with the spectator's extra-cinematic agency, which we can define as the spectator's ability to choose what film they see and to express this choice by buying a ticket for a film, thereby participating in the capitalist structure of the cinematic institution.

On an intra-cinematic level, moreover, stars are mobilised in the service of emotional engagement. As has been well documented, the star's role in a film lies at a point of synthesis between representation and identification.[27] On the one hand, she (or he) is 'performing', playing a part; but on the other hand, her very presence references not only all the other roles that she has played, but also the star persona that she has cultivated. The star functions as an emotional hook, since the spectator's familiarity with the star gives rise to an emotional attachment which exists outside of any diegetic characterisation. This effect has been most famously exploited by Alfred Hitchcock, who cast stars – such as Janet Leigh, Grace Kelly and Cary Grant – in his suspense thrillers in order to heighten audience involvement with characters that were psychologically undeveloped. To illustrate, let us take the example of *North by Northwest* (1959). The film's narrative is entirely concerned with action, into which the audience is plunged straight away. The very lack of a clear background adds to the tension of the predicament in which the lead character finds himself, and character development is kept to a minimum. For this reason the casting of Grant, who the audience may feel it already knows and therefore cares about, allows its members to engage more thoroughly with the film's suspense structures.[28]

With this in mind, it is notable that the two emotional high points of *Code inconnu* are both suspense scenes involving Binoche's character being placed in a tense or dangerous situation: there are clear similarities between Hitchcock's use of Grant over an entire film and Haneke's use of Binoche within these two scenes. But what is important in *Code inconnu* is that the use of a star allows Haneke to forego not only psychological development but also generic development: the director does not have to build up a relationship of loose empathy based on an ongoing use of formal strategies, as was the case in *Funny Games*, but instead relies on the star to function as a minimal way of engaging the spectator's emotions. In this way, he finds a shortcut to the emotional engagement that was dependent on suspense strategies alone in *Funny Games*. Likewise, within the context of Haneke's later genre films, stars do not signal generic qualities (in the way that Fred Astaire signals the musical, or John Wayne the Western); rather, they condense the emotional effects of genre, which leaves Haneke free to draw on generic structures without making the presence of such structures overly explicit (to the point at which they would threaten to overwhelm the films' other frameworks).

Binoche's presence within *Code inconnu* is limited: it is fair to say that her 'smiling face' features much more heavily in the film's promotion than within its diegesis. However, the use of stars comes to play an increasingly significant role in Haneke's subsequent films, going hand in hand with an increasingly marked emphasis on genre: *La Pianiste* has been categorised as both melodrama and, to borrow Barbara Creed's phrase, 'postmodern porn',[29] *Le Temps du loup* as science fiction and disaster movie,[30] while *Caché* explicitly draws on the thriller format once more, as I shall discuss in detail in the next chapter. So while the progession towards generic formats and star performances can be seen as the result of commercial imperatives (*La Pianiste*, *Le Temps du loup* and *Caché* were all produced with French funding and marketed to an international audience), they can, and should, be also seen as part of Haneke's strategies of seduction, both intra- and extra-cinematic.

In this way, Haneke moves further beyond counter-cinema towards a much more integrative form of film-making that takes on Hollywood cinema on its own terms. His use of extra-cinematic structures looks back towards apparatus theory and its concern with the cinematic institution as a whole. But as we saw in Chapter Two, apparatus theory really never engaged fully with this question of why certain audiences view particular films, focusing for the most part on the cinema's internal dynamics. Likewise, the counter-cinema that was contemporaneous with it was characterised primarily by first-generation modernism and forms of reflexivity which never forced the spectator to consider their own relationship to the screen fully. Haneke's use of the star and the genre to encourage emotional engagement refocuses modernist techniques, but his manipulation of the spectator through extra-cinematic strategies realises the implications of apparatus theory in a way that counter-cinema failed to do, prompting the spectator to enter into a social, financial and emotional contract with the film, one which Haneke can then reveal to them.

## La Pianiste

In the combination of genres, stars and modernist frameworks, and the marriage of intra-cinematic and extra-cinematic seduction, there is an underlying formal consistency in the films that follow *Code inconnu*, and for this reason I believe that we can see it as marking the end of the process of negotiation that characterises Haneke's earlier works. After *Funny Games*, Haneke was aware of the risks issuing from generic convention. However, it is not until the extreme modernism of *Code inconnu* produced a similar (although differently sourced) set of problems, that Haneke arguably comes to a realisation of the full significance of generic conventions to his critical aesthetic, if they can be adequately contained within alternative operating frameworks. So rather than dispensing with generic convention, Haneke moves towards an aesthetic in which it is made to coexist harmoniously with principles of first- and second-generation modernism than might be said of *Funny Games*. Each of his three subsequent films – *La Pianiste, Le Temps du loup* and *Caché* – demonstrates an integration of the three frameworks that we have so far seen as structuring Haneke's works (first-generation modernism, second-generation modernism and generic convention) which is much less polarised than in any of the works up to and including *Code inconnu*, and which allows him to resolve some of the problems of response witnessed by his earlier films.

We have seen that critical and commercial responses to *Funny Games* from some camps suggested that the director, in employing the structures of linear narrative, generic convention and extreme reflexivity, had not managed to produce a film that provided a satisfactory alternative to Hollywood cinema. This response was supported by the film's reception within cultish horror circles, with fans reading the film as a variant on, rather than a criticism of, the genre. We hypothesised that these reactions, exactly the opposite of those that Haneke was seeking to provoke, may have prompted his return to first-generation modernism with *Code inconnu*. However, that approach had its own pitfalls: lacking the authorial control of *Funny Games*, *Code inconnu* was overly open to interpretation, and at the same time as both left-wing and right-wing groups appropriated it in support of their respective political concerns, neither party read the film as critical of the spectator, that is of themselves, but only of the other. These reactions to *Code inconnu* also highlight another problem for Haneke: despite his move from Austria to an international forum, his film was nonetheless interpreted as being endemic to a specific national situation. Just as *Der Siebente Kontinent*, *Benny's Video*, *71 Fragmente*, and even *Funny Games*, have been interpreted by the vast majority of critics as 'critiques of Austrian society',[31] so *Code inconnu* has come to be seen in intellectual circles as a comment on contemporary French politics. This despite the fact that Haneke, in almost every interview he has given about that film, has broken his own rule of not discussing a film's meaning and stressed that the film is intended as an examination of a much broader European problem, claiming that the film could have been set in London or in Vienna.[32]

*La Pianiste* offers a particularly ingenious solution to the difficulty of Haneke's films being seen as critiques of specific national situations: its action takes place in a Vienna inhabited by French speakers. The city is thus transformed into something at once self-identical and unfamiliar by the use of a predominantly French cast speaking the French language, circumventing the problem made clear by responses to *Code inconnu* of using a very specific setting. This principle of playing on both familiarity and strangeness extends to the film's generic structure, which in this case is primarily melodramatic.

The film's narrative might seem unlikely material for a reading of the film as part of the melodramatic genre. Based on a novel by Elfriede Jelinek, the film tells the story of Professor Erika Kohut (Isabelle Huppert), a Schubert scholar at the Vienna Conservatory. She is cold, brilliant, demanding, and, we learn in the film's opening scene, she lives at home with her elderly mother (Annie Girardot). When Erika embarks on a relationship with a young student, Walter Klemmer (Benoît Magimel), it transpires that her glacial persona masks a tormented sado-masochist, who agrees to an affair with Walter on the condition that the only 'sex' they ever have consists of a series of macabre rituals prescripted by Erika. Shocked and disgusted by Erika's demands, Walter rejects her emotionally, batters and rapes her, leaving Erika's fate at the end of the film open to speculation.

The film's plot then bears little obvious resemblance to the classic Hollywood melodramatic narratives. But the film's lead actress, Isabelle Huppert, has described the narrative as 'quite simple … a very classical structure. You have three characters that you can easily identify with and you have a normal story'.[33] The promotional description of the film taken from Artificial Eye's 2002 VHS release moreover demonstrates how the film's distributors have, in many ways, marketed it as a melodrama:

> 'The Piano Teacher' is a powerful and controversial new drama from Michael Haneke. Isabelle Huppert gives a performance of astounding emotional intensity as Erika Kohut, a repressed woman in her late thirties who teaches piano at the Vienna Conservatory and lives with her tyrannical mother, with who she has a volatile love–hate relationship. But when one of Erika's students, the handsome and assured Walter Klemmer, attempts to seduce her, the barriers that she has carefully erected around her claustrophobic world are shattered, unleashing a previously inhibited extreme desire.

Indeed, it would be perfectly possible, if a little misleading, to describe the film as 'the story of a repressed woman in her thirties who meets a handsome stranger and embarks upon an affair which will change her world'. Such a description could just as easily be applied to *All that Heaven Allows* (Sirk, 1955) or *Letter from an Unknown Woman* (Max Ophüls, 1948).

*La Pianiste* draws on what we might call a 'traditional' conceit of the woman's film – the inevitability of the heroine's desires as disappointed – in order to align our emotional responses with Erika's. In *La Pianiste*, the protagonist Erika's own perspective is privileged at all times. Although Haneke's style is very remote – eschewing point of view shots altogether – we witness only events at which Erika is present; we see Walter, her mother, her pupils, only when she is with them. In what is almost a reiteration of suspense convention, the audience is moreover aware of the nature of Erika's sexual desires long before Walter is, and so awaits *her* discovery of his reaction, rather than *his* discovery of her secret. In this way, the spectator is encouraged to become emotionally involved with the narrative, as the scopophilic drive is prompted by the film's generic qualities, and the spectator waits to find out what will happen to the character around whom the film's paradigm scenario revolves.

To reinforce the privileged status of characterisation within the film relative to his earlier works, Haneke draws upon and updates classic melodramatic iconography: Erika's emotions are represented by her surrounding environment, giving rise to a highly stylised *mise-en-scène*. But whereas in the films of Douglas Sirk, for example, the characters are lavishly dressed, the sets decadent and almost garish in their range of bright colours, the cinematic world that Haneke creates is, for the most part, one of minimalist modernism. Erika wears a palate of black, white, taupe and brown; sets are composed of clean, straight lines in similar shades. If Sirk's use of colour was intended, as he claimed, to reflect the emotional turmoil of his characters, Haneke on the other hand uses lack of colour to point towards the disaffection that he sees as characterising modern bourgeois society and to portray the dynamics of modern alienation. While Sirk uses deep-focus lenses to lend a deliberate harshness to objects, Haneke switches between long shots and close-ups to depict a dialectic between alienation and claustrophobia. Similarly, Haneke's lighting, rather than bathing the heroine in a soft-focus halo and casting the antagonist in shadows, is stark: natural lighting lending the bleak colours of his sets and characters a cold air. The stillness of his film, almost stagnant in its lack of movement, is the exact opposite of the Sirkian technique of only cutting away to movement, to indicate the whirligig of emotion his characters are on. Haneke's is an aesthetic of clinical precision. Shots are filmed, for the main part, from a fixed point of view, the camera's only movement a restricted and restrictive pan. Haneke's manipulation of classic melodramatic iconography extends to the film's settings. For the majority of the film, Erika is inside: the flat she shares with her mother, the conservatory, the homes of her fellow musicians. When she does venture outside this constrictive world (and even when outside, she is still always inside: a shopping centre, an ice rink, a cinema), she ventures into another world, where her sexual self can be unleashed. This focus on interiors reflects Erika's feeling of claustrophobia, and represents the emotional walls she has built around herself. *La Pianiste*'s aesthetic reflects not hysterical excess but extreme repression, carefully controlled and contained.

Melodrama is thus given the same treatment in *La Pianiste* as suspense is in *Funny Games*: Haneke reduces it to a formal and narrative schema, which notionally draws us into the narrative, but which does not develop in the same way as classical genre film does. As played by Isabelle Huppert, another celebrated French actress, Erika becomes the focal point of the spectator's emotional involvement with the film. This involvement is not straightforward cinematic identification: the film's first-generation modernist aesthetic keeps spectators at a critical distance from the narrative events. The characterisation of Erika is extremely alienating to an audience, which might find it hard to see itself reflected in the cold, closed, sado-masochistic and even repellent figure of a woman who mutilates herself and others, visits peep shows and spies on copulating couples.

Moreover, psychological explanation is either refused, or made so explicit as to merit little comment. In *Funny Games*, we are presented with a scene in which Paul, as a response to Anna's question, 'Why are you doing this to us?' relates Peter's background as an abused child and a junkie, only for the two perpetrators to laugh off the psychological explanation as rubbish. In a similar way, Haneke's incorporation of scenes such as Erika's attempt to engage in sexual relations with her mother is so heavily laden with psychoanalytical overtones that no reading is necessary: such that an article such as J. Champagne's 'Undoing Oedipus: Feminism and Michael Haneke's *The Piano Teacher*', becomes an exercise in cataloguing, rather than decoding, the film's Freudian elements.[34] In this way the film becomes resistant to academic readings which seek a 'deeper', metaphorical meaning, rather than focusing on the individual's response to what is represented on screen.

But we are also distanced from the narrative by Haneke's deployment of second-generation reflexive devices which function as an explicit critique of cine-televisual perception. Throughout the film the cinematic medium – and the process of watching – is foregrounded. The opening scene is bathed in the light of the flickering television and set to the soundtrack of its constant drone: in fact, when Erika and her mother are in their flat, the television is almost constantly on, its invasion into their homes total and unwavering. A later scene sees Erika spy on a copulating couple at a drive-in movie. This scene, originally set in Vienna's Prater Park in Jelinek's novel, constitutes the sole change in setting that Haneke makes to the original novel, and it is crucial to turning the audience's gaze back on itself.

More remarkable still is a scene towards the beginning of the film in which Erika visits a pornographic film viewing booth. Early in the film, we see Erika aggressively enter the space of a porn arcade. She goes into a video booth, whereupon there follows a seven-second shot of a split-screen monitor showing four separate image tracks: each a clip from a generic hardcore porn film. The film cuts back to Erika as she selects an image, then back to the selected porn film on the monitor. The pornographic image track recurs on the cinematic screen twice more, as the film continues to intercut between the diegetic screen and Erika watching it. The camera then lingers on Erika as she reaches into a waste-paper basket and pulls from it the tissues used by a previous occupant to wipe up his ejaculate. She inhales the tissue deeply while watching the film, her face impassive, her very reaction an inversion of the excesses of masturbation.

This scene brings second-generation modernism into play. As we have seen, the use of films-within-films is a recurring device within Haneke's work. Here, it serves a number of purposes in addition to foregrounding Erika's pursuit of passive pleasure. First and foremost, the scene creates a *mise-en-abyme* of the spectator's situation, directly foregrounding the scopophilic urge. The intra-diegetic images on the monitor employ the process of enunciation characteristic of pornographic imagery: direct address imagery.

Direct address imagery is offered explicitly, in Laura Mulvey's terms, 'to be looked at', stressing the addressee's look as opposed to the addresser's intervention, and so is particularly liable to bring the 'fourth look' into play in full force.[35] This 'fourth look' is not of the same order as the other three (intra-diegetic looks, the camera's look at the profilmic event and the viewer's look at the image). In Lacanian terms, this is a look imagined by me in the field of the other which surprises me in the act of looking and causes a feeling of shame. Any articulation of images and looks which brings into play the position and activity of the viewer as a distinctly separate factor also destabilises that position and puts it at risk, for when the scopic drive is brought into focus, the viewer also runs the risk of becoming the object of the look. But this emerges particularly strongly when the viewer's scopic drive is being gratified in relation to an object or scene that heightens the sense of censorship inherent in any form of gratification. The effect of being caught looking gains in force when the viewer is looking at something they are not supposed to look at according to an external system of censorship (as in clandestine viewings), or according to an internal system of censorship (the superego) or, as in most cases, according to both censorships combined. In this way, that fourth look problematises the social dimension, the field of the other. And the social manifests itself as shame, because it has to do with the gaze of the other.[36]

The fourth look is particularly likely, then, to be mobilised by pornography, which presents us with images that heighten the sense of potential censorship. This is important here, for this internal set of images functions as a generic convention as well as a point of contrast. Haneke's film has not only been compared to the melodramatic genre, but as I mentioned earlier, it can also be seen as drawing on some generic conventions, if not of pornography then certainly of the contemporary genre of 'post-porn'.[37] Amongst the films that *Sight & Sound* editor Nick James lists as examples of this sub-genre in his introduction to a series of articles on the depiction of sex and the sexual act in contemporary cinema are *Romance* (Breillat, France, 1999) *Seul contre tous/I stand alone* (Noé, France, 1998), *Irréversible/Irreversible* (Noé, France, 2002), *À ma soeur/Fat Girl* (Breillat, France, 2001), *Baise-moi/Rape Me* (directed jointly by Virginie Despentes and Coralie Trinh Thi, France, 2001), *Intimacy* (Chéreau, UK, 2001), *Idioterne/The Idiots* (Von Trier, Denmark, 1998) and Haneke's *La Pianiste*. The inclusion of *La Pianiste* amongst these films is not, at first glance, particularly surprising. But while the film's content ostensibly aligns it with the other works that he discusses, visually *La Pianiste* relentlessly confines the sexual act to the off-screen space: as James admits, 'there is no real sex in this film'. Its place within the canon of sexually explicit works seems dependent on the film's narrative content, rather than on formal conventions.[38]

So, in fact, the secondary importance of the series of explicit images in the porn booth is that it functions as a prompt for the spectator to make an *imaginary* connection to the conventions of pornography. The intra-diegetic images show pornography in its most raw and basic form: both pornography as a 'norm', and pornography separated from any artistic pretension. Its inclusion thus serves to underline the deviations that Haneke makes from these norms. In the course of the film, the spectator witnesses three narrative instances of intercourse, but in each case the sexual act either occurs in the off-screen space or is obscured within the frame. The pornography booth scene thus also serves to remind us what is implicit in Haneke's film. These images act almost as visual aids, to be recalled whenever the spectator is prompted to imagine what it is that lies outside the cinematic frame.

To illustrate, let us consider one of these intercourse scenes in some detail. Erika and Walter's first sexual encounter occurs in the women's toilets of the Conservatory: a white-tiled septic space bleached in pale light. Erika enters, shortly followed by Walter. He peers over the top of the stall she is using to watch her urinate, although we are not given access to what he sees. When she exits the stall, he kisses her, and they slide to the restroom floor in an embrace, initiating what resembles a classic love scene. The camera, however, remains at a distance throughout, situated at the farthest point from the two lovers in the room. Erika abruptly tells Walter to stop, and stands up again. She unbuttons his trousers, at which point Walter shifts so that he has his back to the spectator, his body blocking Erika's body from view. Walter's black clothing and large frame both resemble and effectively act as the black rectangles that censors often place over genitalia in film, blocking out the act so that we cannot either see her arms or his penis. The camera next cuts to a reverse shot taken over Erika's shoulder so that we are facing Walter, but now the framing has been tightened so that Walter's penis and Erika's hands are outside the lower border of the image frame. Erika then slides into this filmic space beyond the bottom edge of the frame, as she kneels to perform fellatio on Walter. At this point, the circumscribed frame is practically drained of content. Walter's torso is framed against a white background: there is very little movement, and no sound other than his laboured breathing. Indeed, when Walter tries to articulate the aural excesses of pornography ('That's it, I'm coming'), Erika silences him, threatening to stop if he does not keep quiet.

The white doors of the toilets form a background of vertical lines with Walter's body a black stripe across the centre of the screen, drawing our attention to the upper and lower limits of the frame and the space that lies beyond them. Walter's gaze towards this space reinforces the implied presence of the sexual organ and the sexual act, prompting us to follow his eyeline down to the natural conclusion which we cannot see but can easily imagine. The characters' gazes in fact serve as a constant reminder of the sexual act's presence in the off-screen space. When Erika watches Walter masturbate, a series of shot/reverse shots between the two allows us to ascertain their spatial relationship to one another, so that when we are shown a close-up of Erika's face, it is clear exactly where she is looking, and what she is looking at. The technique develops on a similar sequence within *Funny Games*, in which Anna is asked by her tormentors to strip and is subjected to their gazes, but the sight of Susanne Lothar's naked body is refused to the spectator. In this context, it is extremely effective: as reviewer Alexander Walker put it, 'absolutely nothing genital is visible in this sequence, yet "its" presence is painfully tumescent.'[39]

On the other two occasions that Erika and Walter (attempt to) engage in a sexual act, what should be explicit is transformed into something implicit through its non-framing. When Walter rapes Erika, the static camera focuses on the characters' faces: Walter's turned away from the camera for at least half the scene, Erika's impassive as she stares into space. The only noise Walter's breathing, the shot denies us any graphic sexuality. In an earlier scene at the ice rink where Walter plays hockey, Walter's body once more acts as a screen, obscuring Erika's attempts to

**Figure 4.2** *La Pianiste* (2001): Erika (Isabelle Huppert) and
Walter (Benoît Magimel) wrestle for sexual control in the bathrooms
of the Vienna Conservatory.
*Courtesy of the BFI stills department. Permission graciously supplied by WEGAfilm.*

perform fellatio on him. The camera is placed at a distance, so that the
arrangement of both bodies within the frame, their relative lack of
motion and relative proportion to the frame make it difficult for the
spectator to discern what is taking place. But the frame is suddenly
filled with movement as Erika pushes Walter off her and bursts into the
foreground of the frame, vomiting heavily. The 'money shot' here
becomes something disgusting and obscene, not a moment of
satisfaction, but a moment of repulsion and rejection.

These two scenes – one in the bathroom, one at the ice-rink –
demonstrate Haneke's use of modernist techniques to once more create
a moment of 'impact'. Here impact occurs at the point at which the
spectator's desire to see the sexually explicit – the voyeuristic urge – is
either frustrated by the use of off-screen space or directly confronted by
the rescindment of satisfaction. Erika's vomiting re-enacts, in a much
subtler manner, the rewind scene in *Funny Games*: the spectator's
scopophilic desire is fulfilled only for it to be immediately rejected. In
this case, however, the spectator is not confronted by direct address,

and so the effect is less authoritarian, less abrasive, although nonetheless troubling. In part, this is due to the fact that the spectator does not feel himself to be judged by another but by themselves. The criticism that Haneke levels at the spectator is not to do with what they have watched, but with what they would *like* to watch.

The scene may thus give rise to a process of self-judgment. And this in turn prompts feelings of guilt, when the spectator judges themself and finds they are wanting. Haneke's cinematic self-censorship and the unpleasureable feeling of disappointment that this gives rise to ask the spectator to recognise their desire for the sexually explicit, and to consider the moral implications of this. Second-generation modernism in Haneke's version of it renders the spectator complicit with an immoral spectacle and does so within an emotive situation of unpleasure. This combination of unpleasure and complicity cues the spectator to think morally about what they have seen, or, rather, what they haven't seen but wanted to see (most clear in off-screen violence and sex, but also in a more pervasive off-screen condition when the film does not present us with what we want or expect). Once again critical awareness arises from unpleasure: the desire to regain a pleasurable relationship to the on-screen image comes into conflict with the critical awareness of what exactly this would entail – the sight of a graphic and disturbing image – and the spectator is invited into a thought space.

## *Le Temps du loup*

*La Pianiste* is, both critically and commercially, one of Haneke's most successful films to date, and responses to the film suggest, moreover, that the ethical positioning of the spectator that the film enacts is both effective and unobtrusive. Readings such as Robin Wood's 'Do I disgust you? Or, Tirez pas sur *La Pianiste*', while over-emphasising certain social and political aspects of the film, acknowledge both Haneke's critique of the cinematic medium and the ethical positioning of the spectator that arises from the film. Wood recognises that the society Haneke critiques within his film is not a theoretical concept that the spectator (or the theorist) can critically distance themself from, for the reflexivity of *La Pianiste* situates the spectator firmly within its circumference. In his reading, Erika's question, 'Do I disgust you?' is not merely aimed at Walter, but also at the audience, and as Wood so presciently points out, if our answer is yes, then we must ask ourselves whether we, too, are not disgusting.[40] It is, Wood claims, imperative that we recognise not only that Erika is a product of contemporary society, but moreover that we recognise our own contribution to and particaption in that same society.

Given the relative success of *La Pianiste* in achieving Haneke's stated moral aims it is unsurprising that the film-maker reprises the elements that make up its formal construction in *Le Temps du loup*. Once again, *Le Temps du loup* features a recognisable star (Huppert) within a schematically generic set-up: this time Haneke draws on the tradition of the science fiction or disaster film. In a now established manner, he combines these elements with the structures of benign and aggressive reflexivity that we have seen operating in his earlier films. The film's opening sequence, for example, strongly resembles that of *Funny Games*. A tracking shot follows a Peugeot people carrier as it pulls up to a country house. We might presume the setting to be France, since the language spoken by the family arriving in the car is French, but in the modern Eurozone this need not be the case: there are no landmarks to suggest a recognisable locale, and, for those familiar with *Funny Games* and *La Pianiste*, language within Haneke's films is no longer an indicator of locale. However, the scenery looks like Europe, and the people in the car look like well-off Europeans. The husband, Georges (French star Daniel Duval), is terse and authoritative; the two children, Eva and Benny, eager to be released from the vehicle; the wife, Anne (Huppert) concerned and anxious.

Once inside the shuttered house, the family encounter a dishevelled and panicky man wielding a shotgun. He tells them in crude French to get out. Behind him a woman, with a baby who has started to cry loudly, tries to restrain him. Their young son stands behind them. They have the look of refugees or asylum seekers. Georges tells the children to go outside and they obey. In a sequence of rapidly cut shot/reverse shots, he begins to negotiate with the stranger, who questions them about their 'supplies'. The gun goes off. Blood splatters across Anne's face and she immediately vomits. The killer's wife begins to scream, the baby continues to wail. Our point of view is moved outside with the children.

So far, the similarities with the earlier film's opening scenes are self-evident. However, unlike *Funny Games*, which establishes its (simple) plot premise very early on, the film does not explain what we have just seen, either now or later. Instead, we cut to an extreme long shot, in which the spectator struggles to discern the figure of Anne leading the children away from the house with only a bag and a bicycle. The nearest village is apparently deserted and those who will respond to the family's knocking quickly usher them away, despite the fact that they know the family. As they wander about in the increasingly impenetrable darkness, suspense builds, as the spectator tries to establish the nature of the onscreen events. Why are things so strange? What is happening? What has happened?

The indication is that something catastrophic has occurred, an impression which has already been set up by the film's marketing, and even by its title (from 'Song of the Sightseer', part of the ancient German *Codex Regius*), which references a time before Ragnarök, the end of the world. The promotional posters for the film show variants on an apocalyptic vision of a silhouetted figure standing upon blazing railway tracks, and the soundbites added to later prints confirm that the film is 'a remarkable evocation of a world in crisis'.[41] Once inside the cinema, this impression is compounded by the film's plot, which although opaque suggests that the setting for its events is a society that, if not exactly in the wake of an apocalypse, is certainly struggling to cope with the consequences of what Haneke refers to as a 'catastrophe'.[42] Few details are given about the nature of the disaster, but over the course of the film we do learn, for example, that the water has either been cut off or poisoned, and is now a resource in high demand. It becomes a commodity to be traded and controlled by whoever is lucky enough to come across it. Superficially, the film bears a striking resemblance to the genre of post-nuclear apocalypse films that were produced for television in the early 1980s, such as *Threads* (Mick Jackson, 1984) and *The Day After* (Nicholas Meyer, 1983). And at one point we see, pinned to a wall, a copy of a Dürer watercolour of a delicate landscape with what would appear to be the stem of a mushroom cloud on the horizon.

As this brief description of its marketing and plot indicates, the film can be seen to draw at least in part on the genres of science fiction and the disaster film (themselves often heavily overlaid with suspense strategies). It is therefore with reference to this genre in particular that we must investigate the film's approach to its spectator. Before we do so, however, a qualification must be made. The categorisation of *Le Temps du loup* as part of the science fiction, or disaster, genre is somewhat tenuous. Although, as is clear from the above, there is ample material to suggest a formal and thematic link, it is far from self-evident. We can certainly not place the film within a tradition of science fiction in the straightforward way that we can place *Funny Games* or, later, *Caché* in the generic tradition of the thriller, for example. This is primarily because 'science fiction' and the 'disaster film' are rather amorphous terms in themselves. Although genres are always difficult to define, these are unusually so, and both have tended to lack a tradition of critical theory. While there are some exceptions to this absence of theory, such as Vivian Sobchack's *Screening Space* (1988) and the sections on science fiction in Thomas Schatz's *Hollywood Genres* (1983) and J.P. Telotte's *Replications* (1995), even these writings fail to account for the genre's emotional relationship with the spectator. One can perhaps explain this absence of spectatorship theory in genre studies of the science fiction film by having recourse to the fact that, unlike suspense and melodrama, the films that are said by any one theorist or critic to comprise the genre are primarily distinguished by narrative content, rather than by a particular iconography, formal aesthetic or deployment of devices for emotional manipulation. Indeed, even the qualities that we have thus far used to situate the film in relation to the post-apocalyptic film are debatable.

Haneke's deployment of the generic conventions of science fiction and the disaster film is therefore difficult to link to a particular strategy for positioning the spectator, except the initial act of marketing the film as part of a genre and so building up a set of expectations attached to that genre. In this sense, the film's genre is defined more by its extra-cinematic mode of enunciation than its intra-cinematic one, related to strategies of engaging the spectator with the on-screen image. In the case of *Le Temps du loup*, seduction of the spectator with reference to their generic expectations takes place for the most part *outside* the cinema. As regards the film itself, engagement with the film is primarily prompted by drawing on generic qualities from outside science fiction. What Haneke does is to combine elements of the suspense strategies that operate in *Funny Games* – as he does in this opening scene – with elements of melodramatic strategies that operate within *La Pianiste*.

For example, the film's opening scene, which we saw closely resembles that of *Funny Games*, is marked by aspects of that film's form. Rapid cutting is combined with an extremely visceral soundtrack (the wails of the baby, the screams of its mother, the harsh commands of the gunman) to cause a feeling of irritation, which is shattered with the sudden gunshot. Later on, the remaining family members – Anne, Eva and Benny – encounter Georges' killers at a refugee camp. A heated debate springs up between Anne and the gunman. Once more the soundtrack features screeches and wails; other characters, trying to get involved, talk over one another. The scene seems to reach a climax as Anne, screaming, attacks her husband's killer, but suddenly two gunshots go off. The camera pans to two horses being shot in a nearby field, and then cuts suddenly to the sight of a knife being plunged into one of the still-breathing horses' necks, blood spurting out across the screen. The impact is one of sudden shock; the spectator's physical response might be to recoil. Unpleasure arises from the gradual building of tension and the sudden violence that erupts, both too soon and from an unexpected source.

The scenes described above produce impact in a similar manner to *Funny Games*'s rewind scene: generic form and plot structures set up expectations and engage emotion, only for this engagement to be suddenly ruptured by the effects of aggressive reflexivity. However, the film not only engages us on a schematic level, as the earlier work did, but it also begs a deeper emotional investment in the film's characters in a manner akin to *La Pianiste*. Like a suspense film, the science fiction genre uses its characters to explore situations; they can, therefore, function quite effectively as ciphers without the need for any psychological development, and identification is thus sketched in minimally. But Haneke here strengthens the spectator's involvement with the characters, rather than remaining at the level of schema, by introducing stars, for example. This is a development from *Funny Games*, but one familiar to us from *Code inconnu* and *La Pianiste*, and this being the case, we need not say too much about it here; but we should note that Isabelle Huppert is joined here by a well-known cast, including Daniel Duval, Olivier Gourmet, Patrice Chéreau, Maurice Bénichou and Béatrice Dalle, *all* of whom are easily recognisable to European audiences, and several of whom (Huppert, Gourmet, Dalle) are also familiar to American 'art-house' audiences. The spectator's investment in these stars is potentially (depending on the individual level of acquaintance with the actor) redoubled by the dispatch of Duval within the film's first five minutes. Drawing on Hitchcock once more, Haneke shows us that any character – no matter who plays them – is vulnerable, and so our 'fear' for them is increased.

The heightened attachment to the film's characters extends beyond those played by stars to others in the film, notably Anne's children, Benny and Eva. The film depends heavily on the child actors that play these parts: their characters are accorded as much screen time as Anne herself. We see Eva console her brother when he loses his canary, tend to him when he has a nosebleed, and protect him from the sight of a rape at the refugee camp; in an extended interlude, we even see her writing a letter to her dead father, explaining that she now has to be strong for her mother and younger sibling, an instance of psychological elucidation hitherto unprecedented in Haneke's work. In fact *Le Temps du loup*'s Eva and Benny may be the most psychologically developed of Haneke's characters to appear in any film up to this point in his oeuvre. They are joined by the young runaway befriended by Eva, who has his psychology sketched in over the course of the film's narrative. In a scene that verges on melodramatic cliché, he tells Eva that he had befriended a wild dog by bribing it with meat, only for it to bite him when they ran out of food. The implications are that his tough demeanour masks a longing for love and friendship. His loyalty to Eva, who treats him as an equal, becomes his redemption.

The children form the film's moral core, as is most clearly evidenced at its climax, when Benny attempts to sacrifice himself for the good of the group by throwing himself onto a bonfire, only to be rescued by the fascist Jean. This scene is extremely visceral. The crackling bonfire scores the silent blanket of night, and the darkness and shadows play over the harshly contrastive orange flames. Benny approaches the fire and begins to undress. The man grabs the boy, and the two sink to the ground. Jean consoles Benny with the words, 'Everything will work out', as the camera pulls back. The exchange ends the film and acts as a final comment on human nature, suggesting that in humanity's darkest hour there may still be hope. It is by far the most optimistic ending to any of Haneke's films, and it is also the most cathartic. The spectator's fears for the child are allayed, the fascist is redeemed by his act of kindness and his tenderness towards the boy.

The melodrama of this penultimate scene is somewhat anomalous in Haneke's oeuvre and it presents something of a problem within the context of Haneke's project of positioning the spectator ethically. At first glance, this might not be immediately apparent. We have seen that suspense is a minimal way of engaging emotion based on epistemological properties of the narrative; the genre of melodrama however connects emotion with moral character properties. On this spectrum between suspense and melodrama, the central technical element is the concentration of *mise-en-scène* and often camera perspective around individual characters and their place in a plot. Historically, Haneke has drawn upon the melodramatic framework in order to draw the spectator into the film – in *Code inconnu* and *La Pianiste*, for example – before going on to rupture this engagement through the use of first- and second-generation modernism. The scene's close resemblance to forms of classical Hollywood cinema (the suspense and the melodrama) is itself therefore not unprecedented. Curiously, however, the interruption never comes here. Rather the scene is based on a principle of catharsis that aligns our emotional responses with those of the characters throughout.

It is a puzzling thing for Haneke to do at this point in his oeuvre. And the alignment of character and spectator response is not limited to this

**Figure 4.3** Apocalyptic imagery in *Le Temps du loup* (2003).
*Courtesy of Artificial Eye. Permission graciously supplied by WEGAfilm.*

scene. For although the film is pervaded by first-generation modernist techniques which distance the spectator from the narrative, making them work to comprehend the image and distancing them from the diegesis through reflexivity, aperture and opacity, these modernist conventions are given a radically different spin within the context of the film's generic structure: the modernist aesthetic here in fact serves to strengthen identification with the characters. As Adam Bingham astutely points out, to the end of our experiencing the protagonist's predicament, the effect is achieved partly through analogy: the modernist aesthetic places the spectator in a similar position to the one that the characters are in.[43]

Let us look at an example of how this works. Some thirty minutes into the film, Benny goes missing from the barn in which he, Eva and Anne are sheltering. It is the middle of the night. The screen reflects this accurately: no dim lighting here, but a pitch black rectangle. Eva's voice rings out, 'Mum, wake up, Benny's not here,' but we cannot place her visually within the on-screen image; we are as disoriented as the characters themselves. A light flickers on screen; we squint to make out the figures of Eva and Anne as the latter holds up a cigarette lighter. For the following six minutes, we are plunged in and out of darkness with the characters, only able to see by the torches that they make out of burning hay. When Anne, having left Eva to search further afield, spots a glowing beacon, we are equally confused as to its source. When the director cuts to the burning structure of the barn it hits us with a similar force. This scene exemplifies how the modernist strategies that force us to struggle to read the image match diegetic perception throughout the film. As Bingham puts it, 'our disorientation at having a familiar base kicked out from beneath us by Haneke's method matches such a feeling in the characters as their world is ripped from them'.[44] This is perhaps rather a crude way of describing such an effect (and certainly oversimplistic), but it is worth remarking on as a departure for Haneke in terms of how he brings first-generation modernist techniques to fulfil a dual function: at the same time as they distance the spectator from the narrative, they draw them into it, and it is worth noting that on a technical level, there is a significantly greater preponderance of point of view shots than is generally common with Haneke, remarkably aligned with the childrens' perspectives. Close-ups and rapid edits also feature more heavily here than in any film since *Funny Games*.

So when watching *Le Temps du loup*, we feel sympathy for a set of characters who are psychologically rounded (or at least more psychologically rounded than any other character in Haneke's oeuvre), as well as sharing their point of view as a result of the film's modernist aesthetic. This marks a significant change from *La Pianiste*, in which melodrama is reduced to a formal and narrative schema that notionally draws us into the narrative, but that does not develop in the same way as classic genre film would do. In *La Pianiste*, Erika is the focal point of the spectator's emotional involvement with the film, but this involvement is not straightforward cinematic identification; the film's first-generation modernist aesthetic keeps spectators at a critical distance from the narrative events. As we have discussed, the characterisation of Erika is extremely alienating to an audience, and psychological explanation is dispensed with or made overly explicit, so holds little interest for the spectator (or scholar). Here, however, Anne, Eva and Benny become the focal point of the spectator's emotional involvement with the film, and the first-generation modernist aesthetic redoubles this involvement, for it further aligns our perspective with theirs as we, like them, struggle to make sense of what is taking place within the narrative.

Haneke reorients first-generation modernism, using it to bring our experience closer to that of the diegetic characters rather than to provide a critical distance. At the same time, he fails to bring second-generation reflexivity to bear effectively upon this film. For when the moment of shock comes, its effect is to create empathy: when Georges is shot, I am uncomfortable. But when I seek the source of this unpleasure, it lies in the very suddenness of the event, my unpreparedness for it. I share this source of unpleasure with Anne, who was likewise unprepared for the murder of her husband. It is not a complicated explanation, and not one I am forced to consider in detail in order to understand my own reaction. Aggressive moments such as the death of Georges continue, therefore, to emphasise the spectator's proximity to the film, but this proximity is not one of collusion or complicity with the cinematic institution; rather, it is one of sympathy with the pictorial representation, the on-screen character.

Why does Haneke not force us more thoroughly to consider our responsibility as consumers of the spectacle in *Le Temps du loup*? One reason for the apparently anomalous eschewal of second-generation modernism here might be found in the film's history. It is worth noting that *Le Temps du loup* had a very long gestation period, having originally been scheduled for production in the late 1990s, following *71 Fragmente einer Chronologie des Zufalls*. If we were to place the film within the chronological development of Haneke's films, based on when they were written (rather than when they were filmed), it would form a bridge between the trilogy and *Funny Games*: like the earlier films it relies heavily on modernist techniques; like *Funny Games* it introduces a generic structure and encourages emotional engagement with the narrative (even without the presence of stars such as Huppert, the alignment of audience and characters' points of view and the central role that Haneke accords to children would guarantee this).

If we think of the film in this light, however, we must also take into account the fact that Haneke's original script for *Le Temps du loup* – for which the final edit stands at 111 minutes – was three hours long. Haneke described the film's genesis to Nick James, in an interview for *Sight & Sound*:

> The first hour was to have taken place in an indeterminate European capital in which things slowly start to go wrong. There are problems we don't quite understand: the water doesn't work and neither does the electricity. This was to have been set in a ghetto for rich people such as you find in some American and South American cities, enclaves with police protection. Then one of the families decides it would be easier to go to their country house. And that's where the finished film picks up. After 11 September 2001 I felt it was no longer necessary to explain this build-up. It's now easily conceivable we could be faced with a similar catastrophe.[45]

One of the questions we must ask of the film is whether it can stand up to having this beginning excised. The inclusion of the additional footage described above may have enabled Haneke to make a direct link to cine-televisual perceptions (one can only imagine the potential scene in which the family's television, the site of all their information about the world, ceases to work) and it would certainly have served as a clearer link to contemporary society. For this is another problem that the film presents: it seems to be at one remove from the universe that the spectator inhabits. Unlike Haneke's other films, which take place against recognisably Western, industrialised backdrops, *Le Temps du loup* renders modern Europe strange by placing the action outside urban spaces, and setting it after an event that we know has not taken place, whatever this event may be.

This is however not necessarily out of place with the science fiction genre's conventions. As Vivien Sobchack explains in *Screening Space*, the genre 'lacks an informative iconography, encompasses the widest possible range of time and place, and constantly fluctuates in its visual representation of objects'. The visual connection between science fiction films:

> lies in the consistent and repetitious use not of *specific* images, but of *types* of images which function in the same way from film to film to create an imaginatively realised world which is always removed from the world we know or know of. The visual surface of all SF film [sic] presents us with a confrontation between a mixture of those images to which we respond as 'alien' and those we know to be familiar.[46]

Thus, 'the major visual impulse of all SF films is to pictoralise the unfamiliar, the nonexistent, the strange and totally alien – and to do so with a verisimilitude which is, at times, documentary in flavor and style'.[47] Sobchack concludes that within the constellation of generic concerns – which includes nature, science, technology, social and communal organisation – the dramatisation of these concerns centrally depends on the idea of the human and that which is alien or other.[48] Focusing on the 1950s, Thomas Schatz moreover contends that 'the mileu of the Science Fiction is one of contested space, in which the generic oppositions are determined by certain aspects of the cultural community and by the contest itself'.[49] It is a theme reflected in Haneke's film by the characters' disputes firstly over their holiday house, then later over the abandoned railway station that serves as a shelter.[50]

So we can see that the director has, to some extent, succeeded in appropriating the central thematic concerns of the science fiction genre, if not its form. Could it be that Haneke has simply chosen the wrong genre for his project of moral spectatorship to work effectively within? In making his setting too strange, in failing to ground his film in a recognisable (Western) society and to offer a clear sense of what has and might happen, does Haneke abstract the catastrophe, making it (too?) difficult for the spectator to make a cognitive link between the characters' situations and their own within the cinema? Perhaps, but the socio-political relevance of many science fiction films to the periods in which they were made is often one of analogy, which forces the spectator to 'decode' the film. It is not hard to read *Le Temps du loup* as a political analogy; indeed this is precisely the approach that dominates content-based receptions of the film, which argue that *Le Temps du loup* creates a microcosm and sets out to explore different social systems and political principles. The evocations of communism, socialism and capitalism are self-evident and once more the film has given rise to a number of socio-political readings.

There is another, more confounding problem here, which has to do with the spectator's failure not to see the relevance of the film to their situation in the world, but to see its relevance to their situation in the cinema, *as a spectator*. What is remarkably, and perhaps crucially, missing from *Le Temps du loup* is any kind of cine-televisual critique. This seems quite extraordinary when we consider that both science fiction and disaster are genres that generally accord a high status to concerns about technology. J.P. Telotte agrees with Sobchack that the issue of humanity lies at the heart of science fiction, but he links this particularly to the expression of contemporary concerns about the subjection of the human to the powers of technology and science.[51] Likewise the disaster movie expresses a significant concern with technology: according to Doane, catastrophe always has 'something to do with technology and its potential collapse'.[52] Ultimately, she claims, 'catastrophe signals the failure of the escalating technological desire to conquer nature'.[53] More important, however, in relation to Haneke's project is Doane's contention that our experience of 'real life' disasters is marked by a concern with coverage:

> While the vision of catastrophe is blocked at one level, it is multiplied and intensified at another. The media urge us now to obsessively confront the catastrophe, over and over again. And while the railway accident of the nineteenth century was certainly the focus of journalistic inquiry, its effects were primarily local. Television's ubiquity, its extensiveness, allows for a global experience of catastrophe which is always reminiscent of the potential of nuclear distaster, of mass rather than individual annihilation.[54]

The science fiction and/or the disaster film's intrinsic link to technology, as theorised by Telotte, and to the televisual, as in Doane, would seem to make them most apposite genres through which to voice concerns about the cine-televisual invasion of the home and takeover of our forms of perception. And yet Haneke fails to capitalise on the generic affinities with his own interests and to foreground the cine-televisual medium in any way.

Perhaps all one can say is that in *Le Temps du loup* technology is at best conspicuous by its absence: by showing the disarray that a world without television (amongst other gadgets) falls into, Haneke points towards the extent to which contemporary society has become dependent upon it as our primary source of information about the world. If we do not know what is happening, this connects us with the diegetic characters once more, who are similarly struggling to understand how they have come to be in this situation. We might argue then that the film's modernist allegiances lie in no small part with the fact that the emotional alignment of the spectator with the protagonists of the film is part of Haneke's strategy for deconstructing the genre of the disaster film. For Haneke, 'the danger with the catastrophe genre is that it's one of exaggeration, so it makes catastrophe seem attractive – something that we can enjoy because it's so unrealistic'.[55] He describes the aesthetic of *Le Temps du loup* as 'trying to reach people on an emotional level, raising the level of audience identification as high as possible by avoiding overt stylisation or exaggeration'.[56] What Haneke does here then is to return to the aesthetic of consequence which underpinned the modernist episode in *Funny Games*. Indeed it would not be going too far to claim that the whole film is in fact an extension of that scene. Here Haneke aims to reveal the suffering that would be the result of a total disaster, rather than the spectacle that would be its occurrence. The vast majority of our unpleasurable responses to the film arise from our engagement with this suffering, and from the visceral relationship that we have to it, encouraged by Haneke's alignment of the spectator's and the protagonist's points of view.

More significantly still, the film's characters are *all* positioned as victims of the film's aesthetic of consequence in various permutations. At no point are we thrust into a dual allegiance in the way that we are in *Funny Games*, where we are both victim and instigator of the film's violent spectacle. Even when a moment of shock comes – as in the opening scene or in the killing of the horse – this is not connected to a conflict between hero and antagonist. Although the children and their mother are offered up as our main points of identification, no character is singled out as the 'villain' of the piece, as the film's closing scene shows. Impact in *Funny Games* asks us to consider how we might align our desires with those of the torturers (in that we do not want the titular games to end, lest the narrative impetus cease). In *Le Temps du loup*, villains are redeemed by their own turmoil. The family that shoots Daniel are not only the intruders, but they are also intruded upon, and so they conflate the antagonists of *Funny Games* with its protagonists. Even the fascist figure, as we have seen, is capable of kindness. While the psychologies are not particularly nuanced (in that they are left, for the most part, opaque), their situations are. Everyone is struggling with the effects of the unknown event, and so all are deserving, to some extent, of our sympathies.

The film's denaturing of genre and plot could thus be understood as an attempt to provide an antidote to the dramatisation of disaster in media coverage. In a period in which every act of violence is neatly packaged and explained by a newscaster, Haneke's suspension of generic satisfaction offers a meditation on the liabilities inherent in generic responses to and readings of the world. We cannot understand what has happened here because we have not been told. 'Television does not so much represent as it *informs*', Doane has written.[57] *Le Temps du loup represents* but does not inform, and for this reason the film confuses the spectator, leaves them struggling to understand the wherefore rather than the what. In this way, the whole film functions as an extension of the use of off-screen space that we see in *La Pianiste*. In that film, the sexual was confined to the off-screen space, prompting our desire to see it, but simultaneously frustrating it (a treatment of sex similar to the treatment of violence in *Funny Games*). Here, however, *information* is what is confined to the off-screen space, prompting not so much a desire to see, as a desire to know. The problem is thus defined in terms not of morality, but epistemology.

In order to explain *Le Temps du loup*'s failure to co-opt its spectators into moral engagement with the film, we can have recourse to three factors. Firstly, the film has its roots in an earlier period of Haneke's career, in which he had not yet fully resolved his critical aesthetic. This may well serve as an explanation for the other two factors. For secondly, it occupies the paradoxical position of being at once heavily grounded in modernist convention, and at the same time being complementarily structured in accordance with generic conventions, so that, rather than coming into conflict, emotional response and rational response are harmonised. Our critical awareness of the cinematic medium and our need to work at reading the film thus forces us into a position of disorientation that mirrors that of the diegetic characters, redoubling our empathy for them. But thirdly, and (arguably) most importantly, the film fails to explicitly incorporate any aspect of cine-televisual critique. *Le Temps du loup* thus offers the spectator a distinctly unpleasurable experience, but this fails to translate into the moral emotions of shame and/or guilt that *Funny Games* and *La Pianiste* give rise to, since it fails to connect second-generation reflexive structures to a critique of the medium. The film does not therefore coerce its spectator into considering their own position in relation to the film. The spectator does not reflect on the ethics of the process of film-viewing, and hence they cannot become a moral spectator.

## Towards a Resolution

The three films that follow *Funny Games* can be seen as representing a further process of refinement of the three frameworks that Haneke superimposes on to one another in *Funny Games*: first-generation modernism or 'benign' reflexivity, second-generation modernism or 'aggressive' reflexivity, and generic convention. He overlaps these frameworks within the three films, with varying degrees of success for the project of positioning the spectator morally.

*Code inconnu*, we saw, is based primarily on modernist structures which, like the trilogy, place the spectator at an extreme critical distance from the image and so encourage a position of rational awareness. These modernist strategies are combined with some techniques of second-generation modernism, and in a restricted number of scenes Haneke offers a direct critique of the cinematic medium. However, the film eschews generic strategies in all but two scenes. The spectator is not encouraged to engage emotionally with the film as a whole, and so, lacking any desire for pleasure, is not forced to negotiate the conflict between reason and emotion. *Code inconnu* thus fails to position the spectator as a moral agent.

*Le Temps du loup* mobilises first-generation modernism for a new purpose: not only does it place the spectator at a rational distance from the film's content, but it paradoxically leads to a greater emotional investment in the film, by mirroring the diegetic characters' methods of perception. The spectator is encouraged to engage emotionally with the film through the combination of these modernist techniques and the use of a generic structure, in which the manipulative strategies familiar to both suspense and to melodrama are put into play. Both reasoned and emotional response to *Le Temps du loup* are, therefore, simultaneously possible. However, these responses are not thrown into conflict, but are rather harmonised. The spectator feels no need to negotiate between the two, and if they look for the source of the film as an unpleasurable experience, they find it in their sympathy with the characters. This lack of conflict is perhaps due to the absence of an aggressive second-generation reflexivity that directly critiques the cinematic medium and calls the spectator's attention to their desire to watch.

*La Pianiste* is, then, the only one of the three films that approaches the position of moral spectatorship that Haneke achieves for his audience with *Funny Games*. By constructing a *mise-en-scène* that insists upon the connections between the televisual representation of sexuality, degradation and spiritual defeat, Haneke enables the spectator to feel for Erika both compassion and revulsion. The film's reliance on the generic structures of the melodrama encourages emotional investment; its use of first-generation modernism critically distances the spectator from the medium; and it also brings second-generation modernism to bear in several key scenes, an achievement made in part by drawing not only on the structures of the melodrama but also of the pornographic film, a genre which creates a particularly unstable position for the spectator and often threatens to reveal itself as constructed through its mobilisation of direct address imagery. *La Pianiste* can thus be seen as the most successful of the three films in its resolution of the generic, second- and first-generation frameworks, since it calls the spectator's attention to their own desires, and in doing so prompts them to question the ethics of those desires.

# Notes

1. See interviews with Cieutat (2000), and Sharrett (2003).
2. Haneke, in Artificial Eye's pressnotes to the U.K. release of *Code Unknown*, 2000.
3. Haneke, in Artificial Eye (2000).
4. Peter Bradshaw, 'Mind Games', *The Guardian*, Section 2 (25 May 2001): 12–13.
5. Robin Wood, 'In Search of the *Code inconnu*', *CineAction* 62 (October 2003): 41–49.
6. Luc Moullet, 'Sam Fuller: In Marlowe's Footsteps', in *Cahiers du cinéma, The 1950s: Neo-Realism, Hollywood, New Wave*, ed. and trans. Jim Hillier (Cambridge, MA: Harvard University Press, 1985). Moullet's article originally appeared in the March 1959 issue of *Cahiers*. I am grateful to Jim Hillier for pointing out that in *Cahiers* 97 (July 1959), Godard paid Moullet homage of sorts by reformulating this quote as 'tracking shots are a question of morality'.
7. Andre Bazin, 'The Evolution of the Language of Cinema', in *What Is Cinema? Volume 1*, ed. and trans. Hugh Gray (Berkeley: University of California Press, 1967), p. 35.
8. André Bazin, *Orson Welles* (Paris: Cahiers du Cinéma, 2003), p. 58.

9. André Bazin, 'William Wyler ou le janséniste de la mise en scène', in *Qu'est-ce que le cinéma? Tome 1* (Paris: Editions Cerf, 1958), p. 170. My translation.

10. Bazin (1967b), pp. 35–6.

11. André Bazin, 'An Aesthetic of Reality', in *What is Cinema? Volume 2*, ed. and trans. Hugh Gray (Berkeley: University of California Press, 1971), pp. 36–7.

12. Haneke, in Cieutat (2000), p. 25.

13. Haneke, in Cieutat (2000), p. 25.

14. Arthur (2005), p. 26.

15. Bazin (1967a), p. 13.

16. Wood (2003), p. 42.

17. S.F. Said, 'Are We Waving or Drowning', *Daily Telegraph*, (17 May 2001): 24.

18. Sharrett (2003), p. 29.

19. Wood (2003), p. 42.

20. James (2001a).

21. Although *Benny's Video* could nominally be considered a thriller, and does adhere to a linear chronology, neither its form nor narrative development would support a sustained reading of it as part of the genre.

22. See Appendix Two.

23. See, for example, Haneke's interview with Geoffrey McNab for *The Guardian*, in which he states that 'France is the only country in the world that has a large audience for arthouse cinema'. 'There Goes the Neighbourhood', *Guardian* (6 October 2003): 16.

24. David Thomson, *The New Biographical Dictionary of Film* (London: Little, Brown, 2003), p. 151.

25. Thomson (2003), p. 151.

26. It should be noted that when I discuss the use of star actors/actresses and generic iconography in promotional materials, I do not intend to imply that Haneke himself had any hand in the design or distribution of this material, simply that the promotional material condenses the effects of the same icons and iconography within the films and extends it outside the viewing experience.

27. This theory has been notably propounded by Richard Dyer, *Stars* (London: BFI, 1986).

28. Hitchcock states in a 1967 interview with Bryan Forbes at the NFT: '[In] a picture like North by Northwest … you are involved in the adventures of the hero. You worry about him. But with an unknown you wouldn't worry about him so much. If you walk through the streets and see an unknown man lying there waiting for an ambulance after a car accident and you think 'poor fellow.' If you take a double-look and he's your brother it's a very different emotion, you see. So the identification boils down to 'Are you 100% anxious about that particular star?' The lesser known the person, the lesser your interest is'. Bryan Forbes, 'Alfred Hitchcock'. On-line. http://www.bfi.org.uk/features/interviews/hitchcock.html (last accessed 12 June 2008).

29. Barbara Creed, *Media Matrix: Sexing the New Reality* (Crow's Nest, Australia: Allen and Unwin, 2003), p. 58. Creed's term is taken up and elaborated by Lisa Downing in her 2005 study of French cinema's new 'sexual revolution', where she proposes and examines a selection of interpretative strategies for viewing what she terms the 'sexually explicit art film', 'an experimental cinema that blurs the boundaries between art film and porno flick … a genre of film which seeks to dismantle the prohibition regarding the exposure of the body and of "real" sexual activity in narrative film'. Although Downing herself does not include *La Pianiste* amongst those films she discusses, *Sight & Sound* editor Nick James, in his introduction to a series of articles on the depiction of sex and the sexual act in contemporary cinema, does. See Lisa Downing, 'French Cinema's New "Sexual Revolution": Postmodern Porn and Troubled Genre', in *French Cultural Studies*, 15(3) (October 2004): 265–280; and Nick James, 'The Limits of Sex', *Sight & Sound* 11(7) (July 2001): 21.

30. Nick James, 'Darkness Falls', *Sight & Sound* 3(10) (October 2003): 16–17; and Peter Matthews (2003).
31. Frey, 'A Cinema of Disturbance'.
32. Cieutat (2000), p. 29.
33. Huppert made this comment during an interview with Christopher Cook at the 2001 Regus London Film Festival. See Christopher Cook, 'Interview with Isabelle Huppert', available at: http://film.guardian.co.uk/lff2001/news/0,,592339,00.html (last accessed 23 February 2006).
34. John Champagne, 'Undoing Oedipus: Feminism and Michael Haneke's *The Piano Teacher*'. *Bright Lights Film Journal*, http://www.brightlightsfilm.com/36/pianoteacher1.html (last accessed 15 November 2006).
35. Paul Willemen, 'Letter to John', in *The Sexual Subject: A Screen Reader in Sexuality*, ed. Screen Editorial Collective (London: Routledge, 1992), p. 174.
36. Willemen (1992), p. 174.
37. Films which 'take pornography out of its traditional context and rework its stock images and scenarios', Creed (2003), p. 74.
38. James (2001b).
39. Alexander Walker, 'The Piano Teacher' (review), *Evening Standard* (8 November 2001): 21.
40. Robin Wood, 'Do I Disgust You? or, Tirez pas sur *La Pianiste*', *CineAction* 59 (Spring 2002): 54–61
41. Peter Bradshaw, quoted on the Artificial Eye U.K. poster for *The Time of The Wolf*.
42. James (2003), p. 17.
43. Adam Bingham, 'Long Day's Journey Into Night', *Kinoeye Online Film Journal*, http://www.kinoeye.org/04/01/bingham01.php (last accessed 20 January 2005).
44. Bingham, 'Long Day's Journey Into Night'.
45. James (2003), p. 17.
46. Vivian Sobchack, *Screening Space: The American Science Fiction Film* (New York: Ungar, 1998), p. 87. Emphasis in original.
47. Sobchack (1998), p. 88.
48. Sobchack (1998), p. 87.
49. Schatz (1981), p. 223.
50. Sobchack (1998), p. 86.
51. J.P. Telotte, *Replications: A Robotic History of The Science Fiction Film* (Urbana: University of Illinois Press, 1995), p. 86.
52. Doane (1990), p. 229.
53. Doane (1990), pp. 231–232.
54. Doane (1990), p. 232.
55. James (2003), p. 17.
56. James (2003), p. 17.
57. Doane (1990), p. 225.

*Chapter 5*

# SHAME AND GUILT
## *Caché*

---

In the development of Michael Haneke's model for positioning the spectator ethically, *La Pianiste* and *Funny Games* can be seen to represent two high points. In the case of each of these films, the film viewer is co-opted into a position of moral spectatorship through the resolution of three overlapping frameworks, which consist of a 'benign' first-generation modernism (that dominates the Austrian trilogy), aimed purely at a negation of the dominant (American) mainstream cinematic convention; an 'aggressive' second-generation modernism, aimed at calling the spectator's attention both to the film as construct and to themselves as consumer; and a system of generic convention (including the use of stars) that allows for a minimal emotional engagement on the spectator's part with the film's narrative. These overlapping frameworks conspire to create a tension between the spectator's rational awareness of the film as a construct and their emotional involvement in the world that this construct presents, by engaging the scopophilic drive (through the use of generic convention) and then frustrating or rupturing that drive (through modernist techniques). At the point of tension between the active pleasure drive and the modernist obstacles that Haneke places in its way, an impact occurs whereby the spectator becomes aware of themselves as complicit in the cinematic spectacle.

This self-awareness occurs as a result of the unpleasurable emotions which the moment of impact gives rise to, emotions that the spectator is prompted to consider in relation to their own position as a film-viewer. As the pleasure drive is ruptured, the spectator experiences discomfort. In a second moment they become aware of the reason for this discomfort as their instinct to avoid pain leads them to seek its source in order that they might best diffuse it. The unpleasurable experience is redoubled as the spectator comes to the realisation that their initial unpleasure was the result of the frustration of certain desires – desires which, in fact, may be the reverse of admirable. The spectator thus may enter into an experience of the unpleasurable emotions of guilt or shame, as they realise that they are watching something (or want to watch something) that they ought not to be watching (or wanting to watch). In the process of considering these feelings, the spectator enters a moral thought space asking, firstly, why they feel shame or guilt, finding its source in their own complicity with the cinematic medium, and then asking themself whether or not this is justified. They experience an engagement that is both felt ('I feel unpleasure') and thought ('Why do I feel unpleasure?' 'Is this justified?')

At this point, we must look more closely at the sentiments of guilt and shame in order to fully grasp the radical thrust of Haneke's work: radical in its moral critique of the cinematic medium, and radical in its efforts to undermine and reorient the viewer's conventional relationship with the cinematic image. Most films do not hold spectators accountable for, or implicate them in, the on-screen events. Or rather they do, but they work very hard at masking this relationship between spectator and film, so that the spectator remains oblivious to the way in which film interpellates them. This much we have seen in the previous chapters. Haneke's films, however, reveal the ethical imperative in the cinematic viewing situation, and this is one reason – if not *the* reason – for their controversial nature. In earlier analyses of *Funny Games* and *La Pianiste* I have touched upon the significance of the two emotions of shame and guilt to Haneke's ethical project of revealing the spectator's complicity to them. This importance will, I hope, become clearer as we turn to an analysis of Haneke's most successful film, *Caché*.

A film that demonstrates Haneke's most complete attempt to date at a harmonisation of content and form, *Caché*, like all of Haneke's films, is concerned on a narrative level with questions of shame, guilt and responsibility, and with the cine-televisual medium as a form of perception and articulation. It marks the culmination of Haneke's techniques for positioning the spectator morally, functioning as an exploration of and an explanation for the ways in which Haneke's most effective films radicalise the cinematic medium. The film-maker's key thematic concerns are all simultaneously prominent here, constituting both the mainstay of the film's narrative, and its operating structure (the film–spectator relationship). We will see that the film is thus the most complete resolution of Haneke's three frameworks. As a result, it is the most effective of Haneke's films in terms of moral spectatorship. It is also the most reflexive of Haneke's films; that is to say that it reflects upon its own construction and upon its place within Haneke's oeuvre. Of particular interest in this respect is the way in which *Caché* reflects on responses to Haneke's project of moral spectatorship. In doing so, we shall see it goes some way to circumventing the aggressive responses to which *Funny Games* was seen to give rise. Most significantly, however,

*Caché* serves as a contemplation as well as an example of the power of images to prompt the viewer into a position of ethical awareness.

## Narrative Guilt

The protagonist of *Caché* is Georges, the presenter of a literary chat show, who lives with his wife Anne, a literary editor, and son Pierrot in an affluent area of Paris. The film's narrative impetus – and first generic touch point[1] – is provided when Georges receives a series of videotapes showing surveillance of his home and family, accompanied by ominous yet childlike drawings. The content of both the tapes and the drawings is relatively innocuous; the real threats only start when Georges confronts suspected culprit Majid, an Algerian whom Georges had known as a child. When the two are reunited, Georges sees not Majid's humanity but only an intention to do harm. He thus adopts an aggressive stance, warning Majid to stay away from his family.

That Majid poses no real threat to Georges, as the police tell him when they refuse to investigate further, prevents no obstacle to the latter's persecution of this supposed 'terrorist'. Majid is resigned, responding that Georges is bigger and stronger, but that 'kicking my ass won't leave you any wiser about me'. Yet even when the 'kidnapping' of Pierrot turns out to be a misunderstanding – the result of another breakdown in communication – Georges refuses to accept the possibility that Majid is not seeking some kind of revenge upon him and his family. In fact, Georges's very belief in Majid's desire for vengeance implies that Majid has sound reasons for this desire: reasons that Georges does not admit until he is forced to by the events that take place within the film's narrative, including Majid's suicide (which takes place in front of Georges). He eventually reveals, under duress, that as a child he lied to his parents in order to persuade them against adopting Majid, whose own parents had been killed in the Paris massacre of Algerians on 17 October 1961.[2] The images in the drawings are visual reminders of the lies he told, lies which resulted in Majid's consignment to an orphanage and upbringing in privation, a stark contrast to the privileged lifestyle which Georges leads.[3]

As with all of Haneke's films, *Caché* functions on a number of levels, all of which are concerned with the power of images and their ability to call a subject to moral awareness. Even within the brief plot summary above, the thematisation of guilt and responsibility is self-evident, as content-based analyses of *Caché* have been quick to pick up on, many of them arguing for the film as a reflection on Western society's relationship to its past. And the allegory with the French treatment of the Algerians is indeed hard to miss. But, as we have seen, Haneke has long railed against his films being seen as treatments of specific national situations. So while the events that take place in *Caché* might be set against an unmistakeably Parisian milieu, their implications reach beyond that. Christopher Sharrett's interpretation for *Cineaste* takes socio-political readings of the film a step further than most critics, seeing it as a post-9/11 comment on neocolonialism.[4] He claims that the film can be read not only as an allegory of the French-Algerian context, but that the backstory of Majid's parents also evokes the current era of racial profiling, persecution and neofascism, 'with the ball very much in the U.S. court on matters of policing of the colonial domain'.[5] Even this reading may veer towards the overly specific, however. As the director told Christopher Sharrett in an interview for *Cineaste* in Summer 2003, *Caché* may be 'about the French occupation of Algeria on a broad level', but more personally, it is 'a story of guilt and the denial of guilt that faces every one of us'.[6]

Socio-political readings of the film need not be dwelled upon; as we have seen, Haneke's films are always at heart concerned with revealing something not about society, but about the spectator's relationship to the screen. Indeed, at first glance the narrative preoccupations of *Caché* appear to correspond to a general move on Haneke's part away from the direct concern with visual depictions of violence in cinema that characterised *Funny Games* and *Benny's Video* and in favour of a more socio-political bent: Haneke's previous three works – *La Pianiste*, *Code inconnu* and *Le Temps du loup* – have, as we have seen, each been the subject of socio-political readings: the former prompting readings from Robin Wood, amongst others, of the film as an examination of Western society's repressive attitude to sex and sexuality, the latter two perhaps more directly linked to *Caché* in their treatment of questions of migration, race and social hierarchy. However, these three works are simultaneously symptomatic of Haneke's developing notions of what moral spectatorship might be. The question of guilt relates to questions of moral spectatorship in quite a complex way, and it is for this reason that its thematisation within *Caché* is of particular interest.

In order to understand the relationship between diegetic guilt in *Caché* and spectatorial guilt, we need firstly to understand precisely what it is that 'guilt' and 'guilty' mean. There are several nuances in the narrative depiction of guilt that most readings of the film overlook, nuances that need to be drawn out in order to understand fully the film's relationship to the spectator, for the majority of readings of *Caché* display a semantic confusion about the meaning of the noun 'guilt' and its correlative adjective, 'guilty'. The *Oxford English Dictionary* defines 'guilt' in two points:

1. the fact of having committed a specified or implied offence;
2. a. culpability, b. the feeling of this.

We can infer from these definitions that the terms 'guilt' and 'guilty' refer to two distinct phenomena. On the one hand guilt has an 'objective' meaning: one individual or group (such as a court) decides on the basis of evidence whether or not another party is 'guilty', that is, whether he or she is responsible for committing a particular act. On the other hand, it has a 'subjective' meaning, indicating the feelings of responsibility or remorse for one's own actions that an individual experiences. A person therefore might be described as *being* guilty without *feeling* guilty; and equally so, they might feel guilt without having actually committed any objectively illegal offence. It is important to bear in mind this distinction between guilt as an objective responsibility and guilt as a subjective emotion as we will go on to consider it within the context of Haneke's films.[7] For the relationship between the two senses of guilt is one of Haneke's key concerns, both within the film and in relation to the spectator. As Haneke explains:

> You can see the film like a Russian doll with dolls inside dolls inside dolls. The same story can be seen on different levels, can represent different levels: the personal level, the family level, the social level, the political level. The moral question the film raises is how to deal with this question of guilt. All of us have moments of selfishness, moments that we prefer to hide.[8]

This disjunction between the act and its acknowledgement is in fact the crux of Haneke's concern with guilt: it is a concern with the extent to which any one person is able or willing to accept the burden of guilt. There is a distinct contrast in *Caché* between Georges's objective guilt for having lied as a child, and his (lack of) subjective feelings of guilt. In this respect, he is typical of Haneke's guilty characters, whose attitudes to their position in the world are characterised by an ongoing attempt to eschew or deny any responsibility for their own actions. None of *Caché*'s characters express guilt feelings for their actions even though none of them are entirely innocent and so each can be seen to some extent as 'objectively' guilty.

For example, when her son raises his name in conversation, Georges's mother claims to have forgotten who Majid is, and asks what the point is in discussing events that took place so long ago. Similarly, Georges's wife, Anne, is quick to accuse her husband of dissimulation and a lack of trust when he doesn't immediately confess his suspicions about the tapes' source. However, a number of scenes imply that she may be having an affair with her boss, Pierre, and when her son confronts her about it, she responds in a very similar manner to Georges: both dismiss the charges laid against them as 'absurd'. No overt statement is made as to whether or not her son's accusations are justified yet the scene subtly destabilises any notion we might entertain of Anne as the film's moral centre. Her 'crime' might be less serious than Georges's, but her perfidy contributes to a climate of falseness in which no statement, no matter who makes it, seems authentic. Even an anonymous cyclist, with whom Georges collides in the street, is quick to lay the blame for the accident squarely on Georges. Anne's intervention with a measure of temperance – the young man was careless, but so was Georges – falls on deaf ears, as each man hastens to see the other as the guilty party in order to disavow any responsibility they themseves might have.

## Structural Guilt

While the film thus presents to us a cast of characters who are all struggling, in their own ways, against acknowledgement of their responsibilities, these character dynamics announce larger structural forces at work within Haneke's film. Reading *Caché* as analogy, we can say that Anne and Georges take the role of the spectator, while whoever is creating the unknown tapes assumes the position of the artist, or director, attempting to prompt their 'audience' into a realisation of their own responsibility through the use of images. Played by Juliette Binoche and Daniel Auteuil, Anne and Georges are extensions of the character played by Binoche in *Code inconnu*: intellectual, bourgeois bohemians, they epitomise the middle-class audiences that Haneke can depend on to watch his films.[9] While the casting of Binoche and Auteuil – doubtless in part financially motivated, but also a continuation of Haneke's use of stars almost as a generic element – inclines our sympathies for the characters they inhabit, Haneke also holds Anne and Georges up to the spectators as critical mirrors, for their behaviour demonstrates exactly the kind of denial and eschewal of responsibility that Haneke sees as characterising Western audiences' responses to his films. The tapes and postcard drawings sent to Georges meanwhile mirror the effect of Haneke's film on its audience, both functioning as the Sartrean 'footsteps in the hallway', or 'the fourth look', which indicates that someone has caught Georges out, that they are aware of his past actions. Just as Georges is able to ignore, or suppress his awareness of his childhood act as long as no one else knows about it, submerging himself in the trappings of his bourgeois lifestyle, so the spectator can take pleasure in the moral vacuum of cinematic interpellation as long as they are able to suspend their self-awareness. But once the mysterious images introduce the idea of someone who has 'seen' Georges, who is aware of his misdeeds, he can no longer deny that it happened. Both the anonymous tapes and Haneke's film refuse their audience the possibility of escape through fantasy, asking them instead to question their own relationship to the onscreen image.

Majid's suicide is the point at which the two critiques intersect. The visceral suicide is as much an assault on the cinematic spectator as it is on Georges.

In terms of how it pushes the spectator towards moral engagement with the image, the scene functions much like the 'modernist episode' in *Funny Games*. In a series of rapidly edited sequences, tension builds up to Georges's confrontation of Majid. The latter has sent Georges a letter, asking him to visit him in his apartment. We are at a point in the film's narrative when we expect a revelation or plot twist regarding the source of the tapes and letters, all the avenues that Georges has pursued so far having led to dead ends. When Georges arrives at Majid's apartment, however, Majid greets him, then pulls a knife from his pocket and slits his own throat. The camera stays static as blood sprays across the wall and Majid sinks to the floor. It lingers for some six minutes in this fixed position as Georges, horrified, paces in and out of frame. At the centre of the frame is Majid's body, his blood slowly seeping across the floor. The spectator, horrified by the unexpected violence, is then forced to contemplate the image over an extended period, to stare the consequences of violence in the face.

This is one way in which *Caché* asks us to consider our own roles as spectators. Here, as elsewhere, different layers of Haneke's critical framework come to intersect so that they position the spectator in a particularly complex and reflective manner. In keeping with the trend towards genre models that characterises Haneke's later work, the film superficially presents itself as a suspense thriller, drawing on a paradigm scenario familiar from generic classics such as *North by Northwest*, for example, thereby aligning itself superficially with *Funny Games* and, to some extent, *Benny's Video*.[10] Despite its generic resemblance to these films, however, Haneke's use of first- and second-generation modernist reflexivity within the context of this generic framework operates in a manner more akin to *La Pianiste*, prompting a minimal engagement of the emotions on the spectator's part (based on the use of stars and on the incorporation of generic conventions of *narrative*, rather than the overt formal reference that characterised *Funny Games*). Presenting us with the epistemological conundrum of who is persecuting whom and why, Haneke is able to mobilise the pleasure drive in the form of the 'desire to see what will happen'.

This desire is naturally frustrated, however, through the director's very use of first-generation modernist reflexivity, as exemplified by the aftermath of Majid's suicide, and second-generation reflexivity, which offers a more explicit comment on the medium itself. Within the film's generic framework, the film-maker foregrounds the cine-televisual medium more consistently than in any other of his films. It is an achievement facilitated by Georges's occupation as a television presenter: we are repeatedly presented with scenes of Georges hosting and producing his literary television show. In one instance, Georges is narrating to the camera when a diegetic director calls 'Cut!', suddenly rupturing the distinction between layers of filmic reality. And yet clips from the diegetic television show are presented in an entirely different style to the main body of Haneke's film; remarkably, both Georges and his guests are shot head-on, facing the camera, a framing which none of the diegetic scenes repeat.

It is notable that the set of this television show is an exact replica of Georges's study, indicating a further slippage between the represented and the real. The key difference between the two sets is that while both feature wide tables set against *trompe-l'oeil* bookshelves, at Georges' home there is a wide-screen television, placed exactly in the centre of these shelves. This diegetic screen dominates the backdrop to Georges's study, constantly reminding us of the ubiquity of the cine-televisual medium. The point is reinforced as Georges and Anne hold a heated discussion over the sound of the blaring television, on which 'Euronews' cuts between the latest Iraq atrocities and the Palestine situation. In a sequence which recalls similar set-ups in *71 Fragmente* and *La Pianiste*, the two characters discuss the whereabouts of their son, while the television – placed in the background of the set – dominates the scene aurally and visually (situated as it is in the exact centre of the screen, with Georges and Anne at oblique angles). What should be a moment of tension – as the two characters realise that Pierrot is missing – is overwhelmed by the competing image system. But most striking of all perhaps, the images go unnoticed by Georges and Anne, who remain oblivious to the exterior world.

As well as using intra-diegetic cine-televisual imagery to call the spectator's attention to the constructed nature of film – a technique familiar to us from Haneke's early works – *Caché* draws on other, more complex, reflexive techniques in order to throw the spectator into confusion as to what exactly it is that they are seeing. The film opens with a long shot of a house facing a street (notably, the name of this street is the Rue des Iris) in a quiet part of a bourgeois area. There is no movement, and no foreground sound, only the murmur of cars in the distance. As the title credits appear letter by letter across the screen as if being typed, the camera holds the shot. As they finish, some five minutes later, the shot is unchanged. During that time a cyclist passes through the shot, a woman leaves her apartment and then the frame. The camera remains static. 'Well?' a disembodied male voice asks. 'Nothing,' a woman replies. Then a closer shot of the same setting focuses our attention on the house door. A man and a woman leave. The camera pans to follow the man as he crosses the road and then comes back to re-enter the house. We return to the original shot, still static, still

**Figure 5.1** Juliette Binoche and Daniel Auteuil in the Laurents'
study in *Caché* (2005). The diegetic screen dominates the backdrop.
*Courtesy of the BFI stills department. Permission graciously supplied by WEGAfilm.*

empty of apparent significance. Suddenly telltale white lines appear
across the cinema screen: we are watching the image now in the video
fast forward mode. 'The cassette runs for nearly two hours', the female
voice says. We are looking at a film within a film.

As we have seen, this use of *mise-en-abyme* to trouble the cine-
televisual medium is not new for Haneke. In *Benny's Video*, for example,
footage taped by Benny with his video camera is distinguished from
fictional reality by being manipulated from within the narrative –
rewound, put into slow motion, paused – just as we see here. But this
footage is also visually coded as amateurish documentary: it is grainy,
unedited, marked by handheld effects.[11] *Caché* sees Haneke's first use of
high-definition video cameras, which allow him to set up a narrative
device that will mix the images from the videotapes with the images of
Georges's 'life'. In this way, the director formally achieves the maturity
of the metalinguistic style that he has long been developing and which
makes the image itself a central character of his films. However, despite
the narrative similarity with *Benny's Video*, the concern with home video
in *Caché* and its use of intra-diegetic film more closely resembles the
scene in *Code inconnu* in which Anne/Juliette Binoche stars in *The
Collector*. Although close attention to the intra-textual sequence – its
framing, editing and, in the case of *Code inconnu*, its performances –
should, if we are alert, allow us to distinguish it from the surrounding
text, it is most remarkable for initially being unmarked.

In *Caché*, the video sequences are generally marked out from the filmic 'reality' by the use of static cameras, and the alert viewer, after the first few instances of being presented with a scene filmed from a static camera only to have the film subsequently reveal that this is an intra-diegetic image track, will come to equate this form with the use of the intra-diegetic image. Still, even this doesn't allow the viewer any purchase on what kind of images we are seeing, as the line is blurred not only between film and life, but between whether we are seeing an image in the process of being filmed, or being played back. When Georges first visits Majid at his flat, the scene is shown in a classic realist style that incorporates close-ups, shot/reverse shots and a mobile camera. We then watch the scene again and this time the camera is static, the action continuing after Georges leaves the room; it therefore comes as no surprise to us when Haneke cuts to Anne watching the scene on her television. Yet when Georges visits Majid on another occasion the scene is filmed from a static camera in the same position as earlier. This time there is no cut to someone else watching the same scene, no rewind or fast forward, and we see the scene only once: so the spectator must ask themself, is this 'reality', recording or playback? The cine-televisual critique through film form functions in much the same manner as the 'rewind scene' in *Funny Games*, and although it is less abrasive it is more constant. The spectator's ongoing struggle to gain a purchase on what they are seeing acts as a recurring obstacle to the pleasure drive, preventing the spectator from sacrificing self-awareness by reminding them constantly of the film's nature as a construct.

## Authorial Guilt

One problem that poses itself is that the vast majority of the taped scenes are shot from 'impossible' angles: shot from outside walls where bookcases stand, or from a position too high for a handycam operator unless they were standing very conspicuously on the roof of a car. This can't be the case, since Georges tells Anne that he would have seen the cameraman as he passed him. The lines between 'reality' and 'fiction' become blurred in much the same way as occurs in *Funny Games*, but here the effect is much more subtle. Ultimately, the scenes from Georges's 'life' are as filmed just as the tapes are. We know this because the images on the postcards correspond to a series of flashbacks or dream sequences which picture a young Majid vomiting blood and using an axe to slice the head of a flailing cockerel before turning menacingly towards Georges. And yet we learn that these images are not representations of real acts, but of the lies that Georges told his parents in order to prevent Majid's adoption. Majid did indeed chop the head off a chicken, but this was at Georges's instigation, and Georges fabricated the ensuing attack. The precision of the match between the two sets of images is thus such that no one within the narrative but Georges could have created them.

So unless we allow for the distinctly unlikely possibility that Georges is sending himself the tapes (a scenario that would not seem incongruous in a psycho-surrealist film such as Lynch's *Lost Highway*, but which jars with Haneke's understated, realist style which allows little room for psychological development), the search for explanation on a narrative level becomes meaningless. This effect is redoubled by the film's final shot, which sees Georges's son, Pierrot, talking to Majid's son (who remains nameless throughout) on the steps of his school. The shot is taken with a static camera, troubling the meaning of the image still further, raising not only the possibility that the two boys are in cahoots, but that someone else is involved, or that all of the static shots (and even the tapes themselves) are products of Georges's subconscious, along with numerous other permutations. If our emotional relationship to the film is motivated by our desire to know 'whodunnit', then the film's ultimate aperture serves to shift the emphasis within the film from the epistemological question of who is sending the tapes to an existential inquiry into their effect upon Georges. The tapes are merely the trigger for a study of Georges's refusal to acknowledge responsibility for his actions.[12]

What is more interesting, however, about the question of who is sending the tapes is how it ties in with questions about Haneke's own role as director. In addition to encouraging reflexivity on the spectator's part, the search for the source of the tapes allows the director to engage in a process of self-reflection, for the film also prompts us to consider Haneke's role as maker and deliverer of images. This would appear to mark a major departure for Haneke since, prior to *Caché*, Haneke's films have been concerned for the main part with the ethical relationship of the *spectator* to the image. Only *Benny's Video* touches (obliquely) on the issue of film production: Benny is both director and consumer of the eponymous video. Outside this, it seems that there is no place within Haneke's moral world prior to *Caché* for any treatment of the director's role. It is precisely this perceived hypocrisy that came under fire from critics of *Funny Games*, in which, as we have seen, the director's manipulative authority is at its most evident.

In making the driving question of the narrative that of the tapes' source and the motivations of their makers, Haneke seems to be turning his attention for the first time to the director's own role, a move which would allow him, perhaps, to circumvent accusations of double standards. On the level of the spectator–screen relationship, the effect of this short-circuiting of narrative meaning is then to foreground, once more, the constructed nature of the cinematic spectacle. In a sense, what we have here is an extension of Haneke's treatment of psychology in *La Pianiste*, whereby the signposts that would allow for a Freudian or Lacanian reading are so obviously foregrounded (for example, Erika's attempt to make love to her mother, her self-mutilation which literally enacts the castration complex), that any attempt to produce such a reading becomes an exercise in stating the obvious: the point being that our attention is not distracted by the search for such explanations, but is rather diverted towards the relationship of the spectator to the on-screen image. In treating the director's own role for the first time, he is effectively able to dismiss it.

## The Dynamics of Blame:
## Distinguishing between Guilt and Shame

The implication of the ultimate aperture of the ending of *Caché* is that it doesn't matter who the maker of the tapes is, nor what their motivations are: it is not the source of the message, but its effect on the recipient that matters. Benny's parents, the Schöber families of *Der Siebente Kontinent* and *Funny Games*, Erika Kohut and the Anne Laurents of *Code inconnu* and *Le Temps du loup* all reach a new self-awareness through their subjection to violence, even if the ordeals they must undergo to reach this awareness seem perhaps disproportionate to their faults. *Caché*'s Georges Laurent may initially appear the most deserving of his punishment. His crime does not consist in being a self-satisfied and morally disengaged member of the Western bourgeoisie, but rather in a specific act of selfishness with which he shatters another person's life. But after all, this is a child's act, and as John Rawls argues in 'The Sense of Justice', a child cannot fully understand the principle of guilt.[13] Or in Kantian terms, a child exists in the ethical state of nature: it is only when they reach adulthood that they come to understand the morality of their desires and actions and therefore assume responsibility for them. So we must conclude that Georges is punished not for the act itself, but for his attitude to it. He is objectively responsible for committing an immoral act, but he expresses no guilt feelings for his actions and makes no attempt at atonement for, or even acknowledgement of, his part in Majid's fate.

Insofar as *Caché* can be understood as an allegory of the French treatment of Algerians, Haneke is not calling for the French to be punished for the events of 1961, but for them to acknowledge and apologise for what happened in the past. As it concerns Georges, the issue is not the child's crime but the adult's refusal to acknowledge responsibility. For even after being confronted with the tapes, Georges's total denial of his part in Majid's fate falters but does not fail. He eventually admits to Anne the truth of what he did as a child, but this admission does not take place until the film's closing scenes, when Georges has witnessed Majid's suicide and the impending police investigation has seemingly left him no choice but to confess to his wife. Moreover, Auteuil delivers the admission not as a confession, but as a defence: he acknowledges that the act took place but not that he is therefore culpable, and is still able to refer to Majid's death as 'a twisted kind of joke'.

Georges's subsequent behaviour indeed seems little altered. When he is confronted at work by Majid's son, he re-enacts the same scene of denial, accusation and threat that took place with Majid, the two characters placed in a strikingly similar graphic relation, repeating practically word for word the same dialogue. Even the cutting is patterned almost identically. Once more Georges makes the first threat; once more the Algerian tells him that he is stronger, but that strength is beside the point. Only now, his guilt is redoubled: he is no longer only responsible for Majid's life, but his death, as Majid's son points out, accusing him of causing the suicide by his harassment. Georges is dumbfounded, seeing himself as the sole victim of events and suspicious of the son as co-conspirator. Following the confrontation, Georges continues to hide events from his wife, omitting to mention that Majid's son has visited him at work. One senses this is not only, as he claims, to protect her, but also – perhaps primarily – to protect himself. Directly after Majid's suicide, Georges's first act is to take refuge at the cinema – and, as Jonathan Romney astutely observes, one of the films on show at the cinema he visits is Jean-Jacques Annaud's *Deux frères/Two Brothers* (2004), an ironically appropriate choice following his denial of kinship with Majid.[14] In his final appearance on-screen, we see Georges climb into bed with two sleeping pills (or *cachets*, a neat pun lost in translation), shrouding himself in darkness in an attempt to avoid his own bad conscience. Remarkably, it is an act not unlike that of attending the cinema.

Georges's disavowal of responsibility and concomitant aggression towards Majid (and subsequently, his son) points us away from an analysis of the dynamics of guilt and towards a consideration of the experience of shame. Up until now we have not distinguished between feelings of shame and guilt, to some extent conflating the two terms, using them as synonyms. And yet it is noteworthy that, not only in English but also in both the languages that Haneke works with, shame and guilt remain two distinct linguistic concepts: in French the word *culpabilité* is contrasted with the word *honte*; similarly the German word *Schuld* is not synonymous with *Scham*. Is there a difference between guilt and shame? There certainly seems to be an intuitive distinction, as is reflected by these linguistic contrasts between the two concepts. This difference merits further investigation if we are going to posit these sentiments as pivotal to Haneke's project of moral spectatorship. What, we may wonder, are the features of shame, and how do they relate to guilt? What does our capacity for feeling shame reveal about us, about our conceptions of ourselves, the values we hold, and the way in which we see and respond to others?

One potential response to these questions – and one that serves our analysis of *Caché* nicely – is to look at the ways in which blame is directed by each of the two emotions, in order to understand how the relationship of moral spectatorship that Haneke encourages between spectator and film can be a productive one. For as we have seen, the experience of unpleasure prompts a search for its source. When we look to the film, or indeed to the figure of the director as a construct of the film, as the source of our unpleasurable experience, we are effectively blaming him for our unpleasure. This process of seeking someone to blame is what underpins the key question that Haneke's films prompt: why is the director doing this to me? It is a question which entails an awareness of both other (the director) and self (the spectator), and which seeks to understand the relationship between the two in terms of responsibility. And, as we have seen, this search for understanding through self-awareness is the ultimate goal of Haneke's moral project.

## Blaming the Other: Shame and Disavowel

Let us begin by looking at the emotion of shame, an emotion which we contended in Chapter Four dominates spectatorial experiences of Haneke's *Funny Games*. Both shame and guilt involve acute and specific forms of self-awareness. This self-awareness, however, is articulated in different manners in guilt and shame. In both cases, an emotional experience can lead us to consider our own behaviour. And in considering our own behaviour, we often learn about ourselves and our standards of living. We discover that, to ourselves, certain goals are valuable and we have failed to live up to them. The experience of shame and guilt thus often expresses a desire to be a type of being that one can be: a good human being doing fine things.

In this sense, shame is not inherently self-deceptive, nor does it always express a desire to be a sort of being one is not. However, in the case of shame, self-awareness can also lead to a form of disavowal, of deliberate suppression of self-awareness, for shame is an extremely unpleasant emotion, one which we long to be free from. The extremely negative vision of the self that shame offers is perhaps too painful to bear. At its heart, then, shame is a self-involved, egocentric experience. The person in the midst of the shame reaction is often concerned not so much with the implications for others of their failure or transgression, they are more concerned with the implications of negative events for the self.

Since this is the case, narcissism and its associated aggressions are dangers that always lurk around the corner of even a rightly motivated shame. June Price Tangney and Ronda L. Dearing explain that there are two behavioural responses that a shamed individual most often makes. The first of these is withdrawal, escaping the shame-inducing situation and hiding the horrible self from the view of others (as in Georges's flight to the cinema, or retreat into the oblivion of sleep). The withdrawal strategy, however, is apt to be only partially effective. In reality, the shamed, withdrawn individual is still saddled with a loathsome self. 'When it comes to a shamed self,' they state, 'there is some truth to the notion that "you can run but can't hide"'.[15] The second alternative – one that Tangney and Dearing claim is more likely to be effective, at least in the short run – is to turn the tables and shift the blame outward (as in Georges's persecution of Majid). Blaming others (instead of the self) serves an ego-protective function: a shamed person may find it much less objectionable to think that the problem is the other, rather than accept their own responsibility for an event or situation. By externalising blame in this way the previously shamed individual attempts to defend and preserve their self-esteem. The accompanying feelings of self-righteous anger can help the shamed person to regain some sense of agency and control. Anger is an emotion of potency and authority in contrast to shame, which is an emotion of the worthless, the paralysed, the ineffective. Thus, by redirecting hostility, by turning their anger outward, shamed individuals become angry instead, reactivating and bolstering the self, subdued by the experience of shame.

There are two factors that further facilitate the shift from shame to anger: imagery of a 'disapproving other', and the impaired capacity for empathy that accompanies shame. In the first of these, the shame experience also evokes an image of the disapproving other, for shamed individuals have a heightened awareness of and concern with others' evaluations. A shamed person is acutely conscious of what other people might be thinking about them. From there, it is a short step to attribute the cause of painful shame feelings to others who are perceived as disapproving. Feeling shamed, feeling diminished in comparison to others and simultaneously scrutinised and evaluated by others, it is relatively easy to blame the painful experience of shame on the observer. The observing other may or may not be engaging in such negative evaluation of the shamed person; the point is that the phenomenology of shame itself involves a heightened rational awareness of others' presumed evaluations.[16]

The second factor that facilitates the shift from shame to anger is that shamed people lack the empathetic skills to understand how their behaviour or wishes might cause harm to others, and thereby often end up seeing any accusation of having harmed another as excessive and unnecessary.[17] They are therefore apt to feel they are being unfairly treated by those perceived 'disapproving others' who have ostensibly caused their experience of shame. In this way, the imagery of a disapproving other may contribute to the shift from shame to outwardly directed anger.

The ultimate outcome of the shame experience is often then not self-blame, but self-protection. Taking this into account, the narrative content of *Caché* can be seen to enact a further analogy of the spectator's relationship to Haneke's films. On a narrative level, Haneke is not critical of Georges's actions, but of his refusal to acknowledge them, his refusal to seek forgiveness or to make amends. Haneke condemns Georges's tendency to enact the specifically shameful responses of denial and withdrawal, rather than the more responsible response that an acknowledgement of guilt would produce, opening up a horizon of possible responses rather than closing down such options as shame does. As Romney puts it in his review of *Caché* for *Sight & Sound*, the film is an 'attack on a culture of denial, of militant mauvaise foi'.[18]

But this is true not only on a narrative level, for it also has pertinence to the spectator–screen relationship. For *Caché* can be seen, to some extent, as a rebuttal to those critics who fail to acknowledge their own complicity with *Funny Games*, dismissing their attempts to blame someone else – the 'disapproving other' – and revealing them, by analogy, to be morally reprehensible. As we saw in Chapter Three, the immediate effect of reflexivity in *Funny Games* is to create a feeling of shame at having been 'caught' looking: Haneke's audience address functions to signal the gaze of the other which gives rise to a Sartrean experience of shame. This in itself is not problematic; shame of a specific and limited sort can be constructive, motivating a pursuit of valuable ideals, within a context where one already renounces the demands of narcissism (and, on the other side, guilt can, of course, be excessive and oppressive, and there can be a corresponding excessive focus on reparation, one that is unhealthily self-tormenting). But where shame is particularly harmful is in its tendency to transferral, to shift blame – too painful to bear – from oneself onto another. We saw that there are two factors that particularly facilitate the shift from shame to anger: imagery of a 'disapproving other', and the impaired capacity for empathy that accompanies shame. It is in relation to the former that Haneke's authorial persona – which emerges through the film – enhances the film's emotional effect: Haneke becomes the 'disapproving other' whom the feeling of shame evokes. The shamed party seeks out a source to which they can attribute blame, and in the case of *Funny Games* the director is the natural candidate.[19] 'Why,' the spectator asks, 'is *the director* doing this (to me)?' In this formulation, in which emphasis is placed upon the first half of the equation, the concern is with the director as authorial figure, with asking what his motivations are, rather than with the spectator as participant in the film-viewing experience. The answer the spectator all too often hits upon is that the director must be a sadist. This reductive answer reassures us. It saves us from the burden of self-criticism. And it brings the painful process of reflection to a close.

## Blaming the Self: The Acknowledgement of Guilt

Critical responses to *Funny Games*, such as Mark Kermode's, which see the director as sadist, fascist or terrorist, are thus characteristic of a shift from shame to anger. The closing scenes of *Caché*, which see Georges continuing to deny responsibility for his acts, could in this context perhaps be interpreted as a response to critics and spectators, such as J. Hoberman, who refuse to see how Haneke's films are pertinent to themselves. And in this regard, it is not insignificant that Haneke makes Georges a critic: as the director states, 'intelligence is not enough to prevent you from being a coward'.[20] Is Haneke saying that nothing he can force us to watch on screen can make us acknowledge our complicity in the cinematic spectacle, but that perhaps, despite our denials, no wholesale relinquishment of responsibility can be possible once we have been subjected to his structures of reflexivity?

This is one reading of the film's ending, but there is another, much more optimistic alternative to consider. Like *Funny Games*, *Caché* reveals the spectator as complicit and therefore prompts feelings of guilt (or even shame). But unlike the earlier film, it limits the possibility of an externalised blame response by presenting this very type of response within its diegesis. In showing us Georges's denial and aggression – his total inability to accept responsibility for his actions – Haneke makes us aware of this behaviour, and thereby more able to distinguish it in ourselves. In showing denial and transference of blame, Haneke makes it recognisable to the spectator, and so makes it difficult for the spectator to react selfishly in the same way as Georges' does to accusations of guilt.

Haneke supports this attempt at precluding an externalised blame response through what we might call a 'tempering' of his aggressive strategies. This is not to say that Haneke's authorial stamp is reduced within the film: indeed, *Caché* demonstrates the same precision as earlier works, and draws on the three frameworks of first- and second-generation modernism and generic convention to create moments of impact in which the invitation to moral thought arises more effectively than any other of Haneke's films. But Haneke attenuates the aggressive structures of reflexivity that operate within *Funny Games*, such that the director's presence is not as obtrusive. Firstly, the film – which, as we have noted, marks a return to the suspense genre – does not draw as heavily on the *formal* conventions of the genre. To put it simply, *Caché* does not 'look like' a thriller, and it therefore avoids straightforward genre readings, as well as the accusations of hypocrisy that spring from drawing on the formal characteristics that the film sets out to criticise. Secondly, it refuses devices as openly aggressive as the direct address to the audience that Paul makes in *Funny Games*, or that film's rewind scene that so brutally revokes the moment of pleasure. The aggressive reflexive techniques that it operates are much more subtle than those of *Funny Games*, a film which Haneke, retrospectively, describes as the 'exception' in his work. With that film, he states, 'the idea was to give a slap in the face to people who consume violence. But my other films, I think, are a bit more complex'.[21] Haneke does not forego aggressive reflexivity here, then, but rather moderates its effects so as to blur somewhat the presence of the 'disapproving other'. His project of moral spectatorship within *Caché* thus seeks to preclude a denial similar to Georges's on the spectator's part, to prompt them to consider their own responsibilities with regard specifically to the cinematic situation, and to thereby produce not a shame response, but a guilt response.

How does guilt differ from shame? Both emotions involve an acute and specific form of self-awareness. However, in shame, the object of self-awareness is oneself insofar as one imagines oneself the object of blame. In guilt, the object of self-awareness is one's past action, insofar as this action is subsumable under a moral principle with which it is seen to be in conflict. Shame therefore is not only self-aware as a structure of consciousness but it also constitutes a psychological state of self-directed affect. By contrast, guilt encloses the ideal and non-psychological or rational moment of a moral principle. Thus, the distinction between between shame and guilt is between a psychological and an ideal-rational self-awareness.

This distinction between shame and guilt is also embedded in a separate difference which has to do with questions of intentionality. Shame becomes intentionally directed towards the world only when it ceases to be shame and transforms itself into anger. Guilt does not depend on this transformation, since it is already implicitly intentional: the object of one's guilt is one's own action understood as an intentional act grasped from the point of view of a moral principle that only applies to it insofar as it is an act in and upon the world, an act for which one can be held accountable.

Both these ways of distinguishing between shame and guilt are linked by a concern with responsibility and the figure of the other, whether this other is a specific individual or society as a whole. In each of the two formulations, shame is revealed as an essentially self-enclosed emotion, which focuses on the self and its own discomfort or distress. Sometimes these feelings of distress are so strong as to become overwhelming, and this is when the shamed person turns their gaze towards the other, seeking another source of blame. In forming a guilt response to Haneke's films, however, the spectator is implicated in a way that has a rational outlet, and so they can turn their thoughts to themself as moral beings; that is, the spectator can focus on their own social and personal responsibilities. For guilt is an inherently social phenomenon, which entails a sense of the other, but also of the implications of one's own actions and thoughts upon this other, of the world at large. Unlike shame, it requires an understanding of our participation in the social world.

So while shame tends to be an irresponsible, even destructive, emotion, guilt is often a responsible emotion, conducive to self-improvement and self-knowledge. For guilt necessarily entails a sense of ourselves as beholden to others, and to ourselves; it follows logically then that when we experience guilt feelings we are implicitly recognising our own responsibility to others, and sensing that we have somehow failed to fulfil this responsibility. In this case, when the spectator poses the question 'Why is (the director) doing this *to me*?' the emphasis is on the latter half of the equation. The question is formulated in terms of the spectator's agency, their participation in the spectatorial act. The answer they hit upon is that they, the spectator, may be somehow deserving of that unpleasure, and that they have perhaps somehow brought about their own experience of it. The next question they must ask themself is how they have done this. This question opens out on to further questions. And so the spectator begins to engage in a process of self-analysis and moral reflection.

## Moral Sentiments

What can the experience of guilt, in its fullest articulation, offer the spectator of Haneke's films? This is the final question with which we must engage if we are to fully understand Haneke's project of co-opting the spectator into an ethical relationship with the film they are viewing. Let us now move on to an investigation of the precise implications of guilt feelings for the spectator of Michael Haneke's films.

The emotion of guilt has a threefold importance to the spectatorial experience of Haneke's films. Firstly, as we have seen, it arises as an unpleasurable emotion, which prompts the spectator to consider their own position in relation to the cinematic spectacle. In this respect, it produces a similar response to other unpleasurable emotions such as boredom, discomfort and frustration. When we experience these unpleasurable emotions, we seek their source in order that we might rid ourselves of them, and in doing so we begin to engage in a newly cognitive manner with the filmic text.

However, guilt also does something rather different from other unpleasurable emotions. To understand what this difference is, let us return to the moral philosophy of Immanuel Kant one more time. Kant includes guilt within the group of feelings that he terms 'moral sentiments': emotions that are also dependent on a prior awareness of what we deem to be morally right and wrong.[22] Like other emotions, moral sentiments are subjective, and are felt somatically or 'pathologically'. But, Kant explains, they differ in two important ways. Firstly, they involve self-awareness. Unlike more primal emotions such as pain and anger, guilt is a rational emotion, which depends on cognition as well as instinctive reaction. That is, its very 'feltness' depends upon rationality: we cannot experience it unless our faculty for reason is active.

As we saw in Chapter Three, this is what distinguishes guilt, along with shame, from what C.E. Izard terms feelings or drives: motivational states that have a strong innate 'instinctual' component, such as anger and fear. An animal might feel anger or fear, and so seek its source outside itself in order to attack or rid itself of it, but an animal cannot feel shame since it lacks self-awareness; like anger and boredom, shame and guilt are object-directed emotions but, as we have discussed above, the object to which they are directed is the 'feeler' themselves. It is in this sense that the spectator's experience of guilt gains a secondary importance, as a response dependent on the simultaneous occurrence of emotion, or feeling, and reason, or thought, as well as on an awareness of the feeling and thinking subject.

For Kant guilt is not solely dependent on an awareness of oneself. Furthermore, moral sentiments have their origin in causes within our moral reason, and so require prior recognition of the moral law.[23] This is the primary moral sentiment that Kant discusses: respect for the moral law. It is not respect as we understand it in its everyday sense, but rather a complex emotion comprised of two conflicting feelings. It resembles fear of pain, in that it may demand the denial of self-love or the impulse to pleasure; and it resembles love, in the sense that we recognise the moral law as originating in our reason and as being something that we willingly impose upon ourselves. As an emotion, it can be very strong, since it is powerful enough to offset all other emotions and drives.

The other moral sentiments that Kant discusses also depend on respect for the moral law for their effect on the subject. These are: humility – the awareness of our propensity to pursue pleasure immorally; pain – felt when the moral law frustrates our inclination towards the pursuit of pleasure; contentment or satisfaction – the sentiment of moral worth that we experience upon fulfilling our moral duty; empathy – with the joys and sorrows of our fellow human beings and moral agents; hope – the confidence that if we do what we ought to do we will eventually have the happiness that we deserve; and, last but by no means least, guilt – felt when we fail to do our moral duty.[24] Each of these moral sentiments is experienced as the somatic effect of our moral reason impacting on us as human agents with a moral life that is permeated by emotions. So the tension between reason and emotion must already be operating in order for us to feel them.

The Kantian experience of morality serves as an appropriate analogy for the experience of ethical spectatorship that Haneke offers, since both begin with an initially amorphous feeling that is somehow a passive experience, before crystallising into a more precise awareness of pleasure and moral principle coming into tension. In both, there is an atomistic manner of isolating desire and immediate emotional responses from practical reason and morality. The dynamic between the two is characterised by two corresponding processes. Firstly, in both Kant and Haneke there is a temporal shift from one to the other. We initially begin (whether as children or as consumers of entertainment cinema) in an 'ethical state of nature', in which we pursue our desires without thought of what is morally right and wrong. Through experience, however, we acquire rational awareness of moral principles, and of how they conflict with our desire for pleasure. After this transition, from the state of nature to rational awareness of moral imperatives, the dynamic between desire and reason is characterised by conflict. Morality is a process of ongoing negotiation between what we desire and what we believe to be right.

The experience of moral response thus stands in contrast to immediate, instinctual response, as well as to a purely intellectual response. When watching Haneke's films, it is not simply a case of a shift from the latter to the former, as has been theorised by Mary Ann Doane and Jennifer Hammet, for example, who argue that reception is instantaneous, automatic and induced, while the critical act takes place in a second moment, 'a moment made possible by *theory*'.[25] When watching Haneke's films, instinctual response is only anterior to rational response in the opening moments of some films, such as *Funny Games*, before reason has been appealed to through the use of reflexivity. From the moment that the spectator is positioned as a moral agent, instinctive response and rational response are simultaneous and dialectical, combining to induce moral sentiment.

We can characterise moral sentiment as it arises through Haneke's films as the effect of instinctual response occurring at the same time as rational response within the viewing situation, the two circulating around one another. It is the perfect example of what Bresson described as 'production of emotion obtained by resistance to emotion',[26] and it is an experience almost unique to Haneke's films. It is unlikely, for example, that we could experience an emotion such as guilt when watching one of Eisenstein's films, since the impact of montage is expressed in thought as a fixed meaning and so it cannot give rise to individuated self-reflection as we are watching it. Or consider counter-cinema, which precludes *any* possibility of emotional engagement, including the engagement of rational and moral sentiments. By contrast, Haneke's moral positioning of the spectator is based upon the production of moral sentiments which are characterised by this dialectic between the felt and the thought.

Or rather, it is based on the production of something very like moral sentiments, which arises from the simultaneity of reasoned and emotional response. We should be careful however not to see the ethical response that Haneke's films give rise to as a precise articulation of Kant's moral sentiments. The position he offers is analogous with, but not a literal rendering of, the Kantian experience of morality. For one thing, the primary moral sentiment that Kant discusses – respect for the moral law – is not directly relevant to Haneke's project; there is nothing so fixed or rigorous as 'moral law' operating within Haneke's cinematic universe, which is not interested in how people act within society, but how the spectator relates to the cinematic viewing experience. The spectatorial position that Haneke's films provoke is self-focused, rather than other-focused. In order to continue with the Kantian analogy, then, we must reframe 'respect for the moral law' rather liberally as 'respect for one's personal morality in the context of the cinema'. If cinema, as Stanley Cavell supposes, offers us respite from our complicity in the structuring of the world, then it frees us from the perpetual discomfort that Freud describes in *Civilization and its Discontents*, that is the dissatisfaction, the malaise, *das Unbehagen*, that humankind experiences as a result of the fact that we live in a human society (and this despite all the obvious benefits of social organisation). For Freud the expression of this discontent is an unconscious sense of guilt that marks our being in the social world.

Mainstream cinema usually frees us of this sense of guilt by providing us with the rational oblivion that undermines any ability to feel guilt. Haneke's films, however, restore us to this state of guilt, bringing us back to an awareness of our moral values, and so forcing us to engage morally with film in the same way that we engage with society. The director and his film thus act as a force of social conscience for the cinematic spectacle. On entering the cinema and settling down to view one of Haneke's films, the spectator is like the Kantian child residing in an ethical state of nature. During the course of the film, they pass into adulthood, acquire rational faculties and are initiated into the moral world. And, once they have acquired awareness, they are no longer exempt from moral responsibility, for as Kant argues, the only morally indifferent agents are those that are non-rational. Forced to consider their own relationship to the cinematic image, the spectator finds themself conscripted into the Kantian discipline of duty.

## The Ethics of Action and the Ethics of Belief

Haneke's later films, as we have seen, involve a coercive element: the use of generic strategies effectively draws the spectator into the film, making them complicit with the cinematic apparatus. This does not occur in the earlier films: since there is no emotional engagement on the spectator's part, they are not complicit with a narrative scenario. In the later films, however, the structures of first- and second-generation reflexivity, operating in tandem with generic frameworks within Haneke's films, render the spectator complicit with an immoral spectacle and do so within an emotive situation of unpleasure. This combination of unpleasure and complicitness forces the spectator to think morally about what they have seen; or to be more precise, it forces them to think about what they haven't seen, but have wanted to see (a desire prompted by the generic conventions that Haneke incorporates into his films and their extra-cinematic presentation).

Up until this point, our discussion has focused on how the ethical experience of reason and emotion operating simultaneously, which the spectator undergoes when watching *Caché*, mirrors the Kantian conception of how morality is *felt*. But how does it relate to the Kantian conception of moral agency? In Kant, as in Haneke, the moral sphere is separate and in conflict with the natural sphere. For Kant, this conflict must have a pragmatic output: action. But surely we are not, for example, expected to make reparation for our amoral complicity with the cinematic spectacle? When we become aware of our complicity with the cinematic medium, we do not regret our *actions*, for we have not performed an action that hurts another person or infringes on their rights, and nor do we feel our entire person to be morally wrong. This of course may not be true for the film-maker watching one of Haneke's films, who might feel the need to stop making films that interpellate the spectator. A focus of this kind upon the film-maker was the impetus behind counter-cinema: to encourage the film-maker to take responsibility for the product they make, and its effect on an audience of victims. Indeed, the film-maker's response to Haneke's films might not be dissimilar to the discomfort that Joan Copjec and her contemporaries expressed when they realised the negative implications of Baudry's apparatus theory: the moral awareness that came to them in a second moment resulting in a process of ethical deliberation and practical output – perhaps, after all, a more Kantian response than the one that Haneke's films offer their spectators.

But his fellow film-makers are not the target of Haneke's project of ethical cinema; rather, as we have now seen in some detail, his films are aimed at film-goers, who are criticised not for what they make but for what they desire. The spectator has no capacity for real action while in the cinema: when watching one of Haneke's films their activity can only be mental. And yet we have seen that there is an ethical imperative in our relationship to the cinematic spectacle. This imperative is not to do with actions, then, but to do with beliefs or thoughts.

This shift in moral focus from action to deliberation points to a divergence from the Kantian analogy. Kant's moral theory takes as its ultimate end the performance of morally virtuous acts, arising from morally virtuous intentions. Kant argues that our actions are only moral if they match up to the moral law: the universal law that one should *act* as one would wish others to act. The Kantian notion of autonomy that we discussed in Chapters One and Three is understood as dictating the law by which a person acts for themself, rather than following a rule that has come from outside, acting heteronomously. In this respect, Kantian theory is aptly analogised not by Haneke's films, but by narratives of classic realist cinema that the morality critics, discussed in Chapter One, produce readings of. Frank Capra's *It's A Wonderful Life* (1946), to take the example that we used earlier, sees its protagonist, George Bailey, progress from performing morally righteous acts with amoral intentions to achieving a full realisation of his moral responsibility and taking joy in the morally correct acts that he performs. As I have mentioned, Raymond Carney's analysis of this film, in keeping with the tradition of morality criticism, is particularly interested in plot, character and action, and it sees a process of moral deliberation taking place within the film, which is resolved by its close. It does not critique the cinematic apparatus, but rather argues that we 'learn' about morality from watching such a film. Yet the audience watching Capra's film is interpellated into the system of morals that the film plays out, and so all moral 'debate' takes place within the film itself, rather than within the spectator's awareness.

It seems, then, that a Kantian framework gives us a strong idea of the nature of the position of critical awareness that Haneke aims for. But, if we look at the correlation between Haneke's ethical spectator and Kant's moral agent, certain key differences become apparent. Let us recap briefly how Haneke comes to offer the spectator a position of moral engagement with his films. When watching his works, critical awareness has to break with the classic realist apparatus that encourages spectators to engage with moral characters and actions within the diegesis. Active reflection on the spectator's part is thus encouraged by bringing other, more abstract categories, such as the status of the image, to bear on the moral norms embedded in the narrative. The reflection is not one of a spontaneous reaction, as in shame, but rather one of deliberation. However, since there is no action for the spectator to make within the immediate context of him being a spectator, this deliberation is open-ended. The interruption of narrative and emotive engagement with a film produces self-awareness. Complicity with an immoral spectacle causes some kind of guilty unease. The kind of reflective self-awareness that is produced here is not tied to a specific content so that the spectator would inevitably have to think specific thoughts. When watching Haneke's films, we are not led explicitly to judge characters and their actions as melodrama leads us to do.

The films themselves thus give no unambiguous moral judgements. In the Kantian sense, they are not moral, or moralising, pieces of art as Capra's films are. (Indeed, the lack of clear moral statement – of a fixed action to which this moral process of moral deliberation can lead – is perhaps responsible in part for the conflicting readings of and reactions to Haneke's films). As Kant admits, an individual can act morally if he believes that what he is doing is the right action, even though this action might not be acceptable to others.[27] As regards Haneke's paradigm of moral awareness, the model fails to account for its precise effect. For the films Haneke makes and the concomitant position of spectatorship that they offer are aimed not at inciting moral action, but rather moral thought. Their critical aesthetic initiates the spectator into a position of ethical awareness, which has to do with the film's moral content, but is not directly linked to this content in a straightforward manner.

## Ethical Awareness, Ethical Argument

So while Kantian ethics offers a useful model of how the conflict between reason and emotion can give rise to a somatic experience of morality, it can only take us so far. Kantian ethics must have a pragmatic output; this is not a possibility within the viewing situation. Rather, in Haneke, morality results not in action, but in reflection, in a general awareness that does not focus on a specific action or idea in the way that Kantian ethics does. For an elucidation of what exactly this ethical awareness entails within the paradigm that Haneke opens up, we must then turn away from Kant, with his emphasis on the moral act. At this juncture, let us turn instead to Stanley Cavell and the ethical philosophy that he, after Thomas Emerson, has termed 'moral perfectionism'. We can draw on perfectionism to help us understand the experience of ethical awareness that Haneke's films give rise to, since in Cavellian perfectionism, as in Haneke's ethical spectatorship, the morality of any given situation is not linked to action. This is a somewhat simplistic take on the perfectionist position: much of Cavell's writing is devoted to elucidating exactly what moral perfectionism might be, and in this respect any explanation of it within these pages will be somewhat reductive. Nonetheless, its premises offer us a useful perspective on the morality of spectatorship within Haneke's films, and so it is worth briefly surveying these.

As Cavell explains, perfectionism can be said to have been located with Socrates' explanation to Euthyphro that questions which cause hatred and anger – specifically unlike questions of science or measurement – are disagreements over the question of the just and the unjust (we might say of right and wrong), of the good and the bad, and of the honourable and the dishonourable.[28] Citing Plato in *Cavell on Film*, Cavell claims that argument is a key feature of moral discussion. The passage he cites is as follows:

> **Socrates:** But what kind of disagreement, my friend, causes hatred and anger? Let us look at the matter thus. If you and I were to disagree as to whether one number were more than another, would that make us angry and enemies? Should we not settle such a dispute at once by counting?
> **Euthyphro:** Of course
> **Socrates:** And should we not settle a question about the relative weight of two things by weighing them?
> **Euthyphro:** Of course
> **Socrates:** Then what is the question which would make us angry and enemies if we disagreed about it, and could not come to a settlement? Perhaps you have not an answer ready; but listen to mine. Is it not the question of the just and unjust, of the honourable and the dishonourable, of the good and the bad? Is it not questions about these matters which make you and me and everyone else quarrel, when we do quarrel, if we differ about them and can reach no satisfactory agreement?[29]

It is still the case, Cavell claims, that the dominant professional pedagogy in moral philosophy proceeds by taking up the relation of the questions of right and wrong (as most famously presented in Kant), with questions of the good and the bad (as in utilitarianism, exemplified by J.S. Mill). Issues here tend to emphasise matters of moral choice, of what action is to be done, and the reasons for doing it. The emphasis in Socrates' third pair, the honourable and the dishonourable, tends by contrast to emphasise the evaluation of a way of life, and it is this emphasis that he calls perfectionism, epitomised in Emerson's formulation of our moral aspiration to 'our unattained but attainable self'.[30] Cavell explains:

> The soul's journey to itself, as if awakening out of a trance, is not pictured as a continuous path directed upwards to a known path of completion but rather as a zigzag of discontinuous steps, an idea that projects no unique point of arrival but only a willingness for change, directed by specific aspirations that, while rejected, may at unpredictable times return with new power. The path is no more toward incorporation within a given condition of society than it is toward the capacity to judge that condition. The sage in us is what remains after all our social positionings.[31]

How does this relate to questions of agency and thought? Simply put, Cavell, unlike Kant, does not believe that there are any fixed moral imperatives that a moral person will naturally settle on. So we can never be sure of 'acting' morally, for we cannot *know* something morally, we can only *think* something morally; this does not automatically preclude action, but neither does it demand it. That is, perfectionism does not necessarily imply perfectibility. Thus, for Cavell, as for Haneke, moral enlightenment is not a case of reaching a conclusion about what is right or wrong, what actions are good or bad, but rather striving for a state of awareness of the implicit moral nuances of any situation or condition. We must engage in the process of moral deliberation in the knowledge that there are no absolutes, rather than to seek a position of moral certitude which then allows for action.

In *Cities of Words*, his most complete exploration of moral perfectionism, Cavell examines how certain films – part of a genre which he terms the 'remarriage comedy' and which includes, amongst others, *The Philadelphia Story* (George Cukor, 1940) and *Adam's Rib* (George Cukor, 1949) – illustrate aspects of moral perfectionism within their narratives (by following the moral trajectories of the protagonists').[32] At this point his thinking ceases to be useful to us, for it reaches the cul-de-sac that we discussed in Chapter One, whereby Cavell's film analysis becomes overly content-based, overlooking (or at least dramatically oversimplifying) the relationship between the spectator and the images on screen. However, applied to spectatorship theory, and to Haneke's films in particular, Cavell's conception of moral perfectionism can nonetheless yield important insights.

When watching a classic realist film, the moral conclusion we all agree on is generally the one promoted through the ideological apparatus. So watching *It's a Wonderful Life*, we will reach the conclusion that Potter, the cruel capitalist, is evil, and that family and friendship are worthy pursuits that count above all else, for this is the message played out in the film's narrative and with which we are coerced into agreeing through emotional effect and the withholding of critical awareness. But upon watching a feminist film, such as Akerman's *Jeanne Dielman*, we are also coerced into reaching a fixed moral conclusion – that women's everyday experience is indeed worthy of our careful attention – through the effort of intellectual concentration required and unambiguous filming techniques employed. This leads us to a situation where morality is expressed in a fixed world outlook – a moral (or, in Kantian terms, a 'maxim') which gives us a rule to which we can adhere in our future acts. The extreme content of Haneke's films, on the other hand, coupled with the spectator's newfound awareness, leads to a very personal, individuated response. As each moral spectator formulates their own moral response, there will naturally be some conflict, or debate, even if this is only internal, and this very conflict indicates that each spectator is autonomous, rather than constructed heteronomously and homogeneously by an ideological apparatus.

It is the universalising moralism (or moralising universalism) of both classic realist cinema and counter-cinema – made explicit by the pat conclusions that they offer to the spectator – which, according to moral perfectionism, we should mistrust. For if we agree with the film's morality unthinkingly, then we have not fully engaged with it in a moral sense; we have sacrificed our capacity for rational argument to the dictates of the film's moral priorities. By engaging in rational, moral argument on the other hand, whether as an internal debate as we deliberate our response to the film, or with others, as audiences and critics who discuss varying responses to the film and disagreeing about it, we are exercising the capacity for moral deliberation which Haneke opens up for us.

## Discernment, Vice and Virtue

In the perfectionist position, spectatorial autonomy can be characterised not by the spectator's capacity to *act* for themselves, but by their capacity to *think* for themselves, to engage with the morality both of the film's contents and the situation in which they are viewed, rather than following a system of thought that has come from within the film. It is a position perhaps best encapsulated by a quote from Ibsen's *A Doll's House*, a work to which Cavell frequently refers:

> **Nora:** I believe that before all else I am a human being, just as much as you are – or, at all events, that I must try to become one. I know quite well … that most people would think you right, and that views of that kind [i.e., about how a woman's most sacred duties are to her husband and children] are to be found in books; but I can no longer content myself with what most people say, or with what is found in books. *I must think things over for myself and try to get to understand them.*[33]

We can reformulate this way of viewing and thinking about film, based on the Cavellian ideas of rational argument and perfectionism, as 'moral discernment', after the term coined within contemporary philosophy by thinkers working within an Aristotelian understanding of virtue, such as Martha C. Nussbaum and Nancy Sherman. Nussbaum and Sherman have emphasised the capacity for 'discernment' or 'ethical perception' as a key component of moral conduct.[34] In both accounts, discernment takes place at a stage *before* action. The term describes our quality of attention and response to the particular features of a situation. It is, to modern ethicists such as Hector Rodríguez, an important aspect of morality, which goes beyond the mere application of general rules or the assessment of propositions.[35] Two key quotations suffice to demonstrate the salience of definitions of discernment to Haneke's project. According to Sherman, 'discerning the morally salient features of a situation is part of expressing virtue and part of the morally appropriate response ... In this sense, character is expressed in what one *sees* as much as in what one *does*'.[36] Nussbaum, meanwhile, states that what she terms 'moral insight', 'is not simply intellectual grasp of propositions; it is not even simply intellectual grasp of particular facts; it is perception. It is seeing a complex reality ... with imagination and feeling'.[37]

As in discernment, ethical spectatorship is not about being aware of a fact, but about being aware of the moral dimensions of human reality. This does not rule out the capacity for moral action; after all, by initiating the spectator into a paradigm of cinematic discernment that runs counter to dominant forms of interpellation, it may be that the effect of Haneke's films also extends to the spectator's subsequent choice of what films to see and to the way in which they view these films. But it places the emphasis not on action, but on recognition and engagement.

After the spectator has left a showing of one of Haneke's films they should be able – may even have no choice but – to apply their faculty of discernment to other films. The penultimate scene of *Caché*, following Georges's retreat into sleep, implies that once we have been called into moral awareness, it is not possible to return to the ethical state of nature. It opens with a shot of the family home taken from the same barn that we see earlier, in a flashback to Majid beheading a rooster (an image that we now know to be the image of a lie). Looking out on to the courtyard, the camera assumes approximately the same position as the young Georges did in the earlier scene, as we gather from the view of the chopping block, which stands ominously in the foreground within the dark and shadowy interior of the barn. Outside, a car pulls up to the house and a couple gets out. Another couple brings a boy into the yard. Gradually we realise that these are Georges's parents and that the child must be Majid. Sobbing and shouting, he is half-led, half-dragged away from the Laurents and forced into the back of the car, where he is restrained by one of the visitors. As the car drives out of the shot the static camera lingers on the empty courtyard. If this is all seen from Georges's point of view, then is it safe to assume that this is either a memory or a dream? Georges tells his mother when he visits her that he has been dreaming of Majid. At the time this seems a convenient excuse to raise the subject without mentioning the tapes, but this sequence implies that Georges's sublimated awareness of his moral responsibility has finally seeped through into his dreams.

Even when we seek to blank out the responsibility of the world, Haneke seems to be saying with this scene, whether in sleep or in a cinema, self-awareness can resurface. Just so, once called into ethical awareness during their viewing of a particular film, it can be very difficult for the spectator subsequently to return to the cinematic equivalent of the Kantian 'ethical state of nature'. As is the experience of so many film scholars and critics, once we have become aware of what it is to watch film consciously, and conscientiously, it is very difficult to abdicate this position totally. As the viewing of a particularly reflexive, anti-realist film will affect subsequent viewings of other films, so will the viewing of an ethically-committed film such as Haneke's. We noted earlier that if moral reason is operating, then there can be no such thing as moral indifference, and from the first time that the spectator becomes aware of classic realist cinema as a system of ethical interpellation that constructs them in a certain way, that awareness is always with them.

**Figure 5.2** Images of the past haunt the present in *Caché*.
*Courtesy of the BFI stills department. Permission graciously supplied by WEGAfilm.*

Never again can they be completely interpellated by the cinematic institution. The spectator who watches a film that calls them to moral awareness may be transformed irrevocably: from that point on, whenever they sit down to watch a film they are a moral agent and how they view a film henceforth always involves a moral choice. Once aware of the difference between 'passive' viewing and 'morally engaged' viewing, we cannot be unaware of it. We can choose to ignore our moral duties, but this must now be a conscious decision.

The moral spectator could perhaps, if they so chose, put their critical faculties on hold and willingly assume the position in which the cinematic apparatus places them as passive. In this case the moral spectator makes a pact with the cinematic institution, whereby they agree to deliberately suspend judgement for the duration of the film in order to be better entertained by it, to take more pleasure from it. This pact privileges a pleasurable experience over a moral experience of spectatorship. Or, in Kantian terms, it privileges a desire to avoid pain (manifested as shame) over what we know to be morally right (acknowledgement of our responsibility for our actions and their implications). For Kant, this is vice, or moral evil, since the moral spectator is fully aware of the implications of their choice and acts on a settled immoral decision.

To refer to the pleasures of spectatorship as evil may sound dramatic, improbable and unpractical. Nonetheless, it is clear from Haneke's statements as well as the films themselves that he sees these pleasures as morally wrong. Instead of saying that he is 'evil', then let us say that the spectator who allows themself to be interpellated is morally contradictory, that they go against their moral values. Freed from the extreme connotations of Kantian terminology, we are able to see that the charges that we, after Haneke, are levelling against the spectator are no more dramatic than those that theorists frequently apply to the cinematic systems of representation that interpellate the spectator and deprive them of their freedom. For which is the worse crime: to deny someone else freedom or to deny it to oneself? As we saw, Georges Laurent is punished in *Caché* not for the childhood lies that deny Majid a home and family, but for his consistent denial of responsibility for this act, his *mauvaise foi*. And this definition of moral reprehensibility doubly characterises the spectator who seeks to pursue selfish viewing pleasure over moral rationality as reprehensible: in sacrificing critical awareness and submitting to hedonistic oblivion, the spectator not only privileges the pursuit of pleasure over moral goodness, but they also isolate themself, cocooning themself in the cinema and temporarily relinquishing all responsibility to human society, precisely as Cavell describes and as Georges seeks to do in the closing scenes of *Caché*, as he first visits the cinema and then seeks respite in the moral oblivion of sleep.

We have seen that guilt is important to this project of inviting the spectator into moral awareness. Added significance lies in the fact that the unpleasurable experience that Haneke's films give rise to results not from the fact of having *done* wrong but from mere *desiring*. For guilt can be the result of desires, particularly unconscious desires, which would never be acted on. In this case, we may not be judged by another but by ourselves. Thus, Jacques-Alain Miller points out, in Freudian terms the superego censures and punishes us for the sins we commit; but since the superego is also an internal agency, it also punishes us for the sins that we *don't* commit.[38] The relevance to the cinematic spectacle is self-evident, since the spectator's relationship to the cinema is not one concerned with action but with urges: it is our desires that define our relationship to the cinematic image. So, the significance of guilt to Haneke's project of moral spectatorship lies perhaps not with our being made to feel guilt for our actions, since, as we have seen, our capacity for action is limited and so we cannot 'do' our moral duty. Rather, guilt gains its true significance in its relevance to our desires and our thoughts. While we might not need to make reparation to someone for thinking bad thoughts about them, the norms of morality would dictate that we strive against thinking such thoughts. Morality for Haneke is not a process of acting, but a process of overcoming: an overcoming of the desire for oblivion, an overcoming of nature, and an overcoming of cinematic systems of interpellation.

The director describes the reaction to the morally challenging film thus: 'Spectators accustomed to and luxuriously installed in the lies, leave the theatre aghast. Starved for a language capturing the traces of life, and with hearts and minds suddenly opened, the remaining spectators wait for renewed developments of the stroke of luck that has unexpectedly taken place'.[39] The morally virtuous spectator will not only seek out further moral lessons in the cinema of Haneke, but in the works of other film-makers as well. They will exercise discernment, as Haneke's films teach them to do, in the context of these other films. This of course means engaging not only with the moral issues set out within a film's narrative, but making a conscious effort to be aware at all times of their own position as both a consumer of film and an active producer of meaning. Haneke's initiation of us into moral spectatorship might have a very strong effect on how we watch a film. And while it may prevent us from pursuing the passive pleasures of mainstream narrative cinema (and television), the position of moral spectatorship that Haneke creates for the audience has its own rewards. For it teaches us freedom of consciousness, and allows us a position where we neither impose our own experiences on the film, nor allow film to impose itself on us.

# Notes

1. The genre it refers to being the suspense thriller once more, the device of the tapes recalling, amongst others, David Lynch's *Lost Highway* (1997) and David Cronenberg's *Videodrome* (1983), as well as classic thrillers revolving around mysterious missives, such as Hitchcock's *Blackmail* (1929).

2. On 17 October 1961, during the Algerian war for independence from French colonial rule, French rightist forces led a pogrom against Arab populations living in France. The Algerian Front de la Libération Nationale (FLN) retaliated, prompting a bloody purge led by the Paris prefect of police, Maurice Papon, which resulted in the murder of at least two hundred Arabs, many of their bodies simply being thrown into the Seine. The moment also produced the Organisation Armée Secrète (OAS), a group of disgruntled army officers who continued to deny the atrocities and went so far as an attempt to assassinate De Gaulle for being 'soft' on Algeria. Papon was finally tried and convicted, in 1998, though not for the events of 1961 but for crimes that he oversaw in the Second World War, when he signed away more than fifteen-hundred French Jews to deportation and death.

3. Haneke's *mise-en-scène* insists upon the disjunction between Majid's situation and the alternative had he been adopted: for example, his squalid flat is juxtaposed with Georges's elegant townhouse and its accoutrements, to great effect.

4. Christopher Sharrett, '*Caché*' (review), *Cineaste* 31(1) (Winter 2005): 60–62, 84.

5. Sharrett (2005), p. 61.

6. Sharrett (2005), p. 61.

7. I shall henceforth refer to, on the one hand, 'objective guilt' or 'responsibility', and on the other hand 'guilt feelings', which refers to subjective, internal guilt, the experience of culpability, rather than the fact of it.

8. Sharrett (2005), p. 61.

9. Indeed, Charles Gant argues that the film's success at the box office is largely attributable to the casting of Auteuil, who serves as, 'a badge of quality and a comfort zone for audiences hitherto unconvinced by the austere, intellectual Haneke'. See Charles Gant, 'The Cachet of Daniel', *Sight & Sound* 16(4) (April 2006): 8.

10. Paul Arthur ventures a reading of the film based on *Rear Window*'s scenario, in which he claims that the film can be imagined as the scenario of Hitchcock's film, re-presented from the perspective of wife-murderer Thorwald rather than voyeur-sleuth L.B. Jeffries (minus of course, he states, the resolution): 'Except in this case the plaintive cry delivered by Thorwald when he enters the lair of his eager tormentor – "What do you want of me?" – is delivered by the guilt-ridden investigator to a hapless victim, when it should be directed inward at the deceptions propping up his fatuous sense of self'; Arthur (2005), p. 28. It is surely no coincidence that Arthur, perhaps subliminally, draws a link between Haneke's film and the film most consistently cited as exemplifying and analogising the voyeuristic drives that characterise cinematic scopophilia.

11. Peucker (2000), p. 177.

12. Although there is one particularly interesting possibility that presents itself: if we see Haneke's static camera as an accusation of objective guilt, while Georges's dream sequences represent subjective guilt, then this scene, filmed with a static camera, becomes an accusation of objective guilt levelled now at Pierrot and Majid's son.

13. John Rawls, 'The Sense of Justice', *The Philosophical Review* 72 (1963): 281–305.

14. Jonathan Romney, '*Caché/Hidden*' (review), *Sight & Sound* 16(12) (February 2006): 64–65, p. 64.

15. June Price Tangney and Ronda L. Dearing, *Shame and Guilt* (New York: Guildford Press, 2004), p. 92.

16. Tangey and Dearing (2004), p. 93

17. Tangey and Dearing (2004), p. 94. Lest we are tempted to look to Majid as the film's moral core, Haneke implies that even he is not beyond moral reproach. Of the many critical readings of the film, only Richard Porton has been perceptive enough to underline the brutality of Majid's suicide and, moreover, to link it to an expression of shame. If Georges is 'seen' by the Other who is the producer of the tapes, then he himself 'sees' Majid. As Haneke describes it, then, in response to Porton's promptings, Georges becomes the 'disapproving other', for the suicide is both 'a desperate act of self-destruction' and 'an act of aggression directed towards George'; Porton (2005), p. 51.

    As Andrew Morrison's *The Culture of Shame* (Northvale, NJ: Jason Aronson, 1998) discusses, shame is the primary factor 'in generating the "emotional mortification" that leads to suicide', and that suicide is the ultimate resolution of humiliation, mortification and shame (186). The frequent shame-induced fantasy of disappearing, of being 'swallowed up into the earth' is actualised when suicide works. Suicide is then the most effective of all withdrawal strategies, as well as, in this case, a brutal expression of shame-related anger towards the other. It is aimed at inducing a new shame in Georges, a 'survivor shame' whereby the suicide functions as an accusation of blame, based on a principle of empathy (181). The vivid indication of the shame and humiliation which Majid feels, expressed through the brutality of suicide, serves to create for Georges a position of shame as powerful as that felt by the victim.

18. Romney (2006), p. 64.
19. If it seems rather far-fetched to say that *Caché* is directly intended as a comment on earlier responses to Haneke's films, we might consider the remarkable frequency with which the film makes reference to Haneke's body of works. Several shots of Binoche's character are exact repetitions of shots featuring the same actress (playing a character with the same name) in *Code inconnu*. Annie Girardot, who plays Erika's mother in *La Pianiste*, reprises the matriarchal role. Her opening conversational line to Georges is an enquiry as to whether he still plays the piano, an oblique reference to the earlier film. Later in the same conversation, she discusses the loneliness of travelling on the Métro, calling to mind Haneke's suspense scene in *Code inconnu*. But it is *Funny Games* which is most consistently referenced. Georges's first response to the tapes is to ask, 'Whose idea of a joke could this be?', an almost an exact reiteration of Anna's demand to Peter in *Funny Games*, 'What kind of a joke are you playing?' Haneke reinforces this theme of persecution as 'game' or the 'joke' throughout the film, as Georges repeatedly refers to Majid's actions in these terms. The last of these references however makes it clear that Haneke does not intend either film to be taken light-heartedly: 'Sadly,' Georges tells Anne, 'it's no joke'.
20. Porton (2005), p. 50.
21. Said (2001), p. 24.
22. Immanuel Kant, *Metaphysics of Morals*, trans. Mary J. Gregor (Cambridge: Cambridge University Press, 1991), p. 81.
23. To illustrate, let us take the example of attacking a person who has stood on our foot. An animal, feeling pain and anger, might naturally attack the person, in order to prevent a recurrence. It would not feel guilt for this attack since, on the one hand, it is not self-aware and, on the other, it has no concept of moral right or wrong. A person, pained, might similarly lash out. However, it is likely that upon learning that the original offence was unintentional, the assailant would feel guilt if it was one of their prior moral beliefs that unnecessary violence against others is amoral.
24. Cited in Roger Sullivan, *Kant's Moral Theory* (New York: Cambridge University Press, 1989), p. 132.
25. Jennifer Hammett, 'The Ideological Impediment: Epistemology, Feminism and Film Theory', in *Film Theory and Philosophy*, eds Richard Allen and Murray Smith (Oxford: Clarendon Press, 1997), p. 248. My emphasis.

26. Cited in Haneke (1998), p. 556.

27. Kant's moral thought has famously been applied to the problem of abortion with no clear answer as to what is the morally correct action: if person A believes that life begins at the moment of conception and does not abort, A is acting morally; if person B genuinely believes that life only begins when a child is born and aborts then B is also acting morally. There is only a conflict if, for example, A aborts, for that action would be contrary to what her reason tells her is the correct course of action.

28. Stanley Cavell, *Cavell on Film*, ed. William Rothman (New York: State University of New York Press, 2005), p. 324.

29. Cavell (2005), p. 323.

30. Cavell (2005), p. 324.

31. Cavell (2005), p. 324.

32. Stanley Cavell, *Cities of Words* (Cambridge, MA: Harvard University Press, 2004).

33. Henrik Ibsen, *A Doll's House, The Wild Duck, Lady from the Sea*, trans. R. Farquharson Sharp and Eleanor Marx-Aveling (London: Dent, 1958), p. 68. I follow Alice Crary's re-worked translation as given in her article 'Austin and the Ethics of Discourse', in *Reading Cavell*, eds Alice Crary and Sanford Shieh (New York: Routledge, 2006). The emphasis, however, is mine.

34. See Martha C. Nussbaum, *Love's Knowledge: Essays on Philosophy and Literature* (New York, Oxford University Press, 1990), pp. 148–67; and Nancy Sherman, *The Fabric of Character* (New York: Oxford University Press, 1989).

35. Hector Rodríguez, 'Ideology and Film Culture', in *Film Theory and Philosophy*, eds Richard Allen and Murray Smith (Oxford: Oxford University Press).

36. Sherman (1989), pp. 4–5. My emphasis.

37. Nussbaum (1990), p. 152.

38. Jacques-Alain Miller, 'Note sur la honte et la culpabilité', in *La Cause freudienne* 54 (June 2003): 6–19.

39. Haneke (1998), p. 558. The original quote is Haneke's description of the spectator's response to the cinema of Robert Bresson, but I believe one can apply it just as easily to the reception of Haneke's own films.

# CONCLUSION

In the introduction to his book on Michael Haneke's films, Alexander Horwath suggests that Umberto Eco's categories for thinking about mass culture and mass society – apocalyptic and integrative – provide a useful method for thinking about Haneke's relationship to mainstream cine-televisual culture.[1] Haneke's work is apocalyptic, Horwath claims, in that it seeks to implode existing visual forms. But it is also integrative, in that Haneke uses the weapons of mass media – cinema and television – to make his critique: his films are characterised as much by compromise as by ambivalence. Haneke's work is nothing, then, if not paradoxical. But it can also be extremely productive: the very fact that Haneke's work could inspire such extremes of response as we have discussed within these pages is surely one sign of its extraordinarily rich texture.

What I hope this book has demonstrated is that, contrary to what some critics might believe, Haneke is not a 'moralist'.[2] A moralist aims to convey fixed moral conclusions, and they see moral issues in terms of right and wrong. Haneke does not want to instil a particular set of moral values in his spectators, and his films do not promote a particular moral code. As he claims: 'I'd never be a censor because I would never have the presumption to decide what other people should see or not. I polemicise in this area, but I wouldn't sit in judgement'.[3] We have seen that the tensions and uniquely provocative edge to his work are due to the impacted and contending moral and emotional perspectives entangled within his films.

This is why Haneke cannot simply be dismissed with a convenient label, such as fascist or sadist. But it is also why sympathetic critics, such as Christopher Sharrett, err, too, when they try to minimise Haneke's authoritarian persona and to emphasise, instead, his films as socio-political commentaries whose mainstream significance lies only in their content. Haneke's work may be read as such, but to do so is to overlook the significance of Haneke's authorial persona, implicit in both content and form. It has been the goal of this book to show that Haneke's films use this authorial persona as part of their strategy for drawing the spectator's attention to their own self and for forcing a response from them. This response may be one of aggressive self-defence, but it might also be one of humble acknowledgement that they have been judged – and so they, too, must judge themself. Haneke grants the spectator little quarter (no safe vantage point) from which to assess the cruelty and violence of his films. Instead he insists that the sadism depicted in his films, and exhibited to the audience, serves a pedagogical function, for the intention of his work is to place spectators in a position whereby they can lucidly assess the content of the film, and, as we have seen, from which they can assess their own relationship to that content. Haneke means to study the ethics of spectatorship through film, and this study is not meant to comfort or reassure viewers but to enlighten them.

Michael Haneke's films offer their spectator both a warning and a lesson, but it is a lesson that each individual must learn for themselves. As I have suggested at various points in this work, the central question that arises out of Haneke's cinema is 'Why is the director doing this to *me*, the spectator?' This question lies at the heart of Haneke's ethical project of spectatorship, and the process of speculation that follows it constitutes the main goal of Haneke's cinema. To answer it, we must not only question Haneke's intentions, or the intentions of his films, but we must also question ourselves: our responsibilities to ourselves and to others in the world.

## A Coda: More *Funny Games*

I would like here to add a brief coda in which we shall return to the question of Haneke's authorial intentions. In the preceding pages, the commercial development of Haneke's films has been interpreted not only as an attempt to reach wider audiences, but also as an attempt to seduce the spectator into exposing themself to the rigorous punishments that Haneke's films enact. The project is in many ways analogous with the narrative of David Slade's *Hard Candy* (2006), in which a fourteen-year-old girl calling herself Hayley (Ellen Page) plays the flirtatious ingénue in order to seduce a paedophile, Jeff (Patrick Wilson). Once Jeff allows his desires, which Hayley has deliberately drawn out, to emerge, she brutally tortures him in order to force her victim into acknowledging the darker side of his desires. The real subject of the film is not Hayley, then, but Jeff, whose emotional trajectory and dawning self-revelation we follow throughout the film. Hayley remains a cipher, a one-dimensional character that exists only to force Jeff into a position of self-evaluation.

Haneke's position vis-à-vis the spectator is similar to Hayley's towards Jeff. Like her, he tempts his 'victim' with the fulfilment of his desires only to punish them for these desires; the plan would not work

**Figure C.1** Promotional poster for *Funny Games U.S.* (2007).
*Courtesy of the BFI stills department. Permission graciously supplied by WEGAfilm.*

were we not already complicit. Like Hayley, Haneke is a wolf in sheep's clothing: by aligning his films with mainstream models he is not selling out but going undercover. However, also like Hayley, in luring the victim in, he runs the risk of himself participating in the very structures he sets out to critique. And more worryingly, as anyone who has seen *Donnie Brasco* (Mike Newell, 1997) or Sam Fuller's *Shock Corridor* (1963) will know, it is possible to wear one's guise a little too well, and thereby risk becoming the object of suspicion.

And as we have seen, Haneke's most explicitly generic film, *Funny Games*, has been read as a straightforward genre movie by some critics and compared to John McNaughton's *Henry, Portrait of a Serial Killer*, Stone's *Natural Born Killers* and even Wes Craven's *Scream*, with some younger spectators so caught up in its patterns of suspense and stylised violence that they fail to maintain the emotional distance necessary for the position of self-awareness that Haneke aims to provide. His critics have therefore argued that Haneke's position entails an arguable loss of coherence within the film in terms of its ability to construct a solid perspective on the violence it depicts, and it also threatens an inversion of Haneke's radical positioning of the spectator as autonomous whereby that position might seem to become its opposite, namely, a position of overdetermination and subjection, not unlike that which the spectator assumes when watching a mainstream Hollywood film.

It is no surprise then that speculation was rife as to what position Haneke's English-language remake of *Funny Games*, released in 2008, would offer its spectators. Unsurprisingly, the initial response to this rumour on most fan sites was to condemn the director for moving to Hollywood, and the incentive for the move was assumed by many to be purely financial. Of course, by remaking his film in the English language, with internationally recognised stars – Naomi Watts, Tim Roth, Michael Pitt and Brady Corbett – Haneke would able to reach a much wider audience than has ever been possible before, and this is indeed in keeping with the overarching arc of Haneke's development. But accusations of 'sleeping with the enemy' were nonetheless rife.

However, a look at the production conditions for the remake suggested that the director might instead be sneaking in through the back door. For the remake is in fact a U.S./U.K./France co-production and is not managed by a major Hollywood studio (although Warner Independent Productions lent its backing after production had begun) but rather by the smaller, independent companies Halcyon, Tartan and Celluloid Nightmares.[4] Equally so, the casting belies an easy reading of the film as mainstream U.S. product, since Watts and Roth (Anna and George) are Australian and British respectively, while Pitt and Corbett (Paul and Peter) have forged careers starring in independent films, working with directors such as Gregg Araki, Catherine Hardwicke, Gus van Sant and Bernando Bertolucci. This being the case, the production might become a method of infiltrating the United States whilst at the same time opposing what Haneke terms its 'cultural imperialism', working within its terms but not its models. And as more information about the remake filtered through, it became evident that this was no straightforward 'Hollywoodisation' of a European film: *Funny Games U.S.* is a (more or less) shot-by-shot remake (no major storyline and very few script changes were made).

As Stephen Jay Schneider puts it, 'remakes abound in script-hungry Hollywood, where conservatism rules and the chance for a "sure thing" – that is, a guaranteed money-maker, takes precedence over originality and invention every time'.[5] This quote comes from Schneider's 2002 article on the remakes of George Sluizer's *Spoorloos* (1988) and Ole Bornedal's *Nattevagten* (1994). The reason Schneider singles the two films out for attention is that they are rare examples of films that were remade in Hollywood by their original directors – Sluizer's film as *The Vanishing*, in 1993, and Bornedal's as *Nightwatch*, in 1997. Schneider points out that while remakes of overseas productions, and particularly French ones, are extremely popular in the U.S. (*Breathless/A bout de souffle, Taxi/Taxi, Three Men and a Baby/Trois hommes et un couffin* and *The Assassin/La femme Nikita* stand out as recent examples), it is much less common for a director to remake his own film. Hitchcock did it, directing a black and white version of *The Man Who Knew Too Much* in 1934, then a colour version in 1956. Both Walsh and Ford did it as well, the former remaking his 1941 gangster-noir *High Sierra* as a Western, *Colorado Territory*, in 1949; and the latter making *Judge Priest* (1934) as *The Sun Shines Bright* two decades later. Sam Raimi and John Carpenter have also produced 'sequels' that should arguably be better termed remakes, with *Evil Dead II* (1987) and *Escape from L.A.* (1996). It is even more unusual for a non-American director to remake their own film in the U.S., the second time as a Hollywood production, the only examples that Schneider offers, outside his primary material, being Francis Weber (*Les Fugitifs/The Fugitives*) and Robert Rodriguez (*El Mariachi/Desperado*).

We might add to Schneider's list Hideo Nakata, the director of the Japanese horror films *Ringu/The Ring* and *Ringu II/The Ring II*, the latter of which he remade in Hollywood in 2005. Nakata is among a group of Japanese, Korean and Chinese makers of horror films whose work has picked up a cult following in the U.S. and U.K., due in no small part to Tartan Distribution, who market the films under the label 'Tartan Extreme', the same label under which *Funny Games* was released. Following the huge success of Gore Verbinski's 2002 remake of Nakata's *Ringu* (which grossed over $120million at the U.S. box office), Hollywood has hastened to produce further remakes, several of which have been helmed by their original directors, including Nakata's *The Ring II* and Takashi Shimizu's 2004 *The Grudge* (from his 2003 *Ju On*). If *The Vanishing* and *Nightwatch* can be seen as precedents for *Funny Games* as auto-remake in terms of their heritage, the form of his work holds closer allegiances with the East Asian *auteurs* remaking their own films in the U.S. Both Sluizer and Bornedal reworked their material to please the Hollywood studios and their idea of the audiences for the films (Sluizer ironing out temporal gameplay, ramping up the action sequences and tacking on a happy ending; Bornedal upping the amount of sex and violence): the result was distinct box office failure. Nakata and his peers, however, stick more closely to their first works, most notably retaining the original open endings within the remakes. Perhaps coincidentally, perhaps not, they have seen much better returns in English-language territories. With these twin sets of precedents setting up certain expectations of what could almost be termed an emerging sub-genre (on the one hand poor Americanisations of cerebral European art-films, on the other literal translations of generic horrors and thrillers), Haneke could have found a way to take advantage once more of audience assumptions in order to subvert them once more. We

**Figure C.2** Naomi Watts and Tim Roth as Ann and George Farber
in *Funny Games U.S.* The film's casting belies easy readings of
the film as 'mainstream' product.
*Courtesy of the BFI stills department. Permission graciously supplied by WEGAfilm.*

might note here with a wry smile that the star of both *The Ring* and *The Ring II* (U.S. versions) was none other than Naomi Watts – whose weeping face dominates the press material for *Funny Games U.S.* Tim Roth, incidentally, starred that same year in *Dark Water*, the remake of Nakata's *Honogurai mizu no soko kara* (2002).[6]

So despite being superficially the 'same' as the earlier film, *Funny Games U.S.* comes with a new set of intertexts, which cannot help but inform reception of the film amongst certain audiences. The remake itself provides a set of references not present in the case of the original, as do its stars. But additionally, the ten years that have passed between the releases of the original and the remake have seen Hollywood thrillers of the type that *Funny Games* set out to parody thrive, not least in the form of the 'Asian Invasion', and a disturbing sub-genre, dubbed 'torture porn' emerge. Films such as *Saw* and *Hostel* have spawned cult followings and endless franchises (at last count five *Saw* films had been produced, and a third *Hostel* was in the offing), offering graphic depictions of rape and violence which exceed anything seen on screen in 1997. Their aesthetics of excess are also reiterated in numerous video games, and in this respect it is telling that amongst the very few script changes that *Funny Games U.S.* sees are a number of references to gaming culture: Paul's opening gambit to George upon returning to the house is 'Player One, Next Level'; his final declaration before killing him is to tell Anna 'You've failed … Game over'.

Clearly, the forms of visual 'entertainment' that Haneke sees as dangerous and nihilistic are as abundant as at any point in cinema's history, and he clearly sees their audiences as being just as in need of the alternatives he can offer. With the recent slew of Hollywood remakes of 'world cinema' (and most notably of horror films) setting up certain expectations of what could almost be termed an emerging sub-genre, Haneke could have found a way to take advantage once more of audience assumptions. And in this way, he may finally be bringing his cinema of ethics to the very audiences he has always seen as most in need of it: the 'willing consumers of the cinema of distraction'.

## Notes

1. Horwath (1991), p.35. Horwath is referring here to categories originally set out in Eco's 'Apocalypse and Integration', in *Apocalypse Postponed*, trans. Robert Lumley (Bloomington: Indiana University Press, 1994).
2. See Romney (1998), p.6.
3. Falcon (1998), p.10.
4. Pressnotes to *Funny Games U.S.* U.K. release (distr.: Tartan). Made available by Tartan.
5. Stephen Jay Schneider, 'Repackaging Rage: The Vanishing and Nightwatch', *Kinema* 17 (1 April 2002): 24–66, p.26.
6. The appearance of Watts on all the film's publicity material effects an interesting reversal of the original posters, which featured Ulrich Mühe's, contorted in a remarkably similar manner. According to the pressnotes for the film, Haneke's consent for a remake was conditional on Watts starring. This is possibly due to her unarguably excellent acting ability; however, one cannot help but wonder whether she herself does not function as a generic signifier of 'intelligent horror' here. Given that Haneke described the original *Funny Games* as an anti-Tarantino film, it is notable, too, that Tim Roth is cast in the remake, given his roles in Tarantino's *Reservoir Dogs* and *Pulp Fiction*.

*Appendix I*

# MICHAEL HANEKE FILMOGRAPHY

---

1974    *After Liverpool* (TV production)
        89 min
        Directed: Michael Haneke
        Producer: Horst Bohse
        Screenplay: James Saunders (trans. Hilde Spiel)
        Photography: Jochen Hubrich, Günter Lemnitz, Gerd E. Schäfer
        Editing: Christa Kleinheisterkamp
        Actors (main cast): Hildegard Schmahl, Dieter Kirchlechner
        Country: West Germany
        Language: German

1976    *Sperrmüll* (TV production)
        80 min
        Directed: Michael Haneke
        Screenplay: Alfred Bruggmann
        Photography: Henric von Bornekow
        Actors (main cast): Ernst Fritz Fürbringer, Tilli Breidenbach, Karlheinz
        Fiege, Suzanne Geyer
        Country: West Germany
        Language: German

1976    *Drei Wege zum See* (TV production)
        97 min
        Directed: Michael Haneke
        Producer: Rolf von Sydow
        Screenplay: Michael Haneke, Ingeborg Bachmann (short story)
        Photography: Igor Luther
        Editing: Helga Scharf
        Actors (main cast): Ursula Schult, Guido Wieland
        Country: Austria/West Germany
        Language: German

1979   *Lemminge, Teil 1 Arkadien* (TV production)
113 min
Directed: Michael Haneke
Production Company: Schönbrunn-Film, Sender Freies Berlin, ORF
Screenplay: Michael Haneke
Photography: Walter Kindler, Jerzy Lipman
Editing: Marie Homolkova
Actors (main cast): Regina Sattler, Christian Ingomar, Eva Linder,
Paulus Manker, Christian Spatzek, Elisabeth Orth
Country: Austria/Germany
Language: German

1979   *Lemminge, Teil 2 Verletzungen* (TV production)
107 min
Directed: Michael Haneke
Production Company: Schönbrunn-Film, Sender Freies Berlin, ORF
Screenplay: Michael Haneke
Photography: Jerzy Lipman
Editing: Marie Homolkova
Actors (main cast): Monica Bleibtreu, Elfriede Irrall, Rüdiger Hacker,
Wolfgang Hübsch, Norbert Kappen, Guido Wieland, Vera Borek,
Wolfgang Gasser, Julia Gschnitzer, David Haneke
Country: Austria/Germany
Language: German

1983   *Variation* (TV production)
98 min
Directed: Michael Haneke
Production Company: Sender Freies Berlin
Screenplay: Michael Haneke
Photography: Walter Kindler
Editing: Barbara Herrmann
Actors (main cast): Elfriede Irrall, Suzanne Geyer, Hilmar Thate,
Monica Bleibtreu
Country: Austria
Language: German

1984   *Wer war Edgar Allen?* (TV production)
(*Who was Edgar Allan?*)
83 min
Directed: Michael Haneke
Producers: Neue Studio Film, Zweites Deutsches Fernsehen, ORF
Screenplay: Michael Haneke, Hans Broczyner, Peter Rosei (novel)
Photography: Frank Brühne
Editing: Lotte Klimitschek
Actors (main cast): Paulus Manker, Rolf Hoppe
Country: Austria/Germany
Language: German

1985   *Schmutz* (directed by Paulus Manker)
(*Dirt*)
100 min
Directed: Michael Haneke
Producers: Paulus Manker
Screenplay: Michael Haneke, Paulus Manker
Photography: Walter Kindler
Editing: Marie Homolkova
Actors (main cast): Siggi Schwientek, Hans-Michael Rehberg, Fritz
Schediwy
Country: Austria
Language: German

1986   *Fräulein* (TV production)
108 min
Directed: Michael Haneke
Producer: Ulrich Nagel
Screenplay: Michael Haneke, Bernd Schröder (concept)
Photography: Walter Kindler, Karl Hohenberger
Editing: Monika Solzbacher, Monika Schreiner
Actors (main cast): Angelica Domröse, Péter Franke, Lou Castel,
Heinz-Werner Kraehkamp, Cordula Gerburg, Margret Homeyer
Country: Austria
Language: German

1989   *Der Siebente Kontinent*
(*The Seventh Continent*)
104 min
Directed: Michael Haneke
Producers: Veit Heiduschka, Wega Film
Screenplay: Michael Haneke
Photography: Anton Peschke
Editing: Marie Homolkova
Actors (main cast): Dieter Berner, Leni Tanzer, Birgit Doll
Country: Austria
Language: German

1991   *Nachruf für einen Mörder* (TV production)
(*Aftermath of a Murder*)
110 min
Directed: Michael Haneke
Screenplay: Michael Haneke

1992   *Benny's Video*
       105 min
       Directed: Michael Haneke
       Producers: Veit Heiduschka, Michael Katz, Bernard Lang, Gebhard
       Zupan, Wega Film
       Screenplay: Michael Haneke,
       Photography: Christian Berger
       Editing: Marie Homolkova
       Actors (main cast): Arno Frisch, Angela Winkler, Ulrich Mühe, Ingrid
       Stassner
       Country: Austria/Switzerland
       Language: German

1993   *Die Rebellion* (TV production)
       *(The Rebellion)*
       90 min
       Directed: Michael Haneke
       Producers: ORF
       Screenplay: Michael Haneke, Joseph Roth (novel)
       Photography: Jirí Stibr
       Editing: Marie Homolkova
       Actors (main cast): Branko Samarovski, Judit Pogány, Thierry Van
       Werveke, Deborah Wisniewski, Katharina Grabher, August Schmölzer
       Country: Austria
       Language: German

1994   *71 Fragmente einer Chronologie des Zufalls*
       *(71 Fragments of a Chronology of Chance)*
       96 min
       Directed: Michael Haneke
       Producers: Veit Heiduschka, Willi Seigler, Wega Film
       Screenplay: Michael Haneke
       Photography: Christian Berger
       Editing: Marie Homolkova
       Actors (main cast): Gabriel Cosmin Urdes, Lukas Miko, Otto
       Grünmandl, Anne Bennent, Udo Samel, Branko Samarovski, Georg
       Friedrich, Claudia Martini
       Country: Austria/Germany
       Language: German

1995    *Der Kopf des Mohren*
        *(The Moor's Head)*
        120 min
        Directed: Paulus Manker
        Producers: Veit Heiduschka, Wega Film
        Screenplay: Michael Haneke
        Photography: Walter Kindler
        Editing: Marie Homolkova, Michael Hudecek
        Actors (main cast): Gert Voss, Angela Winkler, Leni Tanzer
        Country: Austria
        Language: German

1996    *Lumière and Company* (segment of collaborative film)
        1 min
        Directed: Michael Haneke
        Producers: Ángel Amigo, Anne Andreu, Humbert Balsan, Neal
        Edelstein, Fabienne Servan-Schreiber, Soren Staermose
        Screenplay: Michael Haneke
        Photography: Michael Haneke
        Editing: Michael Haneke
        Country: Austria

1997    *Funny Games*
        108 min
        Directed: Michael Haneke
        Producers: Veit Heiduschka, Wega Film
        Screenplay: Michael Haneke
        Photography: Jürgen Jürges
        Editing: Andreas Prochaska
        Actors (main cast): Susanne Lothar, Ulrich Mühe, Arno Frisch, Frank
        Giering, Stefan Clapczynski
        Country: Austria
        Language: German

1997    *Das Schloß*
        *(The Castle)*
        123 min
        Directed: Michael Haneke
        Producers: Christina Undritz, Bayerisher Rundfunk, Wega Film, Arte,
        ORF
        Screenplay: Michael Haneke (adapted from a novel by Franz Kafka)
        Photography: Jirí Stibr
        Editing: Andreas Prochaska
        Actors (main cast): Susanne Lothar, Ulrich Mühe, Frank Giering, Felix
        Eitner
        Country: Germany/Austria
        Language: German

2000    *Code inconnu: Récit incomplete de divers voyages*
        *(Code Unknown: Incomplete Tales of Several Journeys)*
        118 min
        Directed: Michael Haneke
        Producers: Yvonn Crenn, Christoph Holch, Marin Karmitz, Thilo
        Kleine, Titi Popescu, Alain Sarde, Michael Weber, Bavaria Film, Canal
        +, Filmex, France 2 Cinéma, Les Films Alain Sarde, MK2 Productions,
        Romanian Culture Ministry, Zweites Deutsches Fernsehen, arte France
        Cinéma
        Screenplay: Michael Haneke
        Photography: Jürgen Jürges
        Editing: Karin Martusch, Nadine Muse, Andreas Prochaska
        Actors (main cast): Juliette Binoche, Thierry Neuvic, Alexandre Hamidi,
        Ona Lu Yenke, Luminita Gheorghiu, Walid Afkir, Maurice Bénichou
        Country: France/Germany/Romania
        Language: French

2001    *La Pianiste*
        *(The Piano Teacher)*
        131 minutes
        Directed: Michael Haneke
        Producers: Veit Heiduschka, Michael Katz, Christine Gozlan, Yvon
        Crenn, Bayerischer Rundfunk, Canal +, Centre National de la
        Cinématographie, Eurimages, Les Films Alain Sarde, MK2
        Productions, P.P. Film Polski, Wega Film, arte France Cinéma, arte, ORF
        Screenplay: Michael Haneke (adapted from a novel by Elfriede Jelinek)
        Photography: Christian Berger
        Editing: Nadine Muse, Monika Willi
        Actors (main cast): Isabelle Huppert, Benoît Magimel, Annie Girardot
        Country: France/Austria/Germany/Poland
        Language: French

2003    *Le Temps du loup*
        *(The Time of the Wolf)*
        113 minutes
        Directed: Michael Haneke
        Producers: Veit Heiduschka, Michael Katz, Margaret Ménégoz,
        Michael Weber, Bavaria Film, Canal +, Centre National de la
        Cinématographie, Eurimages, France 3 Cinéma, Les Films du Losange,
        Wega Film, arte France Cinéma
        Screenplay: Michael Haneke
        Photography: Jürgen Jürges
        Editing: Nadine Muse, Monika Willi
        Actors (main cast): Isabelle Huppert, Olivier Gourmet, Daniel Duval,
        Patrice Chéreau, Anaïs Demoustier, Hakim Taleb, Lucas Biscombe,
        Maurice Bénichou, Béatrice Dalle
        Country: France/Austria/Germany
        Language: French

2005  *Caché*
      *(Hidden)*
      117 minutes
      Directed: Michael Haneke
      Producers: Valerio de Paolis, Veit Heiduschka, Michael Katz, Margaret
      Ménégoz, Michael Weber, Les Films du Losange, Wega Film, Bavaria
      Film, BIM Distribuzione
      Screenplay: Michael Haneke
      Photography: Christian Berger
      Editing: Michael Hudecek, Nadine Muse
      Actors (main cast): Juliette Binoche, Daniel Auteuil, Maurice Bénichou,
      Walid Afkir, Lester Makedonsky
      Country: France/Austria/Germany/Italy
      Language: French

2007  *Funny Games U.S.*
      Directed: Michael Haneke
      Producers: Rene Bastian, Christian Baute, Chris Coen, Hamish
      McAlpine, Linda Moran, Jonathan Schwarz, Andro Steinborn, Naomi
      Watts
      Screenplay: Michael Haneke
      Photography: Darius Khondji
      Editing: Monika Willi
      Actors (main cast): Naomi Watts, Tim Roth, Brady Corbett, Michael
      Pitt, Devon Gearhart
      Country: US/UK/France/Germany/Italy/Austria
      Language: English

*Appendix II*

# MICHAEL HANEKE AT THE BOX OFFICE

| Film | Year | Gross per Country | |
|------|------|------|------|
| | | U.S. | U.K. |
| Caché | 2006 | $3,600,000 (approx) | £1,100,000 (approx) |
| Le Temps du loup | 2003 | $61,439 | £45,928 |
| La Pianiste | 2001 | $1,700,000 (approx) | £451,674 |
| Code inconnu | 2001 | $95,242 | £152,289 |
| Funny Games | 1997 | Not released | £33,727 |
| 71 Fragmente … | 1994 | Not released | Not released |
| Benny's Video | 1992 | Not released | Limited release at ICA – estimated figure: £1000 |
| Der Siebente Kontinent | 1989 | Not released | Not released |

(Sources BFI/*Sight & Sound*/Hollywood.com)

# BIBLIOGRAPHY

Allen, Richard. 1995. *Projecting Illusion: Film Spectatorship and the Impression of Reality* (Cambridge: Cambridge University Press).

Allen, Richard, and Murray Smith (eds). 1997. *Film Theory and Philosophy* (Oxford: Clarendon Press).

Althusser, Louis. 2001. 'Ideology and Ideological State Apparatuses (Notes towards an Investigation)' (1970), in *Lenin and Philosophy and Other Essays*, trans. Ben Brewster (New York: Monthly Review Press), pp. 127–86.

Andrew, Dudley. 1971. *The Major Film Theories* (Oxford: Oxford University Press).

Anon. 2000. 'Beyond Mainstream Film: An Interview with Michael Haneke', in *After Postmodernism: Austrian Film and Literature in Transition*, ed. Willy Riemer (Riverside, CA: Ariadne Press), pp. 159–70.

Arthur, Paul. 2005. 'Endgame', *Film Comment* 41(6) (November–December): 25–8.

Artificial Eye. 2000. Pressnotes to *Code Unknown*, available at the British Film Institute Library.

————— 2001. Pressnotes to *The Piano Teacher*, available at the British Film Institute Library.

Baudry, Jean-Louis. 1974–5. 'Ideological Effects of the Basic Cinematographic Apparatus,' *Film Quarterly* 28(2): 39–47.

Bazin, André. 1958. 'William Wyler ou le janséniste de la mise en scène', in *Qu'est-ce que le cinéma?* Tome 1 (Paris: Editions Cerf), pp. 149–73.

————— 1967a [1958]. *What is Cinema? Volume 1*. ed. and trans. Hugh Gray (Berkeley and Los Angeles: University of California Press).

————— 1967b. 'The Evolution of the Language of Cinema' (1950), in *What Is Cinema? Volume 1*, ed. and trans. Hugh Gray (Berkeley: University of California Press), p.23–41.

————— 1971 [1962]. 'An Aesthetic of Reality' (1962), in *What is Cinema? Volume 2*, ed. and trans. Hugh Gray (Berkeley: University of California Press), pp. 16–40.

————— 2003 [1950]. *Orson Welles* (Paris: Cahiers du Cinema).

Benjamin, Walter. 1985. 'Central Park', trans. Lloyd Spencer, *New German Critique* 24(50) (Winter): 32–58.

———— 1996. 'One Way Street' (1928), (trans Edmond Jephcott), in *Selected Writings Volume 1: 1913–1926*, eds Marcus Bruloca and Michael W. Jennings (Cambridge: Cambridge University Press), pp. 444–88.

———— 2004. 'The Work of Art in the Age of Mechanical Reproduction' (1936), in *Film Theory: An Introduction*, eds Leo Braudy and Marshall Cohen (Oxford: Oxford University Press, 6th edn), pp. 791–811.

Bingham, Adam. 'Long Day's Journey into Night', *Kinoeye Online Film Journal*, http://www.kinoeye.org/04/01/bingham01.php (last accessed 20 January 2005).

———— 'Modern Times: Notes towards a Reading of Michael Haneke's *71 Fragments of A Chronology of Chance'*, *Senses of Cinema Online Film Journal*, http://www.sensesofcinema.com/contents/cteq/05/34/71_fragments.html (last accessed 18 June 2006).

Blackburn, Simon. 2003. *Ethics: A Very Short Introduction* (Oxford: Oxford University Press).

Bordwell, David. 1989. *Making Meaning: Inference and Rhetoric in the Interpretation of Cinema* (Cambridge, MA: Harvard University Press).

Bourget, Jean-Loup. 1977. 'Social Implications in Hollywood Genres' in *Film Genre: Theory and Criticism*, ed. Barry Keith Grant (Metchuen, NJ: The Scarecrow Press), pp. 62–72.

Bradshaw, Peter. 2001 'Mind Games' (review of *Code inconnu*), *The Guardian* Section 2 (25 May): 12–13.

Brecht, Bertholt. 1948 [1929]. 'Der Dreigroschenprozeß', in *Versuche 1–12*, (Berlin: Suhrkamp), pp. 280–1.

———— 2000. *The Threepenny Opera*, trans. J. Willet and R. Mannheim (London: Methuen).

Brill, Leslie. 1989. *The Hitchcock Romance: Love and Romance in Hitchcock's Films* (Princeton, NJ: Princeton University Press).

Brown, Geoff. 1993. '*Benny's Video*', *Times* (26 August): 31.

Busson, Raphael. 1993. 'Glaciation des Sentiments' (review of *The Seventh Continent*), *Le Mensuel du Cinéma* 5 (April): 33–6.

Carney, Raymond. 1986. *American Vision: the Films of Frank Capra* (New York: Cambridge University Press).

Carroll, Noel. 1983. *Mystifying Movies: Fads and Fallacies in Contemporary Film Theory* (New York: Columbia University Press).

Cavell, Stanley. 1971. *The World Viewed* (New York: Viking Press).

———— 1979. *The Claim to Reason* (New York: Oxford University Press).

———— 1981. *Pursuits of Happiness: The Hollywood Comedy of Remarriage* (Cambridge, MA: Harvard University Press).

———— 1997. *Contesting Tears: The Melodrama of the Unknown Woman* (Chicago: Chicago University Press).

———— 2004. *Cities of Words* (Cambridge, MA: Harvard University Press).

———— 2005. *Cavell on Film*, ed. William Rothman (New York: State University of New York Press).

Champagne, John. 2002. 'Undoing Oedipus: Feminism and Michael Haneke's *The Piano Teacher*', *Bright Lights Film Journal* 36 (April). On-line: http://www.brightlightsfilm.com/36/pianoteacher1.html (last accessed 11 June 2008).

Chong, Sylvia. 2004. 'From "Blood Auteurism" to the Violence of Pornography: Sam Peckinpah and Oliver Stone', in *New Hollywood Violence*, ed. Steven Jay Schneider (Manchester: Manchester University Press), pp. 249–68.

Cieutat, Michel. 2000. 'Entretien avec Michael Haneke', *Positif* 478 (December) : 22–9.

Cook, Christopher. 'Interview with Isabelle Huppert', *Guardian* website, http://film.guardian.co.uk/lff2001/news/0,,592339,00.html (last accessed 23 February 2006).

Cook, Pam, and Mieke Berninck. 1999. *The Cinema Book* (London: BFI).

Copjec, Joan. 1986. 'The Delirium of Clinical Perfection', *Oxford Literary Review*, 8(1–2): 57–65.

Crary, Alice. 2006. 'Austin and the Ethics of Discourse', in *Reading Cavell*, eds Alice Crary and Sanford Shieh (New York: Routledge), pp. 42–67.

Creed, Barbara. 2003. *Media Matrix: Sexing the New Reality* (Crow's Nest, Australia: Allen and Unwin).

Currie, Gregory. 1996. 'Film, Reality, and Illusion', in *Post-Theory: Reconstructing Film Studies*, eds David Bordwell and Noel Carroll (Madison: University of Wisconsin Press), pp. 325–44.

Dassanowsky, Robert von. 2005. *Austrian Cinema: A History* (Jefferson, NC: McFarland).

Debord, Guy. 1967. *La Société du spectacle* (Paris: Editions Champ Libre).

Derry, Charles. 1998. *The Suspense Thriller: Films in the Shadow of Alfred Hitchcock* (Jefferson, NC: MacFarland).

Doane, Mary Ann. 1990. 'Information, Crisis, Catastrophe', in *Logics of Television: Essays in Cultural Criticism*, ed. Patricia Mellencamp (Indianapolis: Indiana University Press), pp. 222–39.

Downing, Lisa. 2004. 'French Cinema's New "Sexual Revolution": Postmodern Porn and Troubled Genre', *French Cultural Studies* 15(3): 265–80.

Dyer, Richard, 1986. *Stars* (London: BFI).

Eco, Umberto. 1984. *Apocalypse Postponed*, trans. Robert Lumley (Bloomington: Indiana University Press).

Eisenstein, Sergei. 1957 [1929]. *Film Form and The Film Sense*, trans. Jay Leyda (London: Meridian Books).

———— 1998. 'The Montage of Attractions' (1923), in *The Eisenstein Reader*, ed. and trans. Richard Taylor (London: BFI), p.30.

Eisler, Hans. 1947. *Composing for the Films* [co-authored by Theodor W. Adorno, who is not cited in this edition], (New York: Oxford University Press).

Elsaesser, Thomas (with Michael Wendt) (ed.). 1999. *The BFI Companion to German Cinema* (London: BFI).

Engleberg, Achim. 1999. 'Nine Fragments about the Films of Michael Haneke', *Filmwaves* 6 (Winter): 31–33.

Falcon, Richard. 1998. 'The Discreet Harm of the Bourgeoisie' (feature article on *Funny Games*), *Sight & Sound* 8(5) (May): 10–12.

———— 2001. '*Code Unknown*' (review), *Sight & Sound* 11(5) (May): 46.

Farren, Paul. 2001. 'Breaking the Code', *Film Ireland* 80 (April-May): 22–23.

Finney, Angus. 1996. *The State of European Cinema* (London: Cassell).

Forbes, Bryan, 1967, 'Alfred Hitchcock' (NFT interview). On-line. http://www.bfi.org.uk/features/interviews/hitchcock.html (last accessed 12 June 2008).

Frampton, Daniel, 2006. *Filmosophy* (London: Wallflower).

Frey, Mattias. 'Supermodernity, Capital and Narcissus: The French Connection to *Benny's Video*', *Cinetext Online Film Journal*, http://cinetext.philo.at/magazine/frey/bennysvideo.html (last accessed 18 August 2006).

———— 'A Cinema of Disturbance: The Films of Michael Haneke in Context', *Senses of Cinema*, http://www.sensesofcinema.com/contents/directors/03/haneke.html (last accessed 2 November 2006).

Gant, Charles. 2006 . 'The Cachet of Daniel', *Sight & Sound* 16(4) (April): 8.

Goudet, Stéphane. 2000. '*Code inconnu* – La main tendue', *Positif* 478 (December): 22–9.

Grodal, Torben. 2000 [1997]. *Moving Pictures: A New Theory of Film Genres, Feelings and Cognition* (Oxford: Clarendon Press).

Hammett, Jennifer. 1997. 'The Ideological Impediment: Epistemology, Feminism and Film Theory', in *Film Theory and Philosophy*, eds Richard Allen and Murray Smith (Oxford: Clarendon Press), pp. 244–59.

Haneke, Michael. 1992. 'Film als Katharsis,' in *Austria (in)felix: Zum österreichischen Film der 80er Jahre*, ed. Francesco Bono (Graz: Edition Blimp), p.89.

———— 1997. 'Believing not Seeing', *Sight & Sound London Film Festival Supplement* (November): 22.

———— 1998. 'Terror and Utopia of Form, Addicted to Truth: A Film Story about Robert Bresson's *Au hasard Balthasar*', in *Robert Bresson*, ed. James Quandt (Ontario: Wilfred Laurier Press), pp. 551–59.

——— 2000. '71 *Fragments of a Chronologie of Chance*: Notes to the Film (1994),' in *After Postmodernism: Austrian Film and Literature in Transition*, ed. Willy Riemer (Riverside, CA: Ariadne Press), pp. 171–5.

Hegel, G.W.F. 1967 [1807]. *The Phenomenology of Spirit*, trans. A.V. Miller (Oxford: Oxford University Press).

Hess, Judith. 1977. 'Genre Film and the Status Quo', in *Film Genre: Theory and Criticism* ed. Barry Keith Grant (Metchuen, NJ: The Scarecrow Press), pp. 53–61.

Hoberman, J. 1998. 'Head Trips', *Village Voice* (17 March): 89.

Horton, Robert. 2000. '*Code inconnu*' (review), *Film Comment*, 36(6) (November): 18.

Horwath, Alexander (ed.). 1991. *Der Siebente Kontinent, Michael Haneke und Seine Filme* (Wien: Europeverlag).

——— 1998. and Giovanni Spagnoletti, *Michael Haneke* (Torino: Edizioni Lindau).

Ibsen, Henrik. 1958 [1879]. *A Doll's House, The Wild Duck, Lady from the Sea*, trans. R. Farquharson Sharp and Eleanor Marx-Aveling (London: Dent).

Izard, C.E. 1991. *The Psychology of Emotions* (New York: Plenum Press).

James, Nick. 2001a. 'Code Uncracked', *Sight & Sound* 11(6) (June): 8.

——— 2001b. 'The Limits of Sex', *Sight & Sound* 11(7) (July): 21.

——— 2003. 'Darkness Falls', *Sight & Sound* 13(10): (October): 16–17.

Jones, Bronwyn. 'More than a Master of Everyday Horror: The Films of Michael Haneke', *The High Hat*, http://www.thehighhat.com/Nitrate/004/haneke.html (last accessed 26 July 2006).

Kant, Immanuel. 1990 [1785]. *Foundations of the Metaphysics of Morals*, trans. Lewis White Beck (New York: MacMillan, 2nd edn).

——— 1991 [1785]. *Metaphysics of Morals*, trans. Mary J. Gregor (Cambridge: Cambridge University Press).

Kermode, Mark. 1998. '*Funny Games*', *Sight & Sound* 8(12) (December): 44.

Lambert, Gregg. 2000. 'Cinema and the Outside', in *Deleuze and The Philosophy of Cinema*, ed. Gregory Flaxman (Minneapolis: University of Minnesota Press), pp. 253–92.

Le Cain, Maximilian. 'Do the Right Thing: The Films of Michael Haneke', *Senses of Cinema Online Film Journal*, http://www.sensesofcinema.com/contents/03/26/haneke.html (last accessed 18 August 2006).

Lewin, B.D. 1946. 'Sleep, the Mouth, and the Dream Screen', *Psychoanalytic Quarterly* 15(4) (Winter): 419–34.

Margulies, Ivone. 1996. *Nothing Happens: Chantal Akerman's Hyperrealist Everyday* (Durham, NC: Duke University Press).

Matthews, Peter. 2003. '*The Time of The Wolf*', *Sight & Sound* 13(11) (November): 98.

McCann, Ben, and David Sorfa. Forthcoming. *Europe Utopia: The Films of Michael Haneke* (London: Wallflower).

McNab, Geoffrey. 2003 'There Goes the Neighbourhood', *Guardian* (6 October): 16.

Metz, Christian. 1974. *Film Language: A Semiotics of the Cinema*, trans. Michael Taylor (New York: Oxford University Press).

——— 1982 [1977]. *The Imaginary Signifier: Psychoanalysis and Cinema*, trans. Celia Britton, Annwyl Williams, Ben Brewster and Alford Guzzetti (London: MacMillan).

——— 1986. 'History/discourse: a note on two voyeurisms' in *Theories of Authorship: A Reader*, ed. John Caughie (London: Routledge). pp. 225–31.

Miller, Jacques-Alain. 2003. 'Note sur la honte et la culpabilité', *La Cause freudienne* 54 (June) : 6–19.

Morrison, Andrew. 1998. *The Culture of Shame* (Northvale, NJ: Jason Aronson).

Morrow, Fiona. 2001. 'All Pain and No Gain', *Independent* (2 November): 11.

Moullet, Luc. 1985. 'Sam Fuller: In Marlowe's Footsteps' (1959), in *Cahiers du Cinéma, The 1950s: Neo-Realism, Hollywood, New Wave*, ed. and trans. Jim Hillier (Cambridge, MA: Harvard University Press), pp. 145–55.

Mulvey, Laura. 1989. 'Visual Pleasure and Narrative Cinema' (1972), in *Visual and Other Pleasures* (London: MacMillan), pp. 14–29.

Naqvi, Fatima. 2007. *The Literary and Cultural Rhetoric of Victimhood* (Basingstoke and New York: Palgrave MacMillan).

Neale, Steve. 1980. *Genre* (London: BFI).

Nussbaum, Martha C. 1990. *Love's Knowledge: Essays on Philosophy and Literature* (New York: Oxford University Press).

Oudart, Jean-Pierre. 1990. 'Cinema and Suture' (1969), in *Cahiers du cinema: The Politics of Representation*, ed. Nick Browne (Cambridge, MA: Harvard University Press), pp. 45–57.

Perkins, Victor. 1972. *Film as Film* (Harmondsworth: Penguin).

Peucker, Brigitte. 2000. 'Fragmentation and the Real: Michael Haneke's Family Trilogy,' in *After Postmodernism: Austrian Film and Literature in Transition*, ed. Willy Riemer (Riverside, CA: Ariadne Press), pp. 176–87.

Porton, Richard. 2005. 'Collective Guilt and Individual Responsibility: An Interview with Michael Haneke', *Cineaste* 31(1) (Winter): 50–51.

Prince, Stephen. 1998. *Savage Cinema* (Austin: University of Texas Press).

Rawls, John. 1963. 'The Sense of Justice'. *The Philosophical Review* 72: 281–305.

Rayns, Tony. 2001. 'The Piano Teacher', *Sight & Sound* 11(11) (November): 54.

Rebhandl, Bert. 1996. 'Kein Ort. Nirgends: *71 Fragmente einer Chronologie des Zufalls* von Michael Haneke,' in *Der Neue Osterreichische Film*, ed. Gottfried Schlemmer (Wien: Der Deutsche Bibliothek), pp. 309–19.

Riemer, Willy (ed.). 2000. *After Postmodernism: Austrian Film and Literature in Transition* (Riverside, CA: Ariadne Press).

———— 2000b. 'Iterative Texts: Haneke/Rosei, *Wer war Edgar Allen ?*', in *After Postmodernism: Austrian Film and Literature in Transition*, ed. Willy Riemer (Riverside, CA: Ariadne Press), pp. 189–98.

Rodowick, D.N. 1994. *The Crisis of Political Modernism: Criticism and Ideology in Contemporary Film Theory* (Berkeley: University of California Press).

Rodríguez, Hector. 1997. 'Ideology and Film Culture', in *Film Theory and Philosophy*, eds Richard Allen and Murray Smith (Oxford: Oxford University Press), pp. 260–81.

Romney, Jonathan. 1993. '*Benny's Video*', *New Statesman* (20 August): 36.

———— 1998. 'If You Can Survive this Film Without Walking Out, You Must Be Seriously Disturbed', *Guardian*, Section 2 (23 October): 6–7.

———— 1999. Sleevenotes to Artificial Eye VHS release of *Funny Games*.

———— 2006. '*Caché/Hidden*' (review), *Sight & Sound* 16(2) (February): 64–5.

Roud, Richard, (ed.). 1980. *Cinema: A Critical Dictionary* (London: Secker & Warburg).

Said, S.F. 2001. 'Are We Waving or Drowning' (feature article/interview), *Daily Telegraph*, (17 May): 24.

Schatz, Thomas. 1981. *Hollywood Genres* (New York: McGraw-Hill).

———— 1998. *The Genius of the System: Hollywood Filmmaking In The Studio Era* (New York: Pantheon).

Schneider, Stephen Jay. 2002. 'Repackaging Rage: *The Vanishing* and *Nightwatch*', *Kinema* 17 (April): 24–66.

Sharrett, Christopher. 2003. 'The World That Is Known: An Interview with Michael Haneke', *Cineaste* 28(3) (Summer): 28–32.

———— 2005. '*Caché*' (review), *Cineaste* 31(1) (Winter) : 60–62, 84.

Sherman, Nancy. 1989. *The Fabric of Character* (New York: Oxford University Press).

Smith, Susan. 2000. *Hitchcock: Suspense, Humour and Tone* (London: BFI).

Sobchack, Vivian. 1998. *Screening Space: The American Science Fiction Film* (New York: Ungar).

Sullivan, Roger. 1989. *Kant's Moral Theory* (New York: Cambridge University Press).

Suppan, Karl. 1998. 'Die Asthetik der Gewalt in Hanekes *Benny's Video*', in *Visible Violence: Sichtbare und verschleierte Gewalt im Film*, eds Franz Grabner, Gerhard Larcher and Christian Wessley (Münster: Lit).

Tangey, June Price, and Ronda L. Dearing. 2004. *Shame and Guilt* (New York: Guildford Press).

Telotte, J.P. 1995. *Replications: A Robotic History of the Science Fiction Film* (Urbana: University of Illinois Press).

Thompson, Patricia. 2002 'Secret Lives, Hard Lessons', *American Cinematographer* 83(5) (May): 22, 24, 26, 28.

Thomson, David. 2003. *The New Biographical Dictionary of Film* (London: Little, Brown).

Vogel, Amos. 1996. 'Of Non-existing Continents: The Cinema of Michael Haneke', *Film Comment* 32(4) (July–August): 73–5.

Walker, Alexander. 2001. '*The Piano Teacher*' (review), *Evening Standard*, (8 November): 21.

Wecker, Claus. 1993. '*Benny's Video*', *Filmfaust Internationale Filmzeitschrift* 88 (18 Jan): 46–9.

Willemen, Paul. 1992. 'Letter to John' (1980), in *The Sexual Subject: A Screen Reader in Sexuality*, ed. Screen Editorial Collective (London: Routledge), pp. 171–83.

Williams, Linda. 1997. 'Sex and Sensation' in *The Oxford History of World Cinema* ed. Geoffrey Nowell-Smith (Oxford: Oxford University Press), pp. 190–97.

Wollen, Peter. 1982a. 'Godard and Counter-Cinema: Vent d'Est' (1972), in *Readings and Writings* (London: Verso), pp. 79–91.

——— 1982b. 'The Two Avant-Gardes' (1975), in *Readings and Writings* ( London: Verso), pp. 92–104.

Wood, Robin. 1992. 'Ideology, Genre, Auteur' (1977), in *Film Theory and Criticism*, eds Leo Braudy, Marshall Cohen and Gerald Mast (New York: Oxford University Press), pp. 453–66.

——— 2002. 'Do I Disgust You? or, Tirez pas sur *La Pianiste*', *CineAction* 59 (Spring): 54–61.

——— 2003 'In Search of the *Code inconnu*' *CineAction* 62 (October): 41–9.

Žižek, Slavoj. 2002. *Welcome to the Desert of the Real* (London: Verso).

# INDEX

Lightning Source UK Ltd.
Milton Keynes UK
29 March 2010

152058UK00001B/180/P